I Once Was a COWBOY

Sixty Years a Canadian Ranch Hand

Art Hagen

argenta
press

I Once Was a COWBOY

Sixty Years a Canadian Ranch Hand

© 2010 by Argenta Press
First printed in 2010 10 9 8 7 6 5 4 3
Printed in China

The Publisher: Argenta Press is an imprint of Dragon Hill Publishing Ltd.

Library and Archives Canada Cataloguing in Publication

Hagen, Art, 1923–
    I once was a cowboy : sixty years a Canadian ranch hand / Art Hagen.

ISBN 978-1-896124-51-3

    1. Hagen, Art, 1923–. 2. Cowboys—Alberta—Biography. 3. Cowboys—British Columbia—Biography. 4. Ranch life—Alberta—History. 5. Ranch life—British Columbia—History. I. Title.

FC3670.C6H34 2010   971.23'03   C2010-900892-8

Project Director: Gary Whyte
Project Editor: Michelle Nichol
Cover Image: Courtesy of Art Hagen
Back Cover Image: © Joey Boylan I iStockPhoto
Photo Credits: Every effort has been made to determine the holder of copyright for the photographs in the book. Please inform the publisher of any errors or omissions so that changes can be made in future editions. *Photos courtesy of* Blackmer Photography (p. 321, 346); Art Hagen (13, 33, 45, 49, 50, 54, 57, 58, 70, 99, 112, 114, 115, 117, 120, 122, 123, 125, 127, 135, 147, 221, 227, 231, 233, 239, 240, 267, 276, 334, 345, 347, 348, 349); Mattie Hagen (p. 294); Eugene Lodermeier (p. 327); Lenore Oddie (p. 297, 303).

Produced with the assistance of the
Government of Alberta, Alberta Media Fund.

Alberta∎
Freedom To Create. Spirit To Achieve.

PC: 30

CONTENTS

DEDICATION

I would like to dedicate this book to the memory of my parents, Lars and Anna Hagen, the best parents any bunch of kids could wish for. To my sister, Louise, and my brothers Henry, George and Norman. And to the Love family from down the road who shared in my growing-up years. To my daughter, Julie, and her husband, Craig, and my son, Irvine, and his wife, Michelle, for all their wonderful support and encouragement.

To the people who helped in production of this book, Wanda Erickson and my daughter, Julie, for typing the first draft and getting it on the computer. To Ann Jorgensen and my daughter-in-law, Michelle, for proofreading and editing it, while still allowing it to sound like me.

To the memory of my good friends, Wes Newhouse, George Dejonckheere and Jack Ross. Wes, my working partner, was one of the best range cowboys who ever sat atop a cowhorse. George was my travelling partner and could spur a saddle bronc out past the whistle and come back with a grin on his face. Jack was the owner of the Milk River Cattle Company and probably one of the best bosses this hand has ever worked for.

To all of the cowboys, cowgirls, ranchers and folks I knew and worked with. There are too many to mention by name, but I remember you all. To the young generation of cowboys and cowgirls who will pick up the bridle reins and lariats when us old hands lay them down. With faith in God, they will keep the traditions of the range country and the spirit of the west alive forever.

INTRODUCTION

The cattle industry in North America has been here for a long time, from the early days of the open range to the present time of fences and roads. During the days of the open range, there were no fences or facilities for handling cattle; the ranch hands had to rely on each other, their horses and their own ability to use a rope. If a cow critter needed to be treated for an injury or sickness, it had to be roped by the head and the back heels and stretched out on the ground for this to be accomplished. You had to trust your partner, and your horse had to know his job, too. The ranch horse had to be able to work and handle the rope on its own, while the cowboy did whatever needed to be done to the cow.

Cattle had to be trailed long distances from their home range to where they could be loaded onto railcars, sometimes hundreds of miles over rough, wild country, and this could take two or three months on the trail. The cowboys camped out, sleeping under the stars and eating from the chuck wagon. A romantic thought when the weather is nice, the cattle are well-behaved and outlaws are not out to steal your cows.

The railway system expanded, and the cattle drives became smaller and shorter; there were now more places to load your cattle onto the trains to get them to eastern markets. When cattle liners came into play, that, too, became a thing of the past; they could pull right up to the corrals at the ranch and load up the cattle. Cattle drives still happen today, but generally they are short affairs over relatively short distances to move cattle from one grazing location to another when trucking isn't feasible.

Caring for cattle has not changed much: they still need plenty of grass, good water and extra feed in times of drought and in the winter. The ranch hand now, in contrast to days gone by, works with some different options. Modern haying, harvesting and feeding machines have made things much more efficient, and it's easier to care for large numbers of cattle.

The ranchers need to care for their land for ranch survival and success. A good rancher is a steward of the land, a keeper of the range and a guardian of the environment. The ranch hand, too, also plays his part in this. He must move the cattle to ensure the land is not overgrazed and that the water is adequate and clean.

Although the business of ranching is basically the same wherever a ranch hand might hang his hat, he must be able to adapt to the great differences in the country the ranch is settled on. Raising cattle in the hot, dry country of the Rio Grande differs from raising them in the land and climate of the western states nestled under the Rockies. And the lush, green caribou country differs from the snowbound winters of Alberta's Peace Country.

The ranch hand takes on the role of a "road scholar," continually learning as he travels, always seeking to know more and never getting to know all. The cow is a worthy opponent; she has an amazing ability to test her keepers and their mounts. The ranch horse is no slump, either: it can teach humility like no one else. There are hours upon hours of class time on the range, just the cattle, the cowboy, his partner the horse and perhaps an observant antelope or coyote watching the action.

CHAPTER 1

BOYHOOD IMAGININGS

It was one of them very bright summer days in July, in the Kispiox Valley, BC. I could hear the little creek bubbling over the rocks as it tumbled into the small dugout my dad had dug in the creek bed for the horses to drink. The smell of the cedar and spruce trees surrounding the half-acre clearing that made up the yard between the barn and the long log cabin and bunkhouse in my dad's pole camp was sweet to my nostrils, as the late morning sun warmed the evergreens. A squirrel was chattering somewhere among the limbs of a big spruce tree, and some of the birds were singing a little, not like at sunup, when they would really be musical, better than a church choir; the warmth of the sun was slowing them down.

I was seven years old. Lying in luxury in the green grass and shade, at peace with the world. I looked at the clear blue sky, where a few white clouds were moving slowly by, way up there. Just under those clouds, a big bald eagle was floating around in circles, not even moving his wings, but just floating easy, like thistledown. I wondered how he could stay up there without moving his wings, when most other birds had to flap theirs to stay in the air. He looked real majestic up there, like maybe he felt like a king of all he surveyed: the green forest, the creeks and lakes and rivers and the snow-capped mountains in the distance. From way up there, I am sure he saw it all.

Lying there, I was thinking and dreaming of things any young boy might think of, like how high was it to the top of the sky, why did the clouds move on by when it was a plumb quiet day. I did not worry about answers; I liked it just as it was. I guess many small thoughts drifted through my mind, but what I remember clear-like is my dream of being a cowboy when I grew up. I do not exactly know when this notion hit me, but I suppose it was from looking through the pictures in the western story magazines that were numerous in camp.

In those days, there were no TVs and no radios, so the teamsters and loggers used to relax and read a lot after supper before turning in to their bunks. Well, the favourite reading material in all the camps was short story westerns. Those magazines were about the size of an ordinary school scribbler and maybe two or three times as thick. They were of coarse paper with easy-to-read print, usually with a colour picture on the cover and half a dozen or more short stories inside. Of course, all the pictures were of cowboys, horses and mostly long-horned cattle, with a few other breeds mixed in for colour.

The colour covers might show a tall, lean cowboy riding a bronc as easy as sitting in Grandma's rocking chair, or they might show the bronc really powering it on, with the stirrups snapping like whips over the bronc's back and the cowboy sitting on the ground scratching his head and feeling lucky he missed the cactus patch close by. Sometimes, the cover showed a lawman with a star on his chest, beating a bad man to the draw.

Inside, at the beginning of every story, were pencil sketches of real range cow horses, herds of cattle and tall, lean cowhands. Usually two or more of the above or all three would show up. Whoever did the pencil sketching was good at it. Those horses were strong, well-built range horses, rugged and tough. The cowboys pretty well all wore real high-heeled boots with big rowel spurs on the heels. They wore tight-fittin' pants on bowed legs and always had a Colt .45 on one hip in a tied-down holster. They was lean and tall and rugged with square shoulders, some hatchet-faced or lantern-jawed with prominent Adam's apples, short hair and, of course, big hats.

Then there were the *Ranch Romances* magazines. They were made like the others, mostly short stories and colour pictures on the covers and the same pencil sketches inside. They, too, were westerns, but they told the romantic side of western life, as it was before there were any motor vehicles driving around tearing up the grass. The pictures on the covers of these romantics usually showed some really handsome cowboy or a beautiful cowgirl or both, mounted on fine horses.

To say the cowboys were handsome and the cowgirls beautiful was almost an understatement. They looked that good, along with the scenery! I guess the pictures were meant to encourage folks to buy the book.

These books were really good for lonely loggers, teamsters and miners, who were often on the job for weeks on end, away from the civilized world of those days. I found this out for myself, after I learned to read and later went to work. Up till then, I could only look at the pictures and imagine. I will leave the western story scene for now and tell you what stories were like later, after I went to school and learned to read.

In September of the same year that I lay in the grass watching that bald eagle floating on the air currents, I was destined to start school. I was big for my age, but my folks had kept me home an extra year so I would grow as big as possible before I started school. You see, I had three miles to walk to and from school, mostly through big timber along a narrow bush road through the forest. I am sure my parents had many uneasy thoughts sending their seven-and-a-half-year-old boy to school under them conditions, but there was no other way. Dad was working steady, and Mom had my little sister and brothers to care for, besides cooking for and feeding a man.

Art's parents, Lars and Anna Hagen, standing in front of their 1932 Studebaker: "I took my driver's test in that car."

Dad said to me, "I hope you will not be afraid to go alone; nothing will hurt you," and, of course, being the big brave boy I was, I assured him I did not mind and there was nothing to be scared of. I do not think I fooled him, or my mother, either; I was a little scared, but I sure was not going to admit that.

There was one bright spot, however. About halfway to school, on a small ranch about a quarter of a mile off our road, lived a family who were our friends. There were two boys a little older than me, and I used to go around their way, especially in the evenings. That way, I had company half the way home, and it was much more interesting than travelling alone.

My imagination gave me some bad times during those early school years. When I travelled that narrow bush road, it brought on stories that trappers and hunters told when they stopped to visit my folks. I just loved to sit and hear about their experiences when they came back from the north country.

One time, a trapper named Charlie told us about a run-in with a grizzly bear on the edge of the northern tundra country. Charlie was travelling afoot with a pack on his back when he ran into a grizzly digging in the ground looking for grubs to eat. Now, the tundra was open country, with practically no trees, just the odd one. Well, Charlie saw the bear first and tried to go around without being noticed, but no such luck. That old bear spotted him, and being as he just got up from a long winter sleep, he must have been in a bad humour and feeling mean and hungry. He headed for Charlie.

Seeing that bear come, Charlie felt plumb desperate, so he looked around for someplace real quick that might help him. He could have tried shooting the bear but risked only wounding him, instead of making a killing shot. A wounded grizzly is much worse than a healthy one.

By luck, there was a big, jagged spruce stump about 12 feet high that was broken off at the top by the wind. It still had a few limbs from the ground up. Right quick-like, Charlie dropped his pack and made a run for that stump and went to climbing like his tail was on fire.

The bear stopped for a bit and rolled the pack over but decided that Charlie was better, so he came on again. By this time, Charlie had climbed up through them dry limbs on the stump and was sitting on top of it; worst of all, his rifle had fallen to the ground. He had lost hold of it in his mad scramble up that stump. That is sure understandable, because he was in a hurry—and who wouldn't be with a grizzly bear practically pulling on your shirttail?

Well, that old grizzly tried his best to reach Charlie, but, luckily, grizzlies cannot climb. It was nip-and-tuck, though. The bear was big enough that Charlie had to pull his feet up when the bear reached for him.

That old bear was plumb determined and didn't leave for parts unknown for a long while, and Charlie said he'd be damned if he was going to get down and take any chances till that old bear was long gone and short coupled. I have often thought since that Charlie's ass must have been awful tender after sitting on that jagged old stump for so long, but at least he was still alive to tell about it.

Another trapper told of an encounter with a wolf pack up in the northern tundra country. He was heading across the snow-bound wasteland when he ran into a big pack of wolves, hungry and on the hunt. His lead dog was running loose in front, leading the dog team. Some of the real good lead dogs them days were not expected to work as long as they led the team. This was the exception rather than the rule and was the case here.

When they met the pack of wolves, the lead dog had gone a little ways ahead and met with the pack already. Unfortunately, he had been set upon, torn apart and eaten by the ravenous wolves. This gave the trapper a chance to get the scared-to-death dog team stopped and get his rifle off the sleigh.

Of course, the frightened dogs cowered around the sleigh as much as the harness and traces would let them, and the trapper got behind the loaded sleigh and went to shooting into the wolf pack that was busy fighting over the remains of his lead dog.

Well, it's common knowledge, according to the old timers of the day, that when a pack of starved wolves on the hunt smells blood, they go plumb crazy. By shooting into that fighting, snarling, hungry pack, some was wounded or killed and went to bleeding. When the rest of them smelled that blood, being ravenous, they turned on their fallen mates and tore them apart. You might say that trapper fed that wolf pack on themselves until they came to their senses and realized that a rifle was shooting at them and they pulled out for parts unknown.

The trapper said that the only thing that really saved him and the rest of the dog team was that his good lead dog was loose up front, giving him time to unlimber his rifle. If that big pack of hungry wolves had got to the team and him, it would have been game over. He felt very bad over losing his good lead dog; I guess they were close.

The same summer that I was to start school, the newspapers had an article about a cougar cat on Vancouver Island that supposedly killed a woman and a kid. Well, the hunt was on, and I guess they got him. Apparently, the cougar would lay on a big limb over a trail and jump down on its victims.

Now, I could not read this, of course, but I heard the grown-ups discuss it. After asking many questions, I was assured that there were no known cougars in our area and that Vancouver Island was hundreds of miles away. Also, ordinarily, cougars never kill people, but once in a very great while it could happen.

I was also assured that there was nothing to be afraid of with wolves in our country, because there was an overabundance of rabbits and lots of game, so they would not bother anyone, and there were no big packs running around. Well, this assurance turned out to be very true, but, at the time, I was very much aware of having to go to school through all that timber country. To say the least, I was a mite apprehensive and made up my mind to be very watchful, just in case.

School: the time had come. I was about to embark on a career receiving my formal education. I was not too thrilled or excited, but I supposed I was as ready as I would ever be. It was Labour Day, and school was to start the next day.

I crawled into bed that night and, after the lamp was blown out, lay in the dark thinking about the next day. In my imagination, big, grey timber wolves glided among the trees as I was going through the timber to school, but, somehow, they did not bother me. I also had to watch for all those big tree limbs reaching over the road, to make sure there was no big cat waiting there.

Well, I went to sleep and came to in the morning after a good sleep. I got up for breakfast, and Dad said, "I've got to take the team and go right by the school, so you might just as well ride with me, and, being school is only half a day the first day, you can ride with me back." I was sure glad Dad happened to have to make that trip on the first day.

I think now, looking back, he planned it that way. Dad was a real good man. I do not remember if he had something to do by way of the school the next day, but, if I remember right, he had to go by the neighbours' halfway there and so I had someone with me through the timber and so it went till I got going. It helped a lot to get started like that.

Even so, after I got used to going alone, I was pretty watchful. There was one place where the big spruce limbs reached clear across the road. Before I went under them, I would stop and open the big blade of my jackknife. Then I'd run like hell under those limbs, holding the open knife pointed skyward. In my boy's imaginative mind, if a big cat jumped me, he would get the knife blade in the guts and that would fix him. Thankfully, none of this ever happened, and, though it is humorous to think about now, looking back it was surely not funny at the time.

Some things I never told anyone, lest some of the other kids, or anybody for that matter, think I was a scaredy-cat. In addition, I did not want my parents to know. I did not want them to worry, but thinking about it now, Mom and Dad likely had a lot of my misgivings figured out. Since there was no other way, I am glad they did not say anything, and let me be as much of a man as I tried to be. Being as I got through school with no misfortunes, I feel I succeeded.

Going to school was actually fun at times. I learned to ski at an early age, and Dad gave me a pair of skis. He made them and was very good at it. It was mostly downhill from camp to school, and I would just whiz to school in maybe 20 minutes. That was fun; going home up those hills was less fun, of course.

The stock market crashed back in 1929, opening the era of the hungry Thirties just before I started school. I couldn't quite understand it all; with the word "stock" in there, I figured it had something to do with cattle. I guess it did, all right, but how could a bunch of cattle crash? Maybe a stampede, but how could it affect the whole country?

Then they talked about Wall Street falling. Well, I had heard about them big city buildings and figured money was involved, but if the whole "wall" fell, how come they just did not clean up the mess and pick up the money? A boy's thoughts, but I am not too sure I got it all figured out, yet. But then, why worry about the past? It's water down the creek.

Well, the logging operation closed down after that, but we kept on living in the camp. There was hardly any work at all, but somehow the folks kept us fed and watered. Mom was an expert seamstress and made all us kids' clothes; underwear from 100-pound flour and sugar sacks and clothes from any material she could get her hands on. I do not remember going hungry or cold, but at times there was not much variation in the diet.

Whenever there was nothing else to do, which was most of the time during those memorable Thirties, the men spent most of their time hunting and fishing and growing gardens wherever they could find a little patch of ground. Actually, many people adopted the ways of our friends, the Indians, to make a living. I believe the Indian ways contributed greatly toward easing the tough times of the Thirties in our part of the country. We actually had much to be thankful for; in other parts of the country, folks had tougher times.

The good thing about being kids in our part of the country, even in the Thirties, was that life and daily happenings were relatively normal for those of us who were young enough to not really realize the impact of the times. We still went to school and done things any normal kid back in the bush country would do. We learned the value of work at an early age but also had fun doing it and sometimes would get our tails caught in a crack just through being impulsive and not thinking.

Our neighbours who owned the little ranch on my way to school also had some land and a hay and pasture field about a quarter mile past the school. They also had a bunch of milk cows. In the morning, before school, the boys would help milk them. They then took the milk cows with them past the school to the other pasture and brought them home after school on their way home.

One day, I went with my friends to get the cows, and, because we had to take turns cleaning the blackboards and brushes and tidying up the school for the next day, the girls stayed and done that. When we boys came past the school with those gentle milk cows, the girls were finished and were waiting for us, and we all walked home together behind the cows.

About a quarter mile past the school lived a farmer who had buildings on both sides of the road, so he had the road fenced on both sides, forming a lane. At the end of the lane, right at the end of his hay shed, he had a big pole gate, which he always kept shut. There were no cattle guards in them days, just gates, and that effectively closed off the road. I guess nobody minded, really, as there was not much traffic. Everybody just opened the gate to go through.

Well, we kids were following those cows down this long lane from the school, and one of the girls had a lot of homework, being well up in the elementary grades, and so was carrying a big load of books and a lunch kit. She said, "Will somebody pack this lunch kit? I got a lot to pack." I will never know why I said this, but I said, "Why not let ol' Snowball pack it on her tail?"

Well, the idea seemed good. Old Snowball was so gentle, such a nice cow, nobody ever figured she would mind. So, one of us tied the long, curly hair of her tail through the handle of the lunch bucket and let her tail down. The lunch bucket clunked against her hocks, but she did not even get excited.

Being as it was somehow aggravating, she started to switch her tail. Well, maybe Snowball did not mind too much, but those other cows did. When she started to switch her tail, with that empty lunch bucket on it, she was among the other cows—that thing cracked down on the backs of the others and all hell broke loose.

They took off like a herd of runaway longhorns down that lane, with the bull right in front. The gate was shut, but that did not bother that old bull none. He just led that bunch of milk cows right through that pole gate with a hell of a crash, and they were on their way home. Somehow or other, my idea about letting Snowball pack the lunch bucket did not seem so good anymore. We made a mistake.

Lucky for us, the old cow lost the lunch bucket on the edge of the road, still with some long, white tail hair stuck in the handle, just before they got to the buildings. I grabbed that bucket and cleaned the tail hair out of the handle, and we all proceeded down the lane kind of easy-like to where the farmer was, by his broken gate, having heard the crash, and hotfooting it over there. We could see he was downright unhappy, even mad, but being a religious man, all he said was, "What in the world happened to make them cows run that way?" Well, we all could not figure it out, either; by this time we had all become dumber than a sack full of hammers.

I sneaked a careful look at that lunch bucket handle, hoping I had not missed any of Snowball's tail hairs. I had not. We all realized we had done a dumb thing, and by mutual consent we told nobody, and I mean nobody. We did not even talk about it to each other. To this day, I do not think anyone but us knew what caused that stampede. I figure it is safe to tell now, since it has been forgotten so long ago.

Fall turned into winter, with lots of snow, good skiing and good tracking for hunting. During the winter, our neighbours had some fellows staying with them for someplace to live. We were still in the unforgettable Thirties, and these boys helped them build a big new log barn, a really good barn (40 feet by 60 feet) with a big hip roof on it to hold a lot of hay. Come spring they had it up, and, by sometime around the first of June, the roof was on, but the windows and doors were still just holes in the wall.

One day, coming home from school, I went past their place and the boys showed me how the new barn was coming. A couple of strange saddle horses were standing there with their reins on the ground. While we were down beside the wall of the new barn, we heard a calf bawl. We figured one of the cows must have calved, but we could not find either one, and the calf kept on bawling. We could not figure this out, and then I heard my friend laugh. I looked up and almost fell on my ass.

A man with a face that could have come right out of the pages of a western story magazine was looking out the window hole; he was bawling like a calf, with a big grin and his eyes just a-twinkling. He had kind of a narrow face, real friendly eyes, a protruding Adam's apple, short hair and a big hat. I could not believe my eyes.

We went in the barn, and the rest of him matched my western story heroes, right down to the high-heeled boots, big rollered spurs and tight-fittin' pants. The only thing missing was the gun belt and gun with a tied-down holster. He was a cowpuncher named Fred from Nebraska who had worked his way up into our country. In later years, we became good friends.

We had been living in the old bush camp for about five years, since the stock market crash of '29. During that time, my mom and dad had made a deal with another neighbour and acquired a piece of land with about 20 acres of cleared hay land on it.

Also during that time, there was a fella staying with us for a place to live, and he helped a great deal in keeping meat, fish and food on the table. He was also very handy at building stuff, same as my dad. Between them, they built a little homemade sawmill on the new land and cut and sold quite a bit of lumber. They also built a new log house on the place, finished with lumber from the little mill. The house was up but only half roofed over. Dad put a bunk and a stove in there for the summertime for a place to stay close to his work. I often was along to help him.

One day, he was cutting hay in the front field with a scythe and asked if I could make supper. I said sure and headed off for the house. I knew Dad liked beans and rice, so I was about to cook him up a treat.

After an hour and a half or two, I hollered to Dad that supper was ready. He came in and washed up. I had this gourmet feast on the little board table, right in the pots it was cooked in—we didn't have much for serving dishes. Dad said it smelled good and drove his spoon into the bean pot. When those beans hit his tin plate, they rattled like buckshot. He just looked up and said, "Maybe we need to cook them a little more."

We used our forks to smash them up—with a lot of effort, I might add. We managed to eat them with the spuds and back bacon. Of course, the spuds had to be smashed too, also being on the raw side. I never thought to stick a fork in them to see if they were done.

On to dessert, and I was plumb sure that rice had to be good. This was long before instant rice had been invented. I don't know what I did that wasn't right, but I drove a skinny-handled spoon into that rice pot and damned if the handle didn't bend when it hit the top of that rice. I felt pretty bad about my cooking by now, but Dad just grinned and told me not to let it bother me, we all have our turn learning.

Next day, Dad fixed up my cooking just by boiling it some more—even the rice. I will never really figure out how he softened that up, but when he was done, it was all the way I meant it to be: good! So much for my first effort at acquiring culinary skills.

Well, it was getting to be fall: September. School was about to start, and the folks decided to fix up the half of the house that was roofed over and move from the old camp into the new place. By now, my sister and one brother were also going to school, and another brother was ready to start before long. There were five of us kids all together. The new place was only a mile and a half from school, so it was better for us kids.

Anyways, we all got to getting ready for winter, because we moved practically right away. With our own lumber from the little mill, we fixed up two rooms in the part of the house that was roofed over and the kitchen and a big bedroom and then built a chicken house and barn on log framework, using slabs from the mill. It made pretty good buildings. Not too big but good for Mom's chickens and Dad's big logging team and a couple of milk cows he had acquired. Things were looking up. Everything would have been very good, except for one thing: the house and other buildings were fixed up for the winter— but not the winter that set in.

The stove never went out, and still the cold got in there. There was no insulation in them days, except moss in the cracks of the log wall and paper on the boards of the partition walls where we fixed up those two rooms. On the other side was one of the coldest winters I remember. Good thing we had many blankets and us kids all slept in a great big bunk to keep warm. It was fine in the bed; it was bad getting up to go to school, even though the folks had the stove red hot by the time we got up.

For six weeks, it was below 0°F (–18°C) every night, mostly in the –30°F (–34°C) range. I think it was one of the longest winters I can remember. We ran short of hay, and Dad got some from a fellow up the river valley. It was a long, cold 10-mile haul getting that hay home.

One day, Dad got home late, so he just pulled the load over to the hay shed and put the team in the barn; being so cold, he would unload it in the morning. Next morning, he went over to the shed and came back to inform us that a small bay horse had come out of nowhere and was feeding on the load of loose hay. It was Saturday, and us kids were home from school. We insisted if we could please, please keep him, so Dad said sure, if nobody claimed him.

Well, I went with Dad to look at this horse sent from heaven and to help unload the hay. I was big by this time; I think I was in grade five.

It turned out the bay pony was a two-year-old Cayuse or mustang, according to Dad, and sure looked like he needed a home. He had found one, but we kids were sure hoping no one claimed him.

Spring finally came, and Dad asked the police what they thought about the horse and was told that if no one claimed him, keep him, but if someone did claim him, they should pay for his feed. Thankfully, no one claimed him, so before green grass came, Dad got the Nebraska cowboy, Fred, to geld him, and he was turned loose to grow for the summer. Of course, all five of us kids wanted him, so it was decided we would all have him, one-fifth each. Dad green broke him that fall, and he stayed with us the rest of his life.

As we all got older and acquired more horses by trading "shares" among us kids, the horse wound up belonging to my second-youngest brother. Before the trading of "shares," the bay pony helped me embark on a lifelong cowboy career. It was slow to start out with, but, over the years, the cowboy thing was taking shape.

Later, though, things happened that also steered me in that direction—not right away, and I didn't really know it at the time, but for better or worse, I was unknowingly going in the direction my boyhood dreams had portrayed. My dreams must have come true, I think, for, as future events proved, and because I wanted to, I was destined to become a cowboy.

CHAPTER 2

THE MAKING OF A COWBOY

The little bay mustang needed a name, and, after many suggestions and a fair amount of jawing, we decided to call him Bill, you know, short for William. Bill is a nice, easy name to say, and we all agreed that it seemed to fit him real good, so that is the moniker he was known by for the rest of his days.

He had a nice disposition and was a quiet little horse, never bucked and was good to get along with, but that is not to say he did not have a mind of his own. Dad had him well green broke after he had run out all the first summer; he would just do anything and go wherever Dad asked him to. Being as he was so gentle and quiet, he was ready for the kids.

We all wanted to ride him, so our folks said sure, go ahead, but learn to ride bareback first before we could use a saddle. That way, there was no danger of being caught in a stirrup if we fell off. Being as I was the oldest, I took it upon myself to further Bill's formal education and teach him to become a top cow horse. After all, any cowboy worth his salt knew how to train horses, and this was a golden opportunity to get this cowboy thing on the road.

We got along quite well, considering that I was greener than a swamp frog and he was just green broke. This little horse had a good think tank under his ears, and his ideas did not always go along with mine. We could all take turns riding him in the yard, but when it came to leaving home, that was something different.

He would go out along the road till we got to the edge of the hay field. That was far enough. He would insist on going back to the corral. This was a problem. I really was not too good a rider yet, and, riding bareback, I held on to the mane with one hand, the reins in the other, and when he started arguing and spinning in circles, I was about as uneasy as a cub bear on a greased fence rail.

No way was I going to let him get the best of me, so, after arguing for a while and me kicking him in the ribs with my bare heels, he finally went. I rode him a little ways and then turned him around for home to let him know it was my idea. I guess I was on the right track, for it worked some of the time.

I had an "ace in the hole," so to speak. When Dad came home from work, I asked him for advice and was told I was on the right track but that maybe he should take Bill for a little ride. I was told to go catch him and put the bridle on, and when I got back to the house with him, Dad was waiting with a red willow stick about as big as his little finger.

He jumped on bareback and away they went, out on the road plumb peaceful, but when they got to the edge of the field, Bill decided he would try going back home. But that day was a lot different deal. That day, the fellow on his back was a good rider; there was no uneasy balancing act there and no mane hold. Bill quickly got pointed out the road, the red willow was administered to the end where his tail was hanging and there was no more arguing. He just headed down the road, head up and ears pointed ahead, looking for more ground to walk on, and everything was fine. A nice thing about Bill: he never sulked when he got convinced his little tricks did not work. He took it in stride and that was it.

From then on, for a while, I packed the little red willow but did not have to use it, and, before long, it was left behind, that part of his education behind us. He tried it a little bit once in a while, just to see if maybe I'd weaken, but from then on we got along fine, and he was just becoming a very good little horse. Truthfully, in following years I think we learned from each other. In due time, I started riding him with a saddle, my sister and younger brothers could ride him, and he was behaving well. I guess he was what the cowboys would say well broke to ride.

The cowboy business was shaping up, but I had another problem: I did not have a cowboy outfit, like them real cowboys had. If I was going to be successful, I just had to get an outfit. Up till then, I'd been riding Bill with a snaffle bit, which was good, but he was reining and handling real good, so I was thinking I just had to get a fancy bridle, a pair of big rowel spurs, a big hat and a pair of chaps. These things were readily available, except for one thing—money. This was still the memorable Thirties.

Those days the T. Eaton Company used to send out a big mail-order catalogue twice a year, spring and fall. When the fall catalogue came out, I glommed onto it and right away turned to the important part where all the horse gear was. There, sure enough, was a pair of drop-shanked spurs with big rollers. They were the same style as my friend Fred wore; they were a must and they were listed at about $2.25 delivered. They were no ways near the quality of Fred's spurs, but they looked good and the price was maybe within my grasp by spring. Sure enough, there was a real port cowboy riding bit with medium shanks listed at, I think, about $1.89. So far, so good. There was a complete bridle with reins and bit, but at $8.95 it was way over my head.

I decided to buy the leather and make my own bridle and put shiny spots and rosettes on, which would look good at maybe half the price. I would tan my own rawhide for reins. That way, I could afford an outfit in time. I could get a whole handful of shiny spots and glass rosettes for about four bits.

Well, I needed a fair amount of cash, about $8.50 or $9.00 all told, but with good luck in hunting and trapping squirrels and weasels, I should have it by spring. The fur market had come up considerable: squirrel skins had gone from $0.07 a piece to $0.10 and a good, white, prime big weasel was clear up to 75 to 80 cents. Twenty-two shells were 25 cents for a box of 50 shots, so it figured out if you were shooting well, you had to make money. The financial future looked pretty good, and, by spring, I think I had about $12.00 or $15.00. Pretty good winter, huh?

I was looking forward to the T. Eaton's spring catalogue, and it finally came. I turned as usual to the important part and, sure enough, that riding gear was still listed. Down on the right hand corner of the page, I could not believe my eyes, was a cowboy hat—big, wide-brimmed, Carlsbad style, something like Hoss Cartwright wore on Bonanza in later years. It had a five-inch brim and a seven-inch crown with a crease in the front. I right quickly counted up my fortune from my winter furs. I had enough money, maybe a couple of bucks to spare. The first time someone went to town, the order to T. Eaton Co. was in the mail.

Spring was here, the grass was turning green, birds were back for the summer and the usual things, like planting and hoeing gardens, fencing, and milking the cows, were back in full swing. The economy had picked up some, Dad had opened up the camp and logging was getting underway. With Dad away at camp, it fell to Mother and us kids to look after things at home.

Everything went well, and we were getting pretty good sized: I was 14, and my youngest brother was six. With Mom as manager, we made up the crew and things were done. Of course, our mother was the hardest-working part of the crew, but everybody did their part.

I had managed to pass through the eighth grade that spring, so I was out of school, there being no high school close enough to attend and no money to board me out to go to high school in town, so I was home to work. That suited me fine. I never did like going to school, anyway. I do not think my parents were crazy about me not going to high school, but I figured a cowboy would get along just fine on a grade-school education, which I guess I have.

I needed a pair of chaps to go with the outfit coming from Eaton's mail order store. No money, so I would just make me a pair out of cowhide. I knew practically nothing about tanning hides, except that a strong mixture of soap and water would take the hair off, if it soaked long enough. I got me a dried-out yearling hide and took it to the swamp, there to be weighted down with rocks to soak in a water hole until it got soft again. I had to do that so I could fold it to fit in a big tub of soap and water to get the hair off.

After it soaked soft, I got a big tub full of strong, soapy water and put the hide in it, figuring it would take a day or two. A week went by and the hair still did not start to slip. I could not figure out why; the smell of that soap and hide sitting there in the sun should have taken the galvanizing off the tub. I turned the hide every day, even if it was tough to do; I was determined to make them chaps. Luckily, I had a strong stomach.

By the time two weeks had rolled around, the hair was coming loose; I hoped the hide itself was still good, for, by now, the smell of my tannery would have made a dog tuck its tail between its legs and give it a wide circle.

Another day, or so, for good measure, and I decided the time had come. I dumped the whole mess out on the ground, with a lot of choking and gasping and running off a ways for fresh air, and I finally got the hide stretched out on the grass, hair side up, a ways off from where I dumped the tub.

I got a few buckets of fresh water sloshed on the hide to wash it a little, not for cleanliness, mind you, just so I could breathe better. I stretched it out tight by nailing it around the edges to the ground, then got the garden hoe and scraped the loose hair off. It came off clean and looked good, not having rotted, as I previously feared.

The first step in making my chaps was more or less complete, except that the hide wanted to turn hard as it dried. By keeping it clamped down and drying it slow, with a lot of work bending and working it to keep it pliable, I guess I was winning. All this was between my regular work and chores, but I was determined to have them chaps.

I do not remember where I got the pattern for them shotgun chaps; I never did know why they were called shotguns, but I guess I should describe them. Shotgun chaps was quite a favourite style them days; they was something like a pair of leather pants with the crotch and ass end cut out. The front, of course, came up to your waist and had a wide belt, laced together in the middle in front with a shoelace and the belt buckle behind. You just pulled them on, same as a pair of pants, the legs being wide enough to just barely accommodate your boots.

The store-bought ones were of soft, thin leather or Angora goatskin with the wool still on, tanned soft, and usually had a pocket high up on each leg, very good for winter riding. I sure would have liked a pair of them bought ones, but the plain leather was around $20 or $30, and the Angora was around $40 to $60. This being the summer of 1937, they were plumb out of reach, which is why I went through the ordeal of tanning and making my own.

After much drying and working the rawhide to be pliable, I fashioned my chaps and tried them on. They was still a little damp but looked pretty good and was reasonable pliable. I hung them in the cool shade inside the barn, where I figured they would dry real slow and stay fairly soft. A couple of days later, I decided to give them a trial run, but when I went to get into them, it was like putting on a pair of stovepipes. They dried too fast, I guess.

After lengthening my stirrups, so I did not have to step so high to mount and so I did not have to bend my legs, I headed out to gather the milk cows. When the brush scraped across them chaps, going on the narrow trail, it sounded like a saw going though a board. Bill was somewhat annoyed at first but took it in stride after getting used to it.

I had a few sore spots on my legs when I got home, but it seems there is a price to pay for whatever you accomplish. By the end of the summer, after applications of used motor oil and a lot of elbow grease, I finally made the chaps easier to live with. I also made a pair of riding reins out of my home-tanned rawhide that turned out real good, and I used them for many years. I think there is a piece of one of them still around.

The long-awaited parcel with my spurs, riding bit, hat and leather for my headstall finally came. It looked like I was in business. I proceeded to build me a first-class headstall with the leather I got from Eaton's. I had ordered just enough to make it, so there was no room for mistakes, and I did not have any more cash to buy more. This masterpiece had to be right on the first try.

I took the measurements of Dad's bridle to get the right size, and then, after figuring out the design, I made the whole thing out of thin cardboard, so I could trace the pattern onto the leather. This worked really well. Any mistake I made could be made over on paper and the finished size and design traced onto the leather strap for the headstall, eliminating any chance of wasting leather that I could not afford.

The finished product, decorated with coloured glass, rosettes and designs with shiny harness spots, turned out very well. With my new bit on the new bridle and new drop-shanked spurs on my heels and my big new Carlsbad hat, I figured I at least looked a little like a cowboy should. Bill likely felt like

Art, dressed in his first cowboy attire, on Bill: "I was very proud of that hat, at least until it rained."

a Christmas tree with all them decorations, but, after getting used to them rawhide chaps, he was getting so nothing surprised him anymore.

Like I said, he was a really good little horse, and we just went to punching them milk cows. With a little imagination, they could be compared to longhorn range cattle, like in the western stories. After all, there must have been longhorns somewhere that knew their way home, same as milk cows.

A real money-making opportunity came my way in the summer of '37. Dad offered me a job helping him in the bush, driving the skid horse during the summer holidays. I was out of school, but during the summer holidays, my sister and brothers were home to help with the milking, hoeing the garden and chores in general.

What they thought of the idea, I do not know—them having to take care of the things I had been doing. Here I was, making all that money working in the bush, $2.00 a day and board, and getting out of hoeing, gardening and milking, except on weekends. Course it was plain to see that I really missed milking cows and hoeing the garden, but I needed the money, and I'm sure my sister and brothers understood and happily, or maybe reluctantly, took up the slack.

It turned out to be a good summer for me financially. By the time I had to go home when the other kids went back to school, I must have had at least 50 or 60 bucks—not bad for two months working in the bush. I had in mind that I should have a regular pair of riding boots, but they was as scarce in that country and hard to find at that time as teeth in the turkey gobbler. Even if the Eaton's catalogue had some, there was still the matter of money. I had some money from my recent job, but first things first.

My brothers were growing up fast, the oldest at the time being about 11, and becoming mighty hunters and trappers along with me. We all needed more traps, .22 shells and other things for our fur-gathering business, so I decided to buy some needed equipment and ammunition to capitalize on the fur market. Before another winter had rolled around, we had done okay. In the spring, we had gained a few dollars and were looking forward to summer, fishing, playing ball, riding Bill and, of course, reluctantly hoeing the garden and milking cows, but it all fit together.

We lived about six miles from the Indian reservation, and the folks there used to put on an annual sports day in May. This year, they decided to combine their sports day with a stampede, or rodeo, if you will. I sure didn't want to miss that; I'd never seen one before. My folks couldn't take the family, so I talked them into letting me go. I do not remember how I got there.

At first, I went as a spectator, but, when I got there, I discovered that there were no entry fees to pay, so I started thinking about getting in the bareback riding. After all, there were three prize monies up: $5 for first, $3 for second and $2 for third, and you could ride with a two-handed surcingle. The saddle bronc paid off at $10, $7 and $5, but I figured I had better start with the bareback. I had no way to get my folks' permission, but I figured they would not mind me going in the bareback. After all, I was getting pretty big; I had even shaved a couple of times, so I was getting growed up.

Them days in that north country, nobody worried about having a cultivated arena to put on a rodeo—just plain grass sod was fine. I did not see a cultivated, worked-up arena until years later, when I entered the bronc riding at a Canadian Professional Rodeo in 1946, but that is another story.

The arena was the baseball field fenced in with a good rail fence and it was big enough so they could still play baseball with lots of room. All grass sod, it seemed like it was big enough for a pasture. Right behind home plate was built the corrals and a single shotgun chute, kind of like any regular cattle chute, except at the front end where the rider came out was two gates, one in front and one on the side. When the rider nodded his head, both gates were pulled open, and horse and rider were plumb clear. It was really a good setup, except only one horse could be got ready at a time, but then, nobody got too excited if things went a little slow.

Somebody had thoughtfully removed the wooden home plate, but the ground where it lay was tramped plumb bare, no grass, and harder than bare ground in January. Everybody done their best to make a ride past home plate, or at least get to the grass before bucking off.

Well, my turn came to ride and, luckily, my friend Fred was there. He asked me had I rode a bucking horse before, and, when I said this was my first, he did his best to tell me what to do—to use both hands, as it was my first trip, that choice being optional. They were running in my bronc, a strawberry roan stud with a dark mane and tail, which looked about as wild as the hills he had grown up in. There was no doubt in our minds that that pony was going to buck.

Fred was helping me get down onto the bronc, which was standing still in the chute, but when the ass of my pants contacted his back, I felt his muscles tighten and quiver a little. Fred said, "Get up close to your rigging, take a good hold of your hand holds, hit him in the shoulders on the first jump out, lean back and watch his head. Try to get in time, so you do not hit him in the shoulders when his head is going down; when you are ready, nod your head." Well, those instructions were good; I figure I can remember most all of it. I nodded my head, the gate swung open and me and the roan stud was out on the baseball field.

Coming out, I reached and grabbed him in the shoulders with my heels, and if he had any notion about running, that changed his mind. He ducked his head, and it felt like I was on top of a cyclone, but I was still there and past home plate. I figured if I was going to win anything, I had better get to spurring. My mind was in a kind of daze, things were happening fast, but somehow I remember Fred saying, "Spur him when his head's coming up."

I could see this dark mane through the haze in front of me and reached high for his shoulders, but my timing was out; I reached for his shoulders just as his head was going down and he was kicking way up behind. Seemed like a post hammer hit me in the seat of the pants, and I took off over his head and landed on the grass sod. I looked back and, luckily, landed well past where home plate was, onto that nice, soft grass sod. So much for my first bronc ride, but I felt good, even if I didn't make no money. When I came back, Fred grinned and said, "For the first trip, you done pretty good."

Well, it turned out we all enjoyed the stampede—nobody was bruised up too bad. With some races, a baseball game and a soccer game later, it turned out to be a successful sports day. Those folks on the reserve had really organized a fun day; people came from miles, and many folks from the valley community helped with the rodeo part and entered the riding events. It was an annual affair and was looked forward to by everyone.

When I got home, I told my folks I'd entered the bareback. I was a little apprehensive, on account of going ahead without their permission, and quickly added I was in good hands, as Fred was helping me. Dad just grinned and said I should have asked before I left, but being as I rode bareback, he figured it was okay.

"You didn't get hurt?" he asked. I said no, I bucked off clean, and I really didn't figure on riding till I got there and found out there were no entry fees to pay. And, of course, I added that Fred said I done good on my first bronc. I did not really know it, but the rodeo fever was setting in.

CHAPTER 3

TEENAGE CREATIVITY

When the rodeo was over, it was back to the business of daily routine: fencing, chores, milking cows, putting in the crop and planting the garden. Dad was home during spring breakup in the bush, so the spring work all went smooth, with him and the big horses to put the crop in.

We used to plant a big garden, at least an acre or more, counting the garden, spuds and cow turnips. Cow turnips are kind of like sugar beets. We fed them to the milk cows in the winter to increase milk supply as well as to keep them in good condition. Grain was a mite scarce. Everything in the line of crops was cut for green feed. Mind you, we fed some oat bundles. There was no thrashing machine within maybe a hundred miles.

Getting back to that big garden. I think the land in those river valleys north of Hazelton had to be the best garden-growing country on the continent. Just right for rainfall, more than enough at times, and warm summer weather. Everything grew very well. Putting up hay and green feed was a problem some summers—just too much rain.

Besides garden stuff, spuds, hay and green feed, there was something else that grew better than anything: them damned weeds. It was a never-ending job to keep that big garden hoed and free of weeds. Seemed that by the time we had gone across it once, and that took about a week, we looked back to where we started and they would be big and green and growing tall. Dad helped us when he was home, but they just kept on growing. It got so we went to the garden quite reluctantly, but it had to be done.

By now, there were four of us boys wielding hoes, our youngest brother having been introduced to one at the mature age of about six. I guess, to start with, we must have convinced him that it would be fun. That novelty wore off fast.

We had to do something; just thinking about them hoe handles in our hands created a very uncomfortable sensation. Our neighbours had a horse-drawn garden cultivator. Pretty hard to get a chance to borrow that; they used it all the time, as their spud field, cow turnips field and garden was three times as big as ours.

The light finally came on—I had an idea. When we planted the garden, the rows were all straight and about 30 inches apart. I could build a horse-drawn cultivator that would fit like those store-bought ones. By this time, Bill had been broke to harness for odd jobs, so we had the horsepower.

I talked it over with my brothers, and, that one time, there was mutual agreement right away. Anything to get out of hoeing them cussed weeds by hand, we was sure going to give it a try.

The finished product was like a little three-cornered harrow, with homemade walking-plough handles on it, to steer it between the rows. A hook was on the point of the triangle implement to hook Bill onto. We had fashioned crude cultivator shovels—narrow, as they were from whatever strap iron we could find in the blacksmith shop—bent them to fit under the two-by-two wood framework and bolted them in place. There were lots of them; we were not going to leave any weeds unturned. We all worked at it, and it sure was worth the effort. It should have been patented: "The Handy Dandy, Super Duper Garden Cultivator." That is the way it turned out, when compared to those four garden hoes.

Now for a trial run. One of us caught Bill and put his harness on. The harness didn't exactly bring a smile to Bill's face, but being the good little horse he was, he came along to help. Down at the garden, the cultivator was already sitting ready for business. We were sure hoping it would work.

We hooked Bill up, then one of the younger boys climbed onto his back and picked up the short rope reins hooked to his snaffle bit, and we headed down the first row, me holding the handles and steering. When we got to the other end and looked back, what a beautiful sight met our eyes. The ground was cultivated, and hundreds of them big old weeds was lying there, toes turned up, wilting in the sun. Our invention was working. We grinned at each other, and we were even able to smile at them four garden hoes lying there idle.

Our cultivator was light enough for Bill to pull quite easily, and we done the whole garden in about half a day and a better job than we could have done in a week with them hoes. Besides that, it only took two guys, one to ride Bill and one to steer. We used our homemade cultivator for quite a few summers, and when it got too rickety to use anymore, there was money to buy a regular horse-drawn one, picked up in good condition second hand. Growing spuds and cow turnips and the garden was getting plumb mechanized.

Another winter came and went. We were all a year older. Everything was fine, except for one thing—there was a dark cloud on the horizon. Although it was far away, it was very real when we listened to the radio. For the last couple of years, that little guy with the loud voice and little black moustache had been raising hell over in Europe, and his armies had been running roughshod over most of the countries. The decision was made that he had to be stopped, and Britain needed help. All the countries in the Commonwealth rared up and said they were backing England.

Well, Jack Canuck did not lose any time passing the word out for everyone 16 and over to register. He no doubt needed everyone's address and what they was doing, so if this fracas was going to last very long, he would know where to send the invitations to join the party. I, of course, with countless others, got in on the registry, but I still had two more years before I was old enough to be any good.

Anything that was essential to the war effort was put on a rationing basis. That seemed to work well, and one thing for sure, the job market came to life. Where before there was not enough work, now there was more work than people to do it, resulting in people being frozen to their jobs at times, especially if it was essential work. All this started, I think, in August, but I will back up about three months to sports and rodeo time on the reservation in May.

As usual, we looked forward to the big event and, if I remember right, we were all there. That year, I entered the cow or steer riding, whichever kind of critter happened to run in the chute. This event was usually ridden with a loose rope, not a braided bull rope. Nobody had anything like that, but most likely they used a long halter shank gripped tightly with both hands. To make a long story short, I got the opportunity to kiss the grass sod for my efforts.

That year, there were very few bareback entries, so one of the guys marking the judge's card decided to take a bareback horse. Instead of using a bareback riggin', he just took him with a loose rope, two hands. The brown horse poured it on, and he put up a good ride. Somebody hollered, "Get off, you have rode far enough."

He came back grinning and said, "That should be good for second money." Everyone agreed, so he got his card back from whoever was holding it and marked himself in second place, same as the feller judging the other side was doing. It was the one and only time I have ever seen it done that way. Surprisingly, it seemed that everyone was satisfied that he had won second, fair and square, even if he did mark the card himself.

Like I said, the rules at them backcountry rodeos could be flexible enough to accommodate any situation, since it was usually just a fun day, during them times in that neck of the brush. Regular rodeos as a whole were taken serious-like and had rules that were somewhat different, pretty well like they are today.

The saddle bronc riding was won on a very fine-looking sorrel stud. When I seen that horse, I wanted him in the worst way, and I did wind up with him two years later, after he was gelded but still unbroken. In the meantime, it was back to the regular routine. We had really a lot of fun, too, fishing, hunting, riding, skating and skiing in the winter, and even a little cowboying, at times, as our cattle herd slowly got bigger than just the milk cows.

One of my friends, one I grew up and went to school with, had a brother-in-law with a roan mare running on the range that he needed to use. The mare was broke, gentle and plumb docile, but after not being used for a couple of years and raising two colts, she was hard to catch.

My friend and I undertook to get her for the brother-in-law, so we saddled up and went looking for her. She was running on open range with the two-year-old and the yearling still following her. We had a fair idea where she was running, and, after a few miles of riding, we located her, the yearling and the two-year-old with a bunch of horses. Most of the horses were broke, some well broke, some green, and then some had never been touched. We figured if we could get the roan mare with some of the gentle broke horses, we just might talk her into letting us catch her.

It did not work that way. She might have been gentle, but she was a cagey old girl. In less time than it takes for me to tell this, she had us figured out and headed out, taking some of them half-wild, unbroken horses with her, including her two half-grown colts. They ran purty good through the bush trails for maybe a quarter of a mile and then settled down to an all-day travelling pace, the roan mare right out in front.

We stayed right with them, following them for miles, in circles and going straight. I think the roan mare figured on losing us, but we knew that part of the range as good as she did. When we started out that morning, the weather was good, but by the time we had followed that horse herd a few miles, it started to rain. The weather being nice and warm in the morning, we didn't have no slickers or raincoats—I'd even left my rawhide chaps at home—so now we was getting wet, and it looked like we were going to get wetter. It was raining good and steady. Well, a little water was not going to stop us. We went out to get the roan and did not figure on coming back without her. By that time, we had stayed with that horse herd for a couple of hours, and some of them young broomtails were starting to split off. That was okay; we just wanted the roan mare.

Before long, we were just following the three of them—the roan mare and her two colts. They were slowing right down to a walk and slow trot. Being there was no corral within miles, we figured they were getting tired—the old girl might just let us catch her, or else we could just herd them home. Her intentions were entirely different. No way was she figuring on being caught. Then she made a mistake.

We was coming down a brush slope onto a brushy flat with a little creek at the bottom. There were no trails here, and she was picking her way to find a place to cross, kind of following the creek. The creek had cut a trench in the ground on this flat place that was maybe four feet deep and four or five feet wide. In one place, it went on and then doubled right back on itself, forming a U that was maybe 50 or 60 feet long and maybe 30 feet wide.

Following the creek to find a shallow place, she found herself and the two colts in the U with us plugging the open end. Everything came to a stop. We got off our saddle horses, my friend took the halter he was carrying and, being as she was gentle, we figured we'd catch her then. She could not go anywhere, the creek being too deep and wide, and we could plainly see she was not going to try it.

I was carrying a soft lariat rope, plumb raggedy, but being as it was still raining hard and the rope was wet, it had stiffened up some. I built a loop and tried to be ready, in case she made a break for it. She was standing plumb still, and my friend was talking to her and moving slowly to catch her. She stood plumb still till he put his hand on the side of her neck to put the halter on. Just like pulling a trigger, she reared up and made a break for it.

I was still plugging the open end of the U and trying to head her off. She reared straight up on her hind legs to pass me and when she was straight up and down I threw my loop underhand and hoped I would get her.

Somehow, that loop fit like a dog collar, but I was afoot and she was on the high run. I hung on and started dragging on my hip pockets through the small brush. I had only been dragged about six feet when my friend passed me like an arrow out of a bow. He grabbed the rope in front of me, and then we were both skidding through the small brush on our butts with the sticks a-flying, but we weren't about to let her get away. Being well halter-broke, the roan mare quickly came to her senses, stopped, turned and faced us. She had only skidded us through the brush about 20 feet. The jig was up.

Now she was acting plumb civilized, so we led her to where my friend dropped the halter in a mad rush to help me, put it on her and we were ready to head home. We went over to where our saddle horses were waiting, mounted up and headed out, my friend leading the roan mare with the two colts following.

It was raining harder than ever; seemed like the water was running down inside our collars and out through the ass of our pants. My big Carlsbad hat had gone plumb out of shape long before that, after a half dozen rainstorms, all the starch washed out of the brim. I was wearing a black hat that I had recently bought from a mail-order outfit in Colorado. It had been advertised as weather resistant and, of course, I figured that meant waterproof.

It was weather resistant all right, but only to dry weather, wind and sunshine, as I found out that day. The rain worked its way right through it, taking a very large part of the black dye with it. My friend said, "Your hat is leaking." I could see why he noticed it when I got home and saw in the looking glass where my face and neck was plumb black, clear down inside the collar of my shirt.

We was riding along, soaked to the skin—luckily the weather was warm—but feeling real good, as we was not coming home empty handed. I grinned a little and said, "We got her anyways, even if it was a wet trip." My friend grinned back and said, "Yes, I guess we will make cowboys before we make mothers." It had been a good day.

A couple of years before, my sister bought a guitar from T. Eaton Co. and had learned to play it quite well. Among all her other desirable qualities, like riding, milking and being mother's strong right hand in helping with feeding four hungry brothers, she was a wonderful sister with a beautiful voice—she still has—and sang at Christmas concerts, at home and, I think, at some parties. A wonderful sister—we all loved her.

Well, I could sing a little, so I saved up some money and got me a pretty good guitar from T. Eaton Co., and my sister proceeded to get me started. She is younger than I am but more musical and, I think, smarter.

Where she seemed to learn easily, I had to work at it, but I got so I sounded half-respectable. By this time, Wilf Carter was doing very well, and I sure enjoyed listening to him on the radio. For my money, I think Wilf was the best cowboy yodeler who ever shoved his hind legs into a pair of pants. On top of that, he was, and had been, a real working cowboy. I figured, with enough practice, I would sure like to be as good as him. I never did achieve that goal, although I did learn to yodel and learned many of his songs. I had practiced by myself for maybe a year and was getting the hang of it, and I was getting less shy about anyone hearing me.

One evening later that summer, I had the three milk cows tied to the corral fence and was milking them. When the weather was nice, we would milk outside, being much cooler than in the barn. I always used to sing when I milked alone. The cows seemed to even like it. I figured they would give their milk down.

Well, that night, I got going on some of Wilf Carter's yodeling songs. I imagined I was getting this yodeling down pretty good, when in reality it sounded like a coyote with a bad bellyache. Dad was splitting wood at the shed some distance away, and when I stopped to catch my breath, he said, "Arthur, will you please stop that yodeling? Do you want them cows to go dry?"

I realized I needed more practice, a hell of a lot more, and only practiced when I was alone, like during riding or hauling hay. The horses, I think, learned to walk very fast to get home so they did not have to listen to me. I used to practice for hours, real quiet in the living room when everyone else was in the kitchen, just singing to myself and practicing the guitar—no yodeling.

After a while, it made my day when Dad would come in and say, "Sing something for me," which I did, being as he liked it. I was really getting the hang of it. His favourite song that I sang to him many times was "Rosalie Desert Rose." Every time now, when I sing that song, I think of him and the good growing-up years we all had.

The Hagen brothers. Standing are Henry and Art with his new T. Eaton's guitar, and below are Norman and George with Mickey, the family dog.

When Dad opened up the logging camp in 1937, they were skidding timber with horses. One morning, he went out early to feed and harness the team in camp, and there, between the team, staggering around and learning to walk, was a gangly sorrel colt. His mother was not supposed to be in foal, and being she was a big mare and naturally big bellied, somehow or other, no one had noticed. The colt was small when he was born, so I guess it was understandable, but he was surely a catch colt, born out of wedlock, so to speak.

There was nothing to do but build a box stall in the corner of the barn for him, and after four or five days rest, his mother went back to light work and stopped by the barn every two hours for him to nurse. As time went by, he learned to eat oats and hay and grew quite well. As he got bigger, he only needed to nurse at noon during the day, so things got back to normal, and mother and son got used to the routine and did quite well.

For a colt raised in a box stall in a logging camp, he turned out to be a real good horse, very gentle, and grew up to be as big as his mother was. He had a wide white blaze on his face, so we called him Baldy, and in the fall of '39, he was big enough to break for light work and to ride a little.

Bill was broke to harness, so we hooked him and Baldy up together on the Bennett buggy and had a team for light driving as well as doing light work—a very good team for us boys, as the big horses were working in the bush.

Well, the time rolled around again when the spuds had to be dug and the vegetables and cow turnips harvested, about an acre and a half all together. It was a good crop; our homemade cultivator had worked well and was still hanging together. The garden stuff yielded well, having had plenty of rainfall during the summer.

Winter set in, my brothers and sister were back to school, and I was kept fairly busy with chores and feeding the cows and cutting wood. Now that I had a little team to drive, I was able to haul a little feed and groceries to camp. I made many trips over those eight miles, hauling light loads that Bill and Baldy could handle easy, being careful not to overwork young Baldy.

Spring came. We'd had a pretty good winter, us boys still in the fur business, and I got paid a little for hauling freight to camp, so by spring breakup at camp and seeding time at home, things was picking up all around.

During the winter, we had the misfortune of losing one of the big logging horses, Baldy's mother. Two and a half years later, we lost Dad's best logging horse in a bush accident. We had to get a new team. With old Darky and Sandy both gone, Dad had to rely on renting logging horses from the neighbours

Lars Hagen with the old team, Darky and Sandy: "Dad was the best teamster I ever knew; his horses would do anything for him."

for a time. Luckily, they were good and experienced horses, so that went well.

The time had come to get another big team of our own. Some 45 miles away was a wonderfully gentle, well broke, reliable, big team for sale, and Dad and I took the car to look at them and possibly make a deal. They belonged to an old fella who was going to retire, and one thing he insisted on was that they were only for sale if they were going to a good home.

The old fella knew my Dad to be a wonderful horseman, and, after talking for a while, he decided everything was okay and let us look at the horses. He said they were full brother and sister, seven and eight years old, with the gelding being oldest, and weighed about 1600 pounds each. We went out to the little pasture to see them, the old fellow having stated his price.

Well, there was no horse dealing. Doc and Daisy sold themselves that day; the price was very fair. They were a beautiful

Art and Rex the dog in front of Daisy and Doc: "We bought this team 45 miles away; I rode Daisy home and led her brother."

team and turned out to be part of the family. It was hard for the old feller to see them go; he had raised them both from babies. He said, "You'd really take good care of them?" I piped up and said, "You bet; any horse my Dad ever had loved him and about the other way around." That, I think, made him feel better, but it was not easy for him to say goodbye to them two big horses.

I was going to take them the 45 miles home by riding one and leading the other. Dad said to throw the saddle on the gelding, because he was well broke to saddle. I looked at them wide, fat backs and said, "No, I'll ride bareback. Daisy's back looks as comfortable as a chesterfield, and she's broke to ride bareback." That turned out to be a dumb mistake; on the way home I wished a hundred times I had listened to Dad. Daisy's back was comfortable and she was nice to ride, but with no stirrups under my feet my legs felt like they was stretched a foot longer after about 10 miles, and I had another 35 miles to go.

I decided to walk for a ways, but I was wearing a pair of them soled canvas running shoes, and they were a mite small. I do not need to elaborate on what they were like to walk in on a gravel road.

After a mile or two, I crawled onto Daisy to rest my feet and, of course, my legs went right back to hanging and stretching. Was I ever glad to see the stopping place Dad had arranged for me at a fellow's place at 11 o'clock that night, after 25 miles of road.

I sure realized that it pays to listen to your parents, even if you think you are all grown up and know a lot. I never owned another pair of running shoes for 52 years after that, until a bull hit me in the leg during roundup one fall and my foot swelled up so I could not get a boot on. I had to reluctantly buy a pair, and by leaving the laces out, I had something on, so I did not have to travel in only my sock. However, that is another story that I will get to later.

When I got to that fellow's place, he was in bed. I pounded on the door, and he came to the door, hitching up his suspenders. He lit a lantern and we went out to the barn to water the horses and put them in. He had hay and grain already in the feed box, having expected me to show up about nine.

We went to the house, and he said I had better have a sandwich before I hit the hay. He dug out a big loaf of homemade bread, some cold roast and a chunk of cheese. I never, ever had beef or cheese sandwiches that tasted that good. That loaf of bread looked well used before I was done. After a drink of water, I hit the sack and plumb passed out, until Gus hollered to crawl out and come for breakfast.

He figured I was pretty tired, so he let me sleep in clear to seven o'clock. He had already fed the horses long before. I headed for home after thanking him; the sun was shining and

I had only 20 miles left. I got home in good time. I felt a foot taller on account of my legs feeling stretched, but my feet was feeling worse than ever after walking on and off in them damned running shoes. I never wore them again.

After a few days for me and the horses to get over that trip, come about Monday, we headed for camp to skid poles and enjoy a long, hot, dry summer of horse logging. We ended up skidding out of the bush what was eventually to become power line and telephone poles, as most people know them.

CHAPTER 4

A YOUNG MAN'S DREAMS

The same year we bought the new team, there sure was a lot of good hay in the country. It was the hot, dry summer of 1940. Dad and my brothers were putting up the hay for winter feed, and me and a little Swedish feller who worked for Dad was in camp, skidding those power lines and telephone poles onto the big pile that was already on the banks of the Skeena from the winter pole haul. These big piles, sometimes having three to four thousand logs, were stockpiled all year for the annual river drive in the fall.

A clearing was made on top of the riverbank on a side hill with a little flat below to hold the big pile of poles; the poles were rolled over the first bank onto the little flat close to the riverbank itself. As the pile got bigger, it was just a matter of putting skids on top of the pile and rolling over the poles already there and so building the pile by extending it out onto the flat from the side hill.

That was the only way to get a big pile, as there was no big machinery to lift up the logs. We just rolled them on the level, until they fell over the face on the pile. Sometimes, on a big pile, by the time the rolling skids were extended and the pile was finished, it could often be 25 to 30 feet on the face of the pile to the flat below. This was before the big logging trucks of today came into their own.

George giving Daisy and Doc some attention: "They were a beautiful team."

In September, the company hired a crew of river drivers to keep the poles afloat until they reached their destination some 50 or so miles down river. The river drivers would make their way upstream to the farthest camp, where the rolling crew was already putting the poles in the water. From there, all the camps downstream did the same, and the river drivers worked their way downriver, breaking logjams and putting afloat any timber that had hung up on rocks or sandbars. They usually did not get the river cleared until about a month after all the camps had put their poles in the water.

My Swedish partner and I actually put in a good summer. The work was hard, but we were well organized. We singled out the horses for skidding, and we had a horse apiece. Oscar used Doc, and I drove Daisy. Doc would work on his own—just tie his halter shank to the hames and he handled those poles himself, slow and steady. I had to drive Daisy, as she would get in a hurry and run and that would never do as she might get hurt and bust things up. Things worked well; my partner was a good cook, so I looked after both horses, he cooked and we both washed the dishes.

We had a battery radio in camp and, very often, we listened to the Calgary Old Timers, with the pack rats loping forth and back on the roof of the cabin, maybe in time to the music. Them radios were kind of nice; we had not even heard of TVs. We would get music, news and sports. Listening to the announcer, with a little imagination, you could almost see the action.

I remember hearing the Joe Louis–Billy Conn fight for the heavyweight title. I guess they had one of those hanging microphones above the ring; we could hear those big fellers hammering at each other. If I remember right, Billy Conn was a very good boxer, and the judges had him marked quite a ways ahead of the Brown Bomber in points round for round. Things looked good for Billy around the 11th or 12th round. He was real fast on his feet and knew the game, and he managed to have kept Joe from connecting solid.

Oscar and I were listening to that scrap, and it seemed that Joe just might lose on points. Well, they must have been right under that hanging mic, and we heard Billy say, kind of confident and excited-like: "I got you now, Louis." The next instant, we heard a solid thud—Billy had dropped his guard for a split second, and Joe's left came through to Billy's jaw. The fight was over. I do not suppose Billy even heard the referee count. They claimed that being hit with Joe's left would be like being kicked in the head by a workhorse. My partner just said, "Too bad Billy, dat's what you get for being too sure of yourself."

It was sure interesting to listen to, actually. I enjoyed it more when we had to imagine what it looked like, rather than see it on TV. I do not know if Billy Conn and Joe Louis ever did lock horns again.

September rolled around, the camps put their poles in the river, the river drivers were working their way downstream and summer was pretty well over. We were all back home getting ready for winter. Dad was getting next season's logging operation underway, and, after that dry summer, it started to rain. I do not know how all that water got saved up in those blue skies all summer, but when it cut loose in September, it did not know when to quit. It just kept on raining till it turned cold, then it turned to snow and kept right on coming down. We sure enough had a "White Christmas" that year.

That winter I had the big team—Daisy and Doc—on the sleigh haul, hauling poles onto another big new pile on the landing. If I remember right, that big team and I added about 3000 poles to the pile that winter. All the snow made good sleighing, when it got packed down.

Spring finally came, and, with all the snow, it was a wet breakup, so the camp was closed and we went home and proceeded to put in the crops and the garden, and got our fencing and farming done. We got in some fishing and some fun times, did a little cowboying, went to the annual rodeo on the reservation and played a little ball—a regular holiday away from the bush camp for a while.

By now, the home place was taking shape. We put a new wire fence around the yard where the old slab fence was and worked the ground around the house so Mother could have the lawn and flower beds just the way she liked them. She sure planned the yard out nice, with lilac bushes around the yard just inside

The Hagen brothers and some of their friends on a hunting trip in the mountains west of Kispiox Valley.

The home we built. In 1934, we moved in: "Mom lived there for 15 years before she moved into town. We lost Mom in 1967."

the fence and grass and flower beds in beautiful patterns. She just loved working in those flower beds, said it was very relaxing. Her yard and flowers were really something to see. People who came by never failed to admire her beautiful yard.

Mother was a wonderful lady; she seemed to be the special combination of a super mother to us kids, a good wife to Dad and a lover of nature's beauty and all critters. She was caring, compassionate and liked by all who knew her. Mother was someone special in anyone's way of thinking.

Spring breakup was eventually over, and after the usual spring work at home, it was back to the bush. Now that things had dried up, we did more skidding and adding on to another big pole pile in readiness for the annual river drive. As every day was pretty well the same, it could get a mite monotonous, but, sometimes, in the evenings during the summer we would go fishing if we were not too tired, take care of the horses after work and listen to the radio or read western stories.

Bless those old western stories; we all read them and enjoyed them. They took us away from the daily routine to a different way of life, if only in our imagination. Light reading, not serious stuff that laid on your mind but entertaining in the way a western movie would be, just letting your imagination run free. I read about miles of grassland, thousands of cattle and wild horses, top cowhands, great bronc riders, outlaw horses, beautiful women, Texas and Arizona rangers, sheriffs, outlaws and gunmen, good and bad.

I cannot remember much about the stories in detail, except for a few. There was the man known only as Idaho, a roving cowhand and gunman who seemed to be there when someone was in trouble with the outlaw element. Many were the outlaws who hit the end of the trail when they faced him.

Idaho was very fast with a gun. He always drew last, triggered first and saved many good folks and damsels in distress. When it was all over, he mounted his big, brown horse and rode off into the distance, looking for a job and ready to help someone else.

Then there was the two partners who always rode together, kind of a "Mutt-and-Jeff" pair, for one stood six foot some odd in his socks, weighed around 250 pounds and rode a really big horse, described as a cheese-coloured roan. His saddle partner was only five foot something and rode a smaller horse to fit his size, a light-coloured bay. Same as the man known only as Idaho, they roamed the plains, worked here and there and were ready and willing to help anyone who needed help, especially if there was a fight in the offing, whether with fists or guns. I cannot remember their names.

Then there were the big ranches, coping with cattle rustlers, and, of course, a lot of them old ranchers had the most beautiful daughters you could imagine. Them western girls were, for the most part, good cooks and top hands with the cattle, rode good horses and carried a .38 on their hip.

Very often, when outlaws or rustlers or gamblers and bad men tried to take over the outfit, one of these girls would accidentally meet some handsome cowboy riding the range looking for a job. She would take him home and introduce him to her father. After supper, the rancher and he would have a talk, the cowboy wanting a job and usually getting one.

The western stories usually depicted these handsome cowboys as top hands who could ride anything with four legs and hair, handle cattle and rope expertly and were good with a gun. Sometimes the rancher would say, "So, can you hit anything with that shooting iron?" Then, of course, with the crew and the beautiful daughter watching, the handsome young man would pick up a rock in the yard, maybe big as a hen's egg, throw it in the air, draw his gun so fast his hand was just a blur and hit the rock several times before it hit the ground. He always got the job. When the fracas was over and the bad men bit the dust, things would return to normal, and he would wind up as foreman.

Of course, as time went by, the handsome foreman and the beautiful daughter fell in love, and there was a wedding. The rancher could slow down and halfways retire, knowing the young folks would carry on the western tradition, and the whole story ended with everything all right and everyone happy.

Since those days of the bush camps and western stories, I have often wondered why I never met one of those beautiful ranchers' daughters out on the prairie, for I have sure rode a lot of miles of range. Maybe I was born 50 or 60 years too late, maybe not lucky enough. Being still good-looking, I will just keep an eye out, so I do not miss her if she comes riding over the hill on a good horse with the wind blowing through her hair and a smile on her beautiful face. A guy can dream, can't he?

Well, back to reality. Summer was about over, the hay was cut, the poles were in the river and the river drive was on again for another trip down the river for the river crew. It was fall.

I went to town one day to pick up the mail. There was an official-looking letter from the government. Jack Canuck had sent me his personal invite to join the party over in Europe: "Get a medical from the doctor, be ready as telephone and telegraph poles are essential to communications. Keep working, we may not need you right away." I got a deferment till later.

By then, men was hard to get, and they was sure needed to keep the pole industry going. I was granted an extension from army duty to keep on working, along with many others, but we were also frozen to our jobs. Another winter rolled around, with us hauling communications poles out of the bush most every day and piling them on the riverbank.

Spring breakup finally came, and we got a break from the bush work then. The annual spring rodeo and sports day on the reservation was coming up, so we were all looking forward to that. When the big day rolled around, a bunch of us saddled up and headed out on the range to round up some bucking stock. Half of us were looking for cattle that might buck, for the steer riding, and the rest to bring in a bunch of horses.

I was with the cattle crew and got in first. When the horse herd finally came in ahead of a bunch of riders, I was there watching and that good-looking sorrel stud was with them, the same horse the bronc riding was won on two years before. He looked so good, I just drooled at the mouth thinking how great it would be to own him. I made up my mind I was going to find out who owned him and try to buy him.

The rodeo finally got underway, soon as the ball games was over. I entered the bareback riding and got my ear drove into the ground. I was finding out this bronc riding could be a little difficult, especially when you did not get a chance to practice.

Rodeoing and working in the bush were not exactly a good mix from a cowboy's point of view.

That year, there was a strawberry roan gelding that had never been ridden fair and square by anyone. Many good riders coming through had tried him at different times in the past, and he had thrown them all.

First, they put him in the bareback, and he did not buck very hard, so of course everyone figured he was slowing down, so they put him in the saddle bronc riding. Well, that was more like it; the roan gelding seemed pleased, and everyone who had tried him in the past had used a saddle. He did not disappoint anyone this time.

He stood in the chute while he was saddled, gentle-like, as if he was ready to take Grandma for a little ride to get the milk cows. The rider climbed down onto him, got his feet in the stirrups and nodded his head. Them gates on the shotgun chute swung open, and he stepped out and dropped his head. He just exploded under that cowboy's hip pockets, and about the third jump them same hip pockets was sitting on the baseball diamond.

At the end of the rodeo, the cowboy who had won the saddle bronc riding offered to try to ride him for a collection from the crowd. A rancher's wife also offered to ride a big red poll bull that was gentle but was also a good bucker, for a collection. All this as an added attraction for the day. The woman rode first and, being a good rider, made the whistle. Then it was the bronc rider's turn.

He was a good rider, and some folks figured, that day, the roan gelding just might get rode for the first time. Well, same as before, the gelding stood in the chute, plumb quiet; he was a gentle horse, broke to harness—he just wouldn't let nobody ride him. The sun was setting in the west, and while he was rigged out, he was quietly watching some horses grazing outside the fence, around the ball field that was serving as an arena.

The rider eased down into the saddle, set himself and nodded his head. Same as before, the gate swung open, the roan stepped out, down went his head and he just exploded. The rider was still in the saddle on the third jump, so the roan gelding bore down. I have never seen a horse buck like that—he went so high in the air, rolled over on his side in midair, and I figured for sure he was throwing himself. The setting sun was shining on his belly and when he came back to earth, all four feet was under him and he was getting tougher every jump. He and the rider parted company right then. As far as I know, no one ever rode him successfully with a saddle.

The collection amounted to about $7, which the lady bull rider and the bronc rider split. Course, that was not too bad for them days, as the bronc rider only got $15 for winning the bronc riding during the regular contest, on another horse.

There have been some notorious bucking horses in North America through the years past: Scarface and Tumbleweed, Midnight and Five Minutes to Midnight, Snake and Devil's Dream, Badger Mountain and Stormy Weather, Yellow Fever and Blue Bill, just to name a few. I am firmly convinced, looking back over the years and seeing a lot of those good horses buck, even riding a few, that the little 1300-pound roan gelding that I drove on the hay mower and dump rake could hold his head up proudly as an equal with the best of them. There is no doubt in my mind that if Old Dutch had been on the rodeo circuit, he would have been a famous bucking horse in the same class as Midnight. He might even have matched Midnight's success of being retired as a saddle bronc without ever having a cowboy stay on him long enough to qualify for a score.

My mind was still on that beautiful sorrel with a perfect white diamond on his forehead and another smaller diamond on his nose, the two diamonds connected by an even white strip along his face. I did some inquiring and found out he belonged to an old-timer living in the village on the reserve. He had been gelded and was for sale; the price was $55. I did not have $55 right then, but I had to go back to work in the bush right away, as spring breakup was about over. I was hoping that no one else would want him, as he was an unbroken bronc, only halter-broke.

I did not get back until on toward fall. After the poles were in, I saddled up Bill and rode down to the reserve to do business with the Indian old-timer, named Richard, who owned the sorrel. He was an old friend of Dad's, couldn't speak much English, but his daughter who spoke good English interpreted for him.

I figured on doing a little horse dealing and offered him $50 for the sorrel. He just shook his head and said, "Damned fine horse, $55." The look in his eyes told me there would be no dealing, the price stayed. I was not going to miss this horse for $5—the $55 was a fair price, and I just thought I'd try my hand at a little dealing. I gave him the $55, he counted it, put out his hand, we shook on it, he said deal and I said deal. He said, "He is yours now, you ketch him." I owned the sorrel gelding. I went out on the range and caught him, broke him to ride and he turned out real good, a hell of a good walking horse and smooth to ride.

I was still frozen to my job, so it was back to the bush for the winter, which passed quite uneventfully. Except for a log dropping on my foot, making me pretty lame for a month or so, and falling off a logging sleigh and cracking a couple of ribs, the winter passed with the usual work going on. I was not hurt enough to have to go to the doctor or lay off work. As I was on the sleigh haul, I did not have to do much walking, and, though it hurt some, I was able to keep on working and was back in comfortable shape by late winter.

Well, the usual spring breakup came, and we went home to put in the crop and garden, getting ready for another summer. It was sometime in June that I had an experience that I never will forget.

Baldy, the colt born in the bush camp, was by now full-grown, well broke and a good workhorse. He was running out on the open range somewhere on the reservation, and we needed him. I saddled up my sister's sorrel gelding and went out looking.

I met a neighbour, a small rancher who lived along the river, and asked if he had seen our horse. He said he had not, so I said, he must be down on Stony Flat, along the river. The rancher said he had a two-year-old colt down there that would likely follow my horse and asked me to leave him behind if at all possible, so he would not get too far from home. I said okay.

I got down to Stony Flat, and there was Matt's colt, all alone; our horse was not there. Sure enough, the colt started to follow us, and being he was a big, lazy, easygoing colt, I figured I'd just let my horse, Mike, lope away from him. That worked real well; the colt did not bother to follow that fast, and we were leaving him behind.

Well, Mike was a real travelling horse and liked to lope, and we were heading toward home as it was getting close to sundown. We were loping along slow and easy, and all of a sudden Mike caught his front feet on a hogshead—you know, those grassed sod humps in the ground, look like grassed-over anthills.

He turned end over end and landed on his back. When I felt him go, I jumped somewhat sideways so he did not land on me. When he got up, somehow that oxbow stirrup had not come off my right foot and he got up with me hanging up. There I was, the right stirrup had come over in front of the saddle, twisted and locked my foot solid, leaving me hanging on his left side with just my shoulders touching the ground and my left leg waving in the air. I thought for sure I was seeing the sunset over the mountains for the last time. I got this view from under his belly.

Strange as it might seem, I was not scared at this moment but was sure he would run. We were in a two- or three-acre clearing surrounded by second-growth poplars, with cow trails going through them. It does not take no genius to know what would have happened to me if he had run. He was quite a lively, high-strung 15-year-old.

Mike stood as still as a rock. The long bridle reins had fallen on the ground in front of him; seeing them, I crawled on my hands, talking mighty nice to that old horse, and managed to get hold of them. I felt a little better now—maybe I could keep him in a circle in the clearing if he did run, so I wouldn't get busted up in them trees, and hang on his side somehow and get loose.

Old Mike did not move out of his tracks, so, having the reins over my arm, I climbed up my own leg until I got hold of the left stirrup. From there, I managed to grab the long, front saddle laces and finally the horn. Do not ask me how I managed to do this—I was desperate.

With me hanging on his left side, with my right hand on the horn, I had to double up and use my left hand to free my right foot from the stirrup, which was twisted up on his withers. I do not know how long this all took; it seemed like a long time, for I did not know how long he would stand.

I finally got my foot loose and fell on the ground. Through this whole thing, that sorrel horse never moved.

There was another hogshead right under his nose. I crawled over, sat on it and rolled a smoke. Where I had been plumb cool while all this happened, I now felt jittery, realizing that this had been too close for comfort. I finished my smoke, stood up, hugged that old horse, and said, "Thanks Mike, you just saved my life." I checked the cinch, stepped up on him and loped for home. Since then, I have made sure the stirrups will come off my feet under any conditions.

CHAPTER 5

DESTINED TO BE A COWBOY

It was late fall of '43 and we were getting ready for another winter in the pole camp. I went into town and picked up the mail, and there was a personal invite from Jack Canuck to come and join the fracas over in Europe. No ifs, buts or maybes. There was a railway ticket enclosed to Vancouver and the Little Mountain Barracks. The army bus would meet me at the Vancouver railway station on the morning of January 20, 1944; be there.

We had enough communication telephone and telegraph poles stockpiled that Jack Canuck figured I was needed in uniform instead of in the bush. At the appointed time, I left for Vancouver a-singing, "In the Army Now." I pulled into Vancouver—the bus was there and hauled a whole bunch of us, pretty well all working guys like me, to the barracks to get settled in for training. The first thing on the agenda was going through the health inspection system. That proved to be an interesting and sometimes embarrassing thing for us backwoods country boys.

We got into a big room where the doctors were working, and the first order was to strip off our clothes and put them in separate piles along the wall, where we eventually got back to put them on. When they said strip off your clothes, that is just what they meant. We were all lined up buck naked like the day we were born.

One fellow, being shy-like, more than the rest of us, left his shorts on. In no time an officer said, "Get them off. You ain't got nothing under them shorts to hide, anymore than the rest of them. There is a pile of towels there, grab one and wrap it around your belly, all of you guys."

Well, that made us feel less embarrassed, on account of they had women working in there on all the paperwork, and they was parading by forth and back in the course of their duties. They never paid any attention; I guess by then they'd seen enough bare butts to last them for the rest of their lives.

You talk about a medical inspection; those doctors never overlooked anything inside or out. Eyes, ears, throat, teeth— they shone flashlights down your throat to see clear down to your gizzard and then turned you around and said bend over and looked up your butt end. Seemed to us like they were trying to see daylight through our teeth from the bottom up.

Well, we finally were done, and they told us to go find our clothes and get into them. We zeroed right in on our clothes piles; it was nice to get out of them towels. The towels were okay for me, being skinny, but some of them big fellers were not so lucky. The towels was small enough they didn't go all the way around some of them big guys, so they had to kind of shift them when the women came by, coming and going to different offices.

Some fella in uniform showed us where to get some bedding and a place to sleep. We went to some guy called the quarter-master to get blankets. By the size of him, I thought he was big enough that he did not need the other three quarters. Size means nothing in the army; they welcome you whether you are pint-size or overgrown, as long as you are in good shape.

In my case, they called me back to some of those doctors, a couple of days running. The first time through, they put that air-squeezing gadget on my arm and was looking at something similar to a big thermometer. I had no idea what they were doing. The next day, they done it again and said to go lie down in the other room for an hour, and they tried me again. I still did not know what it was all about, and they did it again the next day. I was starting to wonder what it was all for, maybe there was something seriously wrong that they were not telling me. I felt fine and did not suppose it was anything that might make me cash in my chips.

In the evenings, after we lined up and were fed at the mess hall, we would wander down to the cantina and put in a little time before turning in, playing the jukebox and maybe having a drink. They played one of Wilf Carter's records that I think everyone liked, because he sang "I Bought a Rock for a Rocky Mountain Gal" all night. We had to hit the sack at 10:00 PM because that was lights out.

Then somebody came and told me to go to one of the offices where the girls were working. An attractive young lady smiled and said to come in; I told her my name, and she said she needed some information and papers to fill out. I figured it had something to do with being sworn into the army. I had been to see one of them army head shrinks the day before. He was a nice fella and said I would do fine, as my attitude was good.

While this good-looking gal was typing them papers, I was looking over her shoulder and saw something about two cracked ribs. How'd they know that? It happened two years before and didn't hurt no more, same as a bone in my left foot that still hurt me a mite, but I didn't tell them.

Well, I guess them doctors did not miss nothing with their poking and prodding. She was done and I signed a paper and figured they would fit me with a uniform. She handed the papers to me and told me to go in to some officer to be cleared.

The officer looked at the papers and pulled out a little brown slip that said rejection on it and 4F. He said, "Go on home and go back to work; I guess you are not in good enough shape for us just now." He gave me another slip and told me to get in line at the paymasters to be paid for my time. I got $1.50 a day and board, a return ticket home and a ride on the bus to catch the

Henry atop Dusty: "I bought Dusty from a fellow out on the Kispiox Reservation; it was my first horse-dealing venture."

train. My army career was over. I did not know why. I figured I was in top shape but got it kind of figured out after I went back to work in the bush.

The rest of the family was surprised and, I think, pleased to see me walk into the yard at the farm after only being gone less than two weeks. Dad did not have anyone to replace me, so I still had a job in the bush.

When I got back to work, I got plumb tired and stumbly by the end of the day and my back would hurt. After sleeping all night, I was fine, but by evening I was all wore out again and kind of light-headed. Well, this went on for about a week, so Dad said to take a day or two off and go and see the doctor. I did just that; he overhauled me and said he could not find much wrong.

Then he put that air gadget on my arm and was looking at that overgrown thermometer. After a couple of tries, he said, "It is out of the bush for you, and I do not want you to do a damn thing for two weeks." I said, "How come?" and he said, "Your blood pressure is excessively high, and it will take a lot of rest and medicine to bring it down."

He gave me a bottle of pills and said to take four a day—morning, noon, supper and bedtime—and remember, no lifting or work. I said, "What is high blood pressure? I am plumb green about them things." He thought for a while to try to explain, then he said, "Suppose you've got a pressure pump, pumping water through a half-inch hose at say 10 gallons a minute—you can figure there's some pressure on the side of the hose." I said, "Yes, I can see that."

Then he said, "Now suppose somebody drives over your hose and breaks it. You still need 10 gallons a minute of water, but you only got a 3/8-inch hose to replace it. It stands to reason that there's going to be a lot more pressure on the sides of the small hose to produce those same 10 gallons a minute and harder on the pump." I said, "Yes, I can see that."

"Well," he said, "that's how high blood pressure works. For some reason, your blood veins and arteries shrink and get smaller, and your heart is the pump. Those pills, along with lots of rest, will relax your blood vessels. That will give things a chance to be right again. Don't forget what I've told you and get careless. Come and see me in two weeks."

Well, I done as he said, and in two weeks, I was a lot better. He let me go to work and try cowboying and ranch work and said to come back in another month, and I was pretty well straightened out. Been cowboying and arguing with that blood pressure ever since. He was a damn good doctor and explained in language a fella could understand, instead of them long-barrelled professional words some of them used.

After that, it did not take a genius to figure out what them army doctors' decision meant. I guess my boyhood dream of being a cowboy had come true, or at least was started, for I had a hell of a lot to learn to become a good hand. But I never figured I would get started for a reason like that. I have been a cowboy and ranch hand ever since, for more years than I like to count. Still in good shape, healthy, happy, still riding and okay, yes, still watching my blood pressure and taking medication, but that is okay; keeping in shape is the main thing.

I headed east on the train to a town called Burns Lake, where there was supposed to be some small cattle ranches. After getting a room in the only hotel there, a small hotel with a false front, I inquired around. The hotel man said there was a small ranch north of there, along Francis Lake, that was looking for a man. As luck would have it, the owner came to town the next day. I got the job and a ride back the 17 miles to the ranch.

It was a small outfit, more of a farm than a ranch. I done everything—feeding, choring, cutting wood—but not much cattle business. I never stayed too long. The folks was nice people, the grub was really good, but the pay was low, and when he sent me out to work in the bush cutting rails, I figured I'd better listen to the doctor and bid that outfit so long after a couple of weeks.

I headed back west and went to see an old rancher living in Smithers. He had a pretty good cow outfit 35 miles east of town. I got on with him but had to wait two weeks until he got back from the Kamloops bull sale. He said, "If you can find a short job for two weeks, when I get back, the job is yours." It was a regular small cow outfit, I suppose about 150 head. It was what I was looking for.

In the meantime, I had to find a job, so I could eat and have somewhere to sleep for two weeks. It was still cold, and there was snow on the ground, sometime around the middle of March. I had a room, so next morning, I went to downtown Smithers and looked around.

I went into a gas station and asked the guy in there if he knew anyone around who might need a man for a couple of weeks. He said, "Go and ask that guy at the gas pump who's filling his gas tank." I went out, talked to him and explained the situation, and he said, "Sure, I can use you for a couple of weeks, as I have lots of odd jobs to catch up on." I asked what this job was worth; he said $2.00 a day, room and board. I said, "How about $2.50?" and he said, "Let's match for it." He dug a nickel out of his pocket and said to call it in the air as he flipped the coin. I chose heads and, of course, it came up tails.

I worked for him for 16 days and made $32.00, but his wife was a hell of a good cook and I had my own room in the house, so I put in a good two weeks. He was a nice fellow, good to work for. There was only one thing wrong. He was a dairy farmer, so I had to pull milk-cow teats twice a day, which is not exactly my favourite pastime.

Even though I spent two good weeks at that dairy farm, I was plumb happy when that old cattle rancher got back from the bull sale, and I went to work for him. Again, I was lucky; he was good to work for, too. No more money, but no dairy teats to pull; he had regular cattle and horses and was a straight cattle rancher. The rancher was a bachelor; he lived in town on an acreage in a big old house and drove the 34 miles to the ranch when he felt like it or needed to. I'd be the only one at the ranch, as he had moved the cattle to another place of his to feed for the winter, and, though it was early spring, they wouldn't be back till after calving time.

He picked me up at the hotel one morning, and we headed for the ranch. A nice, well-kept place, good house and outbuildings, big hip roof barn and good corrals and a nice little creek running through the barnyard. He showed me around and said, "You are on your own, just phone me if you need anything, or want to know something. There are half a dozen yearling colts in the barn to finish halter-breaking and a good old roan mare for you to ride, for now. Just look after everything; Jake will get you started before he leaves, and there is lots of grub in the house, you just have to cook it. Have to get back to town, see you in a few days."

Well, Jake showed me how to take over when he left, which was late that afternoon. I had nothing to do but settle in and do some cooking till the next day.

Next morning, I went down to the barn to look after all the colts and saddle the mare if I might need her. Them yearling colts was all standing in tie stalls plumb quiet, and I figured it was going to be easy. Jake must have had them pretty well halter-broke to be standing in the barn, tied up so quiet-like.

Well, I went to lead them to water, handle them, curry them, brush them and try to handle their feet. I could hardly get them out of the stalls; they were plumb gentle but only broke to be tied up, and I could not lead them out of their tracks. They were just used to coming in to be fed and knew their own stalls and were tied up for the night. They would just brace their feet and would not move, until you took their halters off and they would run out to the creek for water. I'd halter-broke a few young horses at home but none that would just stand there braced till you took their halters off.

Now, I was still pretty green, and I had run into something there I never ran into before. I got through that first day by turning them out loose, and, at night, I opened the door of the barn; they all came in for feed and went into their own stalls to eat and get tied up for the night.

One thing for sure, Jake had gentled them very good, but he was gone and the boss wanted these gentle boneheads so they would lead nice. They were yearling workhorse prospects that now weighed about 800 pounds—me being maybe 145 pounds at the time, I was no match to try them by straight strength. They would not even pull sideways, just bent their necks and braced themselves. I could not help but wonder what Jake had done, besides getting them plumb gentle, which of course was good.

Well, I was doing a lot of figuring to decide what was the best way to handle the situation. Being kind of green did not help either. I got lucky; after I'd had supper, I noticed that Jack, the ranch owner, had quite a well-stocked bookcase. I browsed through it for something to read to pass the evening and stumbled onto a big old veterinary book about three inches thick. Damned if half of that old book was on training horses, I think probably written by Professor Beery, the fella who started the Beery School of Horsemanship, which, as far as I know, is still operating.

I spent all evening on that book. It was illustrated, so I learned a lot of different halter-breaking rope hitches that really worked. When I tried them, I had the colts leading in less than a week. The boss was pleased and figured I was a fair hand. I let it go at that. I was not about to tell him that the old book in his own bookcase had saved the day for me. It turned out to be a good learning experience, and I use those old ways to this day, when I have to.

One day, the boss came out from town and decided there was a three-year-old mare in the horse herd that should make a fair saddle horse. Had some workhorse blood in her but not too big. He said, "We will get her in, and you can try her; she is gentle."

We could not catch her, so we had to run her into the chute to get a halter on her, as I was not much of a roper at that time. "Hell," he said, "we got her in the chute, let's saddle her." I did not have no rigging yet, so we got a ranch saddle out of the barn and got it on her. I tied a piece of rope to the halter shank to lengthen it, and, as she was halter-broke, we let her out of the chute and into the corral. She buried her head and tried to buck the saddle off, but with me hanging onto the lengthened halter shank and pulling her sideways, she quit easy.

"Well, she looks pretty good to me," old Jack said. "Put a bridle on her and get on her." I was green, but I could ride pretty good, so I said, "Okay, where is the snaffle bit?" He said, "I do not have one rigged up; this will do," and he handed me a regular bridle with a port racking riding bit on it. It did not look too good. At this stage of the game, it is hard to pull a horse around with a port racking bit till they learn to neck rein. This was the very first time that mare had ever enjoyed the scenery looking through a bridle. She accepted it pretty well and, after a while, quit trying to chew the bit and spit it out and just stood there with the saddle and bridle on.

Jack said, "Go on, get on her, she cannot buck you off in this little corral." I said, "Okay. I do not like the bridle because I do not figure I can have any control, but she cannot go anywhere except around inside the corral."

I was lucky; she just humped a little and went to walking and trotting wherever she wanted to in the corral. I figured that was good, she was getting used to being ridden; a few days in the corral, and we would get along fine.

We were coming around in the small corral for about the third time, looking good. "Hell," Jack said, "she is fine," and opened the gate to a 100-acre field, turning us out of the corral before I could even protest that it was too soon.

Well, I figured, the wreck was on, and I was right in the middle of it. I did not have any control except by handling the reins real gentle to not get her on the fight. I was able to keep her slowed down nice and easy as we headed into that big field. I managed to keep her going half-straight to the bottom end of the field and then, when we got heading back for the corral, I figured I was in for a ride, figuring she would make a run back to the other horses.

I guess I was wrong, for she behaved good and, of course, I was not trying to make her do anything she did not want to. She wanted to go to the corral, and I was sure willing to let her. I could not do anything else with that bridle on her.

We finally got back in the corral, and I said to Jack, "Shut the damn gate before she changes her mind," which he did. I got off her, and Jack said, "I told you she would be easy to break." I did not know, except she did not try to buck me off. I just let her go where she wanted, did not have a choice. She sure as hell was a long ways from broke, but the boss was satisfied.

I still did not think he used very good sense, turning me out in the big field on a green bronc that had been introduced to a saddle and hard bit bridle only an hour before. Being somewhat green, I think I was damn lucky, or God must have sent his best angel to help me. I am still willing to give him credit for that. For the way it was done, I should have got in a man-sized wreck, but it all turned out okay.

Jack was right on one point: the mare turned out real well as time went on. I went back to a snaffle bit and gentle hand and rode her quite a bit. It was a couple of months and a lot of miles later that she bogged her head and gave me one of the toughest bronc rides I have ever had. Mind you, I was not worrying about any rules, just staying on her any way possible. When she finally quit, I was still on her, had lost one stirrup and we were both plumb out of wind. I just sat there for a while then carefully got off, checking the saddle and cinches. I climbed back on her, we went to work and, to the best of my knowledge, she never bucked again and became a damn good cow horse.

It was getting close to branding time; we had to bring the cows and calves back to the home ranch from the other ranch where they were fed all winter and calved out. It was a fair distance, but the boss took me in the truck to show me the way. The next day, I rode down there and stayed the night.

Next morning, an old top hand cowboy and I proceeded to move those cows and calves home. We followed a dirt road, being it's brush country. All went well, and I was learning quite a lot from this old cowhand about moving cows and small calves.

After a few miles, there was a turn in the road and I smelled a strong, unpleasant smell. My new, broke mare did not like it too well, neither. I said to Old Dutch, "What in the hell stinks so bad?" He just grinned and said, "Don't you know? There is a sheep farm just ahead."

We came around the turn in the road, and there it was. The cows didn't seem to mind and kept going, but my mare had never seen a "woolly" before, and there was a couple of hundred of them just inside the fence, watching us go by and chewing their cuds and bleating. I never could figure out how they could chew and bleat at the same time.

Well, my mare was getting a little panicky with the sight of that bunch of woollies and the fragrance arising from that sheep yard. Old Dutch rode over and said, "I will trade sides with you; my old horse does not mind them." I was glad to trade sides and get on the far side of the cowherd before something exciting happened, like having a runaway through that bunch of cows and calves, or getting bucked off on my ear. From then on, everything went fine. It was slow going, but we got to the ranch and put the cows in a small field for a couple of days to rest before branding.

Branding was on the coming Saturday. The boss hired a cook for the day to feed the branding crew. A bunch of neighbours came to help. I watched and listened and helped where I would not seem too green, as this was my first big branding with a crew. On the farm, we just had a few head, which was somewhat different. All went well, with the odd beer now and then; everyone was sober, and the drinking would have to come later if anyone wanted to.

We were all through, except for a yearling bull that needed castrating, dehorning and branding. Well, a couple of the boys stretched him out and got him done. They told me to open the corral gate and let him right out into the yard. As I was doing that, they were turning him loose, and he was not in what you could call a good humour. He spotted me in the middle of the open corral gate and, I suppose, blamed me for all that had happened to him, and he took a bead on me.

Well, I realized he was plumb serious about wanting a piece of my hide, so I headed for the open yard to outrun him. I ran pretty near a hundred yards across that yard, not looking back and figuring he was blowing snot in my hip pockets.

Well, I won the hundred-yard dash, climbed up on the fence and looked back—no bull and all the boys standing at the corral laughing their guts out. A fella named Pete said, "You should be in the Olympics, the speed you got. That bull quit you after the second or third jump and went out the side gate." I had to admit, it must have looked funny, me running for my life across that yard all alone with no bull after me. It took a while before they would let me forget it.

Branding being over, it was back to regular everyday stuff. One day, Jack the boss said, "That old snubbing post in the small corral beside the barn needs to be replaced; the old one has rotted and is going to break. Cut down a jack pine and make a new snubbing post—you'll have to dig out the old one, but the ground is good, no rocks—and peel it." I said okay. I replaced the post, dug down about four feet and tamped it good. It looked good; I was proud of the job.

The boss phoned out from his house in town and asked how I was making out. I said, "She is all done, got a brand new shiny snubbing post; all I have to do is peel the top end. I left it so it would not be so sticky to handle. I peeled the bottom end that is buried in the ground. I will peel the top end first thing in the morning."

He said, "Good, I will come out and give you a hand. We will get that cow in with the bad hind feet and trim her up before you put the cows up on the summer range." We had to get her in, rope and snub her to the post and stretch her out on her side to work on her feet—there was no doctoring chute. Those days, those things were done with ropes. He said she was a gentle old cow and would not give us any trouble.

The corral we were going to be working in was an old exercise pen for a workhorse stud he used to have, so it was built real sturdy out of logs six to eight inches through, about six feet high and some 40-odd feet across, with the new snubbing post right in the middle and no corners. It was plumb round.

We opened the heavy outside gate and went to get the cow out of the other pen. We were afoot, but the old cow seemed gentle and handled well. Now the story changes.

When she realized that she was locked in that round corral all alone, she got a mite panicky and not so docile. I had a 40-foot rope and got her by the neck as she was running by, on the first try. That did not suit her too well, and she was getting plumb unfriendly.

She saw Jack across the corral and went for him. Jack was heading for the top rail of the fence on the high run, screaming to me, "Snub the son of a bitch!" I'd already thrown a dally onto that new snubbing post, but it was June and the sap was running in all the trees; I'd just peeled the top of the post that morning and it was still slipperier than an Olympic skating rink.

I was bracing my feet and managed to slow that cow down, with the rope sliding around the post; my feet were skidding, the cow was pulling, wanting to get at Jack, and he just made it up the fence before she got there. By then, she was just about as unfriendly as a cow can get. Jack was 68 but was more like 18 that day. She turned her head and spotted me hanging onto the rope by the snubbing post, and, being as she could not get Jack, I would do fine. The dally was still on the post, and I backpedalled as fast as I could to take the slack out of the rope and try to get her snubbed to that post. I succeeded, so I thought.

That cow weighed about 1200 pounds; I was about 150 pounds at the time, and she still wanted me bad and kept on a-coming. My boot heels were making a number 11 in the dirt, skidding toward her, that rope spinning on that greasy post like a well-oiled pulley.

Jack was hollering, "Hang on to her, boy!" I did not need no encouraging. I did not dare let go or she would get me. With her pulling, I was sliding right into her unfriendly face. My guardian angel must have been on the job, again, for by some miracle the rope locked over itself on the snubbing post with about a foot to spare, with her blowing snot on my belt buckle.

Well, it was a stalemate. What do we do now? I could not let go when she was still serious about getting a piece of me. As luck would have it, the sliding door from the corral to the barn was open a small crack, about an inch or two. Jack said, "Hang on to her," and jumped off the fence and made a run for the door.

As soon as she saw him move, she forgot about me and tried him again. I managed to slow her down enough that Jack beat her, got in the barn and shut the door. She had her back to me, so I dropped the rope and made it to the top rail of the fence. Well, she ran around that little corral a time or two and stopped at the gate, still dragging that 40-foot rope.

I looked down, and the rope was right along the fence below where I was sitting. I climbed down outside of the fence, careful-like, not to attract her attention, and reached through. I got the rope easy-like and tied the end to a big log in the fence. Well, she came up the other side of the corral and, of course, the middle of the rope caught the snubbing post. She was still ringy, but with the end of the rope tied to the corral, the corral was not going to move. She wound herself up short, going around and around that snubbing post. We got her.

We just got another rope and snared her back feet, stretched her out and Jack trimmed her feet, with me kneeling on her neck, after we had loosened the rope so she could get her wind. I opened the gate, took the rope off her front end, Jack untied the heel rope from the corral fence and kept the dallies. When we were ready, he dropped the dallies and climbed up on the fence and I ran for the other fence and climbed it. I looked back. The old cow got up quiet-like and walked out the open gate as if nothing happened. She was not locked in that damn corral anymore. Since then, I have seen the odd old cow go plumb haywire if it is locked in a corral all alone but be plumb gentle otherwise.

A few days later, I was alone at the ranch. I saw a cowboy riding in from the north. He rode into the yard and we introduced ourselves. His name was Roy, and he had a small outfit south of the ranch. He said there was not much doing, so he figured he would ride down and get acquainted with the new fella Jack had hired, being as we were going to be neighbours. It was about 11:30 in the morning, so I said, "Get off and rest your saddle and have some dinner." We put his horse in the barn and went to the house, where I proceeded to make something to eat.

I had dinner just about ready when the boss drove in. We said hello all around, as they knew each other. Jack said to me, "Help me pack the groceries in." I said sure, and when we got out to the truck, he asked, "What's Roy doing here?" I said he just rode down to visit, as he said he was not busy. The boss said that he must want something and doubted if Roy intended to borrow or pay for it.

I asked, "Do you mean he could be a little light-fingered?" The boss said, "That is just what I am thinking. You watch him close." I said, "I'll be damned. He seems like such a nice fella." Jack just kind of grunted and said, "Sometimes them nice fellers are the ones you have to watch. Anyway," he says, "he is sure welcome to stay for dinner, which is okay, so let's go eat."

After dinner, we went down to the corral to look at the mare I was working on and riding, all three of us. I thought the boss was hoping Roy would ride off right away, but he was in no hurry. He allowed that the mare should make a good saddle horse and then we all three sat in the grass in the shade of a building and bullshitted for an hour or so. I said I should go and fix that broken corral rail. Jack said to leave it until the next morning, when it would not be so hot.

I guess he had his reasons for keeping me there, as he soon said, "I've got to meet a guy in town in an hour and a half, so I got to go. Come with me a minute; I want to show you something that needs fixing when you got time."

We got to the truck; Roy was still lying in the shade. Jack said, "I just wanted to tell you to stick to that feller like a burr on a wool blanket till he leaves, even if it takes the rest of the day. I don't want him to ride away with most of the ranch tied behind his saddle." That was the boss, outspoken and straightforward.

Well, he headed for town, and Roy and I rested in the shade till pretty near 5:00 PM. A very restful day, you might say. He finally said, "I'd better hit the trail, don't want to be late for supper. The wife will have it ready by the time I get back." He stepped up on his horse and rode away.

I watched him ride till he was out of sight. I thought about my suspicious boss and if what he had told me could possibly be true. He was such a nice feller, it seemed. I do not remember ever seeing him since.

It was suppertime, and I had not been in the house more than a half hour. The phone rang and it was the boss. "Has Roy left yet? Did you stay right with him till he left?" I replied, "Yes, I watched him ride out of sight heading towards home." "Good!" Jack said, "You've done a good day's work."

A few weeks later, I had to leave and go home and help with the haying. It ended my first cowboy job away from home, but it was just the beginning of many miles a-horseback, looking after other ranchers' cattle. I rather hated to leave. For all of Jack's outspoken ways and straightforward rough language, at times, I think he had a heart of gold and was one of the better bosses that I have ever had. I learned a lot, and I will never forget him.

CHAPTER 6

BACK ON HOME RANGE

It was a little after the first of July when I arrived back on home range and the hay was ready to cut. The weather was good so we were done early as we had lots of help, with the four of us boys and Dad and the big team of horses.

There was a small ranch along the river north of our place that had a lot of hay yet to cut and stack. The hired man had left, so I went to work for George for the rest of the summer. George hired another young fella and an old friend of his, too, so we would get the hay cut and stacked while the weather was still good. In that country, if it started to rain, sometimes the wet weather would last a while. We were lucky that summer and had mostly good weather to finish his haying.

We were quite a crew, me and the neighbour boy, the boss and his old friend, Ed. Though they were good friends, the boss and Ed (both in their middle 60s) was always arguing in a good-natured way. Ed was always smoking his old pipe. He had chewed the stem off till it was only about half its original length, and half the time it was plumb cold and hanging upside down.

One day, the young feller asked him why he smoked that cold pipe. Old Ed growled and said he liked that old pipe and, besides, he would not burn any haystacks down and it was handy when he wanted it. I never could figure out what comfort or satisfaction he got from that old chewed-off pipe, out cold and hanging upside down.

Ed was a good man, even if he was a little growly, hard of hearing and liked doing things his way. Even so, he was good to get along with, when you got to know him. We actually had a lot of fun along with the work. Those two old-timers had some good stories to tell from the early days, and we young fellers learned a lot from them.

One day, we were pulling hay up into the barn, with the team hooked to a cable that was attached to the harpoon fork, a device stuck in a pile of hay to lift it into the barn loft. There was a long rope hooked to the harpoon fork's trip mechanism so you could jerk the rope when the hay cleared the slide and let it drop in the loft. The cable the horses were hooked to ran through a pulley in the peak of the loft and then down to another pulley hooked close to the ground so the horses could pull on a level line.

Setting the fork into the load on the wagon and setting the mechanism that turned the hinged teeth on the bottom of the harpoon fork crosswise to hold the hay till it cleared the slide left the 50-foot rope lying on the ground beside the wagon to uncoil as the horses pulled the load up till it cleared the slide. Somehow or other, the boss did not notice the coil and stepped in it, just as Ed started the team to pull the hay up.

Well, the rope somehow tangled and crossed on the boss' foot and he started up the side of the wagon on the hay hanging upside down by one hind leg. His weight tripped the fork out of the hay. Ed did not think he had taken the slack out of the cable and kept the team going. We all hollered for him to stop. Being hard of hearing, he thought, I guess, we had on a big load and urged the team to keep going.

By now, the boss was going up and over the hay. Realizing that Ed had not heard right, I ran like hell up to Ed and hollered "Whoa!" to the team. Ed growled, "What in the hell is wrong?" I said, "George got his foot caught in the trip rope and you are

pulling him up into the barn by a hind foot." Ed was as sympa-
thetic as hell and growled around his cold pipe, "Why in the
hell can't he watch were he put his damn feet?"

Anyway, he backed the team up; we pulled the cable back
and got George back down from the hay slide. George never got
hurt at all. It was somewhat humorous, and George even laughed
aloud that he had better watch where he put his feet with Ed
driving the team on the harpoon fork. Ed just glared at him,
sucked on his cold pipe and ignored George's attempt at humour.

Haying finally was done, and Ed and the other young fella
went home. George kept me on to get ready for winter. We had
to round up and ship cattle. I guess he had about 100 head, and
we had to wean and ship the calves and some dry cows.

Just like any ranch, there was lots of stuff to do before winter
set in. One was to dig the spuds, of which he had planted about
a half acre. One day in late September, George had to go to town,
and I had to start digging and sacking spuds. I used the team,
took the coulter, a round disk that cuts the sod, off the walking
plough and went down the rows ploughing the potatoes out.
Worked well. The plough was set to go deep enough to go under
the spuds, and the mouldboard, the iron that turned the ground
over, just turned the ground upside down and rolled the spuds
out. You had to scratch around in the dirt to get them all, but it
was a hell of a lot faster and easier than digging with a fork.

When I came in for dinner, the boss's wife asked me to keep
an eye open for George's good railroad watch he'd lost in the
same field two years before. After dinner, I ploughed another
row out and was kind of watching the spuds roll off the plough.
One of them looked different to my glance. I stopped the team
and scratched the dirt where I saw it, and damned if it wasn't
George's good watch. I very carefully tried the stem in case it was
stuck; it turned easy and, after a couple of winds, started to run.

It had lain in the ground two summers and one winter and run as good as it did before it got lost. They were sure pleased that it turned up. It was a pocket watch and had a gold case, worth quite a bit, even in them days. Railroad watches must have really been good to take that.

Quite a few of the old-timers carried those railroad watches. They allowed that they wanted to know the right time, if they carried a watch at all. Them days, as far as I knew, they were all pocket watches and amazingly accurate. They had to be. Railroad men all carried them as in them days there was no cell phones or two-way radios, and the trains ran on a strict time schedule.

My dad had one, and he would only check his time in the telegraph office or railroad station. One time the radio told the time, it was not the same as Dad's watch. He said the radio was wrong and would not change his watch. Two weeks later, he went to town to the telegraph office, and the watch was right on time. I never knew him to change it.

The railroads and telegraph were on the same synchronized time. Those days, telegraph was the only way to communicate along the railroad for any distance in case of an emergency. The emergencies those days consisted of side tracking an oncoming train to avoid a collision, or if the time schedule was crossed up somehow, or for a snow slide.

The fall work was done on the ranch with no mishap, so I went home. As my blood pressure was okay again, I went to work in the bush for the winter. Come spring, there was the usual spring work to do when the camps were shut down because of spring breakup. Then, of course, the annual stampede on the reservation was on in May. We could not miss that great event.

I had not had any kind of bucking horse practice, so I got in the cow riding, hoping to cash in on the $10 first prize that was up. The cow had other ideas, being as I was not much of a cow rider.

A long halter shank worked as a handhold. She was a waspy, ring-tailed old girl. To make the story short, the $10 eluded me, and I wound up with some green grass stains on my shirt. They were still using the fenced-in ball diamond for an arena.

We had an accident of sorts that year. A bronc rider from up the line came and entered in the saddle bronc riding. He was wearing a real nice pair of angora chaps. Those angora goatskin chaps were built for warmth, not bronc riding. That was okay, except they had a very wide, fancy, tooled belt that was cross-laced at the front with five or six holes laced like a pair of boots. They had a narrow belt on the back that buckled behind.

Someone said to this young fella, he should take that leather lacing out and put in an old rotten shoelace, in case the saddle horn got under his chaps belt, so it would break. The fella just grinned and said, "It'll be good; it fits tight so the horn can't get under."

Well, he got his horse, and about halfway through the ride, he almost bucked off over the horse's head. When he caught his balance and straightened up, the saddle horn got under that wide belt. Now he could not get bucked off; he was tied on, and that sorrel bronc kept pouring it on, with the saddle horn punching him in the belly every jump.

The horse started to weaken in his bucking, and one of the boys on horseback managed to get there and get the halter shank and snub the bronc to his saddle horn, and they got the rider off. He was one sore puppy. They wheeled him off to the hospital 12 miles away, where he stayed for three weeks. He was a tough son of a gun. He healed up as good as new, but I will bet he never rode a bucking horse in them angora chaps again.

With the reservation stampede and big dance over, we all headed back home to do what we did best: work.

One day in late May, somebody noticed a lot of smoke at the upper end of the valley. Someone evidently had a campfire that got away. Forest fire! We were all conscripted to fight fire by the forest ranger. It was close to a field we cut hay in, about 10 miles from home, so of course we all went.

It did not turn out to be too big a fire; we got it contained in about three days. It burned about a section of timber and brush and was not too big but hotter than hell. A few of us watched the burned area, and the ranger kept his eye on us for about a week. We cut burning logs and put them, and stumps in the burned area, out. I do not know what the big deal was; he was just particular, I guess. There was nothing to burn anymore, and the fire was slowing going out, just smoking here and there. I suppose he figured we had to earn our money the hard way, instead of just watching it go out. After all, the government was paying us so good: thirty-five cents an hour and board.

One day, we had been out early and patrolled the burned-out area. The fire was out, except for a few smoking stumps in the center of the burn. Everything was fine, as safe and secure as grandma's flower beds.

Well, the day was warm and sunny, and we had just got done sawing a three-foot cottonwood windfall into six- to eight-foot lengths with a crosscut saw by hand so we could roll the short log lengths over to put out some smoking bark under them. We were all getting tired from the work and long hours. Right close by was a small piece of ground that, by some miracle, the fire had gone around. It had a big spruce tree, also untouched by the fire, in the middle of it, with a nice bed of dry spruce needles under it. The ideal place for a little rest, which we all decided we needed. We lay down on the bed of spruce needles for what was intended to be about 15 minutes.

Pete, one of the fellers, said, "It is so nice here, and I am so tired, I could go to sleep." He grinned and said, "We had better not doze off, or, sure as hell, the ranger will come along and catch us." Another fella had his dog with him and said, "Don't worry, that half-breed dog of mine will wake us up if the ranger gets close." The dog was half border collie and half German shepherd.

We did not intend to, but damned if we didn't all fall asleep, including the dog.

It was a good thing I was a light sleeper. Some dry brush crackling woke me up. It was the ranger, less than a hundred yards away and coming right at us through a dry willow thicket on the outside of the fire perimeter. I reached out, grabbed the fella's arm next to me, and whispered loud, "Come to life, you guys, the ranger is coming." In less time than it takes to tell it, us six guys had scattered in seven different directions and was digging in the ashes to make like we was working.

I think the ranger knew we had been lying down, might have even seen us through the brush, because he was grinning and asked how everything was. We assured him the fire was out and everything was fine. "Well," he said, "it looks like the job is done, so you can all leave, except I would like one man to patrol the area for a week or so in case an old log or root smoulders underground, crosses the fire line, breaks out in fresh brush and starts up again. Any volunteers?" We were all tired of that firefighting, but finally the feller with the dog said, "Okay, I'll patrol till we're sure all is safe."

After he had left, Pete said I woke up so fast, I ran a hundred yards before I got my fire axe on my shoulder. Another fella said it was a good thing I stumbled over that good watchdog and woke him up, too. He might have kept on sleeping and gave us away. The fire was out, and our firefighting experience was over.

Another month, and we were haying. The weather was good, so all went well and we were done in good time. Dad had a huge pile of poles on the river back at camp, the product of the previous winter operation. The Timber Co. sent word to get the poles in the river, as the river drivers were coming. He had to hire

10 or 12 men to get them poles in the water, and he needed a cook. Who would cook?

Well, cooking for a crew was not exactly a favourite occupation anyone wanted, so things got quiet. Dad said to me, "You can cook pretty good, how about it?" I said okay. "Good," he said, "same wages as the logging crew."

I dragged my butt out of bed 4:30 the next morning, fired up the old wood stove and proceeded to put breakfast together for 12 hungry loggers. I cooked a big pot of coffee and another big pot of rolled oats mush, along with a pan full of bacon and eggs and hotcakes.

The hotcake griddle held eight hotcakes at a time. I was just staying ahead, them guys just eating them hot off the griddle as fast as I could make them. My god, I thought, if those guys got that hungry sleeping, what is it going to be like when they come in at noon after working all morning? I was about to find out.

By noon, I had cooked up a bucket full of spuds, a big pot of beans with bacon and onions, a bunch of biscuits and a pile of meat. When the crew went back to work, I was faced with a big pile of dirty dishes, and my culinary efforts had plumb disappeared. My one consolation: there was a half of the boiled spuds left to fry for supper and half the beans to warm up. Otherwise, it started from fresh, and they would be back hungrier than hell by about 5:30 pm. What a disheartening reality to tie into another pile of dirty dishes in the evening.

After two weeks, I had sure as hell made my mind up to not become a chef or even a cook of any kind.

The poles were in the river, ending another season, and it was time to start all over again.

Late that fall, I hired on at a lumber camp operating a sawmill for a retired bronc rider who had decided to go into the lumber business. It was a small mill, commonly known as a portable mill, as it could be taken apart and moved to various places in the bush where the timber was. As every aspect of the actual logging was done by hand and horsepower, it was cheaper to cut roads into the bush to truck the lumber out than haul logs any distance. It actually worked well.

There was a great number of small sawmill operations throughout the northern bush at that time, and most folks made their living, full time or part time, working in the bush. There were many small farm operations in the country, but income from seasonal bush work in winter was, in a great many cases, a welcome and necessary financial addition to the overall farming income. The retired pro bronc rider was cooperating fully with the reservation people to put on a pro-style rodeo in the spring, and we were looking forward to that.

Pete, my friend since the forest fire, and me were both working in camp, and as we were both aspiring young bronc riders, we needed some practice. We set up a bucking barrel that winter to toughen up on, and when spring came, we talked the owner into letting us practice on some of the workhorses that would buck, as there was a round corral at camp.

The boss did a little bit of horse-trading on the side, and one day, he showed up with a half-wild, young mustang stud in the corral. I do not know how they got him there. We were at work, and he was in the corral when we got back to camp for supper. He was not halter-broke to lead.

We found out later that the former owner had raised him, and he had been following his mother since he was little. He rode the mare to camp, into the corral with the two-year-old stud following, and left him there. The young steed was a little shy but seemed half-gentle. We packed water and feed to him and just left him, except to try to be friends so he would come gentle.

Come Sunday, we were not working, so Pete and me decided to play with the young stud, gentle-like, and try to lead him around the corral to get him halter-broke. We got him along the fence, and he stood and let us put a halter on him. Someone must have worked with him a little previous. Damned if he did not lead from the fence to the middle of the corral.

We figured it was going to be easy, but in the middle of the corral, he stopped and refused to move another step. Coaxing and pulling the halter, no way, he would not budge and went to sulking and laying his ears back.

He started so good, we were in no hurry to put any nerve hitches on him. I pulled on that long halter shank, and he just braced his feet and would not move. Pete happened to be packing an extra halter, and he said, "Maybe he'd move if I slap him on the ass with it, to get him started again." I said, "Try it, maybe it will work."

The stud was madder than we realized. We had not roughed him up at all, and when Pete slapped him, he came straight at me like a shot, with ears back and his teeth bared and mouth wide open. I tried to outrun him to the fence, but his teeth hit me between the shoulder blades and knocked me flat on my face.

Then he reared up and tried to stomp me, but my guardian angel was on the job, and he landed with one foot on each side of my ribs and proceeded to bite a chunk out of my back. He had enough pressure on my back with his teeth; he held me down, and I could not get up, so he went to chewing on me.

It happened so fast, he got a few bites in before Pete came running at him, clobbered him over the neck with the halter and ran him off. I was not hurt, but my back was mighty sore; lucky, I had a T-shirt on. Pete said, "Let me look at your back," and pulled my shirt up. He said, "He broke your hide, good, right through your shirt. We better go to the cookhouse and put something on it." I walked pretty straight to keep the shirt off the bite.

Hap, the boss and retired bronc rider, helped me off with my shirt and, after looking at my back opened like that, he reckoned I would live. He said, "Lay face down on the kitchen table and arch your back, so the medicine does not run off. I have some stuff in the other room that will fix you up."

While he was getting the cure-all, I leaned over the kitchen table and arched my back. He came back with a bottle and said, "Hang tough, this might sting a little." Well, when that turpentine hit the hole where the stud had chewed on me, nobody needed to tell me to arch my back. I think I bowed up like a bottom side of a wagon wheel. Hap said, "Lay still, give that stuff a chance to soak in and work and you will be as good as new in no time."

After a while, it quit burning, kind of like a branding iron cooling off. Hap's wife tore up a clean white piece of pillowcase, made a pad and taped it on with some tape out of the first aid kit. That bronc rider knew what he was doing, no infection, and I was feeling fine in a day or two, a little tender, that is all. I was glad of that. I did not really look forward to another splash out of that turpentine bottle.

The pro rodeo on the reservation was coming up in about three weeks, so I was well healed up to enter the bronc riding, and we was all looking forward to that event. There was a fella filming a documentary for the National Film Board called *People of the Skeena,* and it turned out he filmed the rodeo as a part of the documentary—but that's the beginning of the next part of my story.

CHAPTER 7

RODEO RIDERS AND ROUGH STOCK

The fella filming the documentary *People of the Skeena* was staying at the camp while he was photographing and working on his documentary for that area. He took pictures of the bucking barrel in the evenings to get ready for the upcoming rodeo on the reservation.

The day finally came when the first professional-type rodeo in the area was to become a reality. As there were really no professional-type contestants, we all did the best we could. Our boss, Hap, was the only professional man there, and he had his hands full making it all work; with only amateur help, and having retired from active competition, he did not enter any event.

He got an older cowboy, who knew rodeo and was a fair and very good man and knew all about marking a judge's card on a point basis for the riding events, to judge on one side. On the other side, the only one we could get was a rancher, who was very fair and knew a good ride when he saw it but had never marked a judge's card on a point basis, considering points on a percentage basis for horse and rider, but he knew the rules in general.

When it was all over, they had to do some figuring to match the cowboy's card on one side—marked in points for the ride, for example, maybe 64-67-72-74—for each contestant against the old rancher's markings with the other side. He marked his card, for example, fair, poor, good, damned good, or okay ride.

The one thing they both had in common was the buck-offs. The cowboy marked a B.O. for bucked off. The rancher would probably put down fall off, hit the dirt or bucked off. That part of the judging was identical, even if worded different. By matching the cowboy's points with the rancher's opinions, they got it figured out, and everyone was satisfied.

We had to start somewhere, and with that as the beginning, by now there must be hundreds of professional-type rodeos in that north country. I do not remember much about who won, except my friend Pete won the bronc riding, and I made second. My sister and a friend got in the cow riding and made good rides, but I do not remember if they won anything. The crowd sure gave them a big hand for trying.

As the rodeo was only four or five miles from camp, Pete and I went there a-horseback. After it was over, we rode back to camp for something to eat and to clean up for the big dance that night, before riding back. Of course, we both celebrated some with Johnny Rye on our good fortune of first and second in the bronc riding.

It was plumb dark before getting on our way on horseback. I said to Pete, "Put what is left of Johnny Rye under your heavy outside shirt; we might need it before the night is over." We never gave it a thought that we was going on the reserve.

We got down on the river flat, about mile from the dance hall on the reservation. It was darker than the inside of a cow, and Pete said, "My damned lace in my left stirrup leather broke; my stirrup is falling off, and we have to fix it." No flashlight, but we had a few matches.

We were struggling in the dark to get it fixed, when a car pulled up behind us, the driver stuck his head out the window and hollered, "You boys having trouble?" It was the provincial police and a sergeant of the Mounties. We said we would be okay, just broke a lace in the stirrup leather.

He said, "I got lots of time; I will shine the lights on you until you get it tied together." That was very good of him, but it had just dawned on me: there we were on the reserve with my open bottle of Johnny Rye under Pete's shirt, and Pete was not quite 21 yet, at the time underage.

I whispered to Pete, "Stay behind that horse, I will finish fixing the stirrup," when the constable said, "Can I help in any way?" They was both damn good guys, but right then we sure didn't need no close-up help, so we said, "Thanks for the light, we got it fixed." They drove past us and said, "See you at the dance."

We considered those two lawmen to be friends, but that open bottle of Johnny Rye could have sure turned that into official business in a hell of a hurry. I guess Lady Luck was good enough not to put a damper on our fun night ahead.

We hid Johnny Rye behind a big rock before getting to the dance hall. We went back just at daybreak to have a little sip; someone saw us in the damn light, and he was thirsty, too. When we came back after the dance, going home about sunup, we realized someone had helped Johnny Rye escape.

Next time I went to town, I ran into the provincial police constable. We stood and bullshitted for a while as usual, when he grinned and said, "You and Pete must have been pretty well oiled when you got to the dance." "Well," I said, "I do not know about being oiled. We did have a few drinks before leaving camp." He said, "They must have been damned big drinks." I said, "Why do you think so?" "Well," he said, "if not, how come you tried to ride your horses into the hall?" I said, "How did you know that?" and he said, "Did you not see my car right there? Jimmie and I were watching you."

I said, "How come you guys never said anything?" He said, "We did not need to. That bunch of big Indian fellows was doing

Art staying on High Cloud, at the 1946 Kispiox Stampede: "I won second place, and in later years I ended up with him as a saddle horse. I called him Dime."

such a good job of stopping you, we just sat back and enjoyed the party."

I was sure glad we had stashed Johnny Walker behind that rock. It would have been just our luck to have that crock fall out of Pete's shirt right by the police car. By the way, the police cars them days were not marked, but Tony was right: in our oiled condition, we failed to recognize his car, although we knew it good. Damned good for us those two lawmen saw the humour of the situation. It turned out to be a damned good dance; everybody had fun, and nobody got in any kind of trouble. The rodeo was on a Friday, so we had the rest of the weekend to heal up.

I worked at the sawmill camp till haying time, and after the hay was up, I heard of a pro rodeo coming up in the middle of August in the city of Vernon in the Okanagan Valley. As I'd become a member of the Pro Rodeo Association—actually, it was called the Cowboy Protective Association—I was eligible to compete and figured I'd give it a try. I was actually fighting a headwind, with all the top contestants there, including some champions, but had to start somewhere.

I caught a ride on the Greyhound, did not need no saddle, as that part of the circuit had a half dozen brand-new committee saddles that everyone had to ride. Being brand new and slick as a polished hardwood floor, many cowboys, including me, bucked out of them too soon, before the whistle blew. They had some good stock; I think most was run in out of the hills, but there were some good horses there that had bucked in rodeos before, quite a lot. A little different from the present-day rough stock strings that are hauled in, in cattle liner trucks.

I was there the day before, watching the crew paint yellow numbers on the horses' hips for the draw. There was an old bay horse standing in the arena, plumb gentle. The rodeo manager just walked up to him and painted a big yellow number five on each hip. The old horse never moved, and some young feller from town said, "Why would they paint him? He is too old and gentle to buck." Well, next day would see whether he was right or wrong.

They did not have no Brahma bulls there, so they had steer riding instead. A rancher up the valley supplied the steers, two-year-old prime black Angus steers, fresh from the range. They trailed them in. No cattle trucks to speak of, them days.

I was sitting in the office when the rancher came in after corralling the steers. The arena director and manager asked how many he brought. The rancher said 21. "Holy cow," the manager said, "we got 21 riders. What we will do for re-rides?" The rancher just grinned and said, "There ain't going to be no re-rides."

I was up in the first section of saddle bronc riding next day, still green and all alone. I did not know anyone. It was my first big rodeo. My horse was in the chute, a big fat bay mare. I got the committee saddle on her, climbed aboard and nodded for the gate.

Soon the gate opened, she reared up and threw herself flat on her side on the ground. I got my leg out of the way before she hit and stepped off and said to the arena boss, "We will have to put her back in the chute." He said, "To hell with her, she will probably do it again. I will get you a re-ride horse."

My re-ride horse was a good-looking sorrel gelding, about 1400 pounds. I got that new slick saddle onto him but set it too far back. Lack of experience, I guess, but it made him harder to ride. I nodded for the gate, and this horse came out a-charging. Even with the saddle set too far back, for riding bucking horses, I figured, I had him rode and was doing okay.

One of the people told me afterwards that I was riding him, looking good. He was a damn good bucking horse, and, at about seven seconds, he threw one at me I could not ride. I hit the ground on all fours. Well, I hurt my leg landing, enough to make me limp. I was coming back to the chutes, and someone said, "He must be hurt." Well, I could not figure that out; they must have seen someone come limping back before. Someone else said, "They got the saddle off him," and I realized it was the horse they were talking about.

Apparently, after bucking me off, the buck shank fell on the ground, and, with his head down, still bucking, he stepped on it and his momentum threw him heels over head. He landed on his back on that new saddle and broke his back. I felt bad when one of the Mounties had to go out and shoot him to put him out of his misery, and he was dragged out of the arena.

I was back at the bucking chutes taking my chaps off, when the rodeo boss picked up a halter and went back in the corral and caught the old bay horse he had painted the number five on the day before and led him into the chute. A damn good rider had drawn that old veteran, who stood plumb still in the chute while being saddled, just like some old horse being harnessed to plough the garden.

When the rider nodded for the gate, the old horse just turned out slow-like, walked a couple of steps out, then dropped his head and poured it on. The rider lasted maybe three or four jumps, and as soon as he hit the ground, the old horse stopped.

The rodeo boss just walked out and took the saddle and halter off, and the old veteran trotted to the catch pen. I guess it was well worthwhile, painting that number five on that old boy's hip.

The steer riding also was an interesting event; very few steer riders made the whistle on those two-year-old black Angus. Those days, everyone had to ride 10 seconds to the whistle, instead of eight seconds, like nowadays.

I got to know two brothers, both bronc riders, who had a ranch at Loon Lake. They needed some help for haying, so I got a job from them for two or three weeks, driving a team on a mowing machine, until the next rodeo came up on Labour Day in Kelowna.

My first big rodeo had become history. All of us teamsters had to take our turn crawling out of our bedroll about 4:00 in the morning to wrangle the workhorses for the haying operation. On the third morning at the hay camp, it was my turn to wrangle.

Jack, one of the teamsters, told me the night before that the wrangle horse in the corral was gentle, a good horse, and when you found the horses, that old horse would pretty near corral the horses. That old horse's saddle, blanket and bridle were hanging on the fence, and Jack thought the stirrups were set about my length.

I was young, tired and slept like a log. It was plumb dark when Jack reached over and shook me awake. "It's 4:00 AM, time to get the horses in."

The bunkhouse was small, so our beds were only a couple of feet apart. I dragged myself out of bed. The dawn light was just coming, and I could make out the old wrangle horse in the corral as if he was a shadow.

After getting him saddled, I climbed aboard and felt like I was wedged in the saddle. Being used to riding a 16-inch seat saddle—my own, which was still in a sack under my bed—that form-fitting wrangle saddle with a high front and five-inch straight-up-and-down cantle and 12-inch seat felt a mite tight. Not to say nothing about the small, high horn that wanted to punch me in the belly every jump when the horse loped.

With that rig and being still dark, I took my time. Sure did not want to take a chance of my horse stepping in a badger hole and falling. I would have had a hard time getting clear with that tight-fitting saddle.

The old horse spotted the herd of workhorses in the dark and proceeded to head them for the corral. I was kind of a passenger, my first time in that pasture. Usually those horses automatically headed for the corral, but something spooked them, a coyote, or wolf maybe, and they headed in the wrong direction.

The old wrangle horse was on the job; he took off like an arrow from a bow, got around the horse herd and headed them for the corral. I was glad when I shut the gate and could get out of that little saddle. Had a tender spot on my belly where that high horn had got me when we turned the horse herd.

That was the only time the horse herd spooked whenever I wrangled. That little saddle was okay when they came in easy-like. Then of course, I was getting used to it, but I believe it is the tightest-fitting rig I ever rode.

The weather for haying was ideal. The boss went to town for groceries one day. After he came back at suppertime, he said it took him longer than he figured. The whole town was pretty well closed down as everyone was down by the river trying to stay cool. It was 115°F (46°C) that day. He had to go and hunt up the storekeepers by the river to come and give him his groceries.

Remember those gentle workhorse colts back in chapter five that I had to get halter-broke, so they would lead, and how that horse-training instruction book I found in the bookshelf pretty well saved the day for me? Well now, I was in that hay camp, and one evening, Boulon, the hay crew boss, and me was sitting on the porch outside the cookhouse after supper. I got to telling him about this book that I thought Professor Beery had wrote; I said it was almost unbelievable what that man could do with it, looked like it had probably been wrote around the turn of the century. He said, "Believe it, I saw Professor Beery work one time and put on a demonstration when I was just 14 years old." Close as I could figure out, that demonstration would have occurred sometime between 1915 and 1925.

This is the way Boulon told it to me. Boulon had been raised around the little cow town of Williams Lake in the Cariboo Country in British Columbia.

Seems that Professor Beery started the Beery School of Horsemanship, which I believe is still in existence. He had started a program that supplied a course folks could take by correspondence on a countrywide basis. He was travelling the country, promoting and trying to gain interest in his program and in the course of his trails stopped in Williams Lake for a few days.

One evening, he went into the saloon, figuring, I guess, there probably would be cowboys, ranchers and horse people in there, where he could interest folks in his program. Turned out there were quite a few people there and, of course, we have to bear in mind that, them days, every aspect of the range and cattle country depended on the horse.

I guess, according to Boulon, it was somewhat hard to convince those cowboys that you could gentle and break a range bronc the gentle and easy way, without a fight on your hands. As far as they could see, the only way was to get aboard and ride the storm, until the horse quit bucking. Then, if you were a good enough rider, lots of miles and wet saddle blankets later, you would wind up with a good horse.

One of them supposedly made the remark, "I'm from Missouri; you've got to show me."

Professor Beery just smiled and said, "There must be lots of unbroken range horses around here. If some of you boys would like to run in a totally unbroken four- or five-year-old tomorrow morning, I'll put on a demonstration tomorrow afternoon and show you what I mean."

They took him up on his offer. They knew of a big black, about five years old, running with a small herd not far from town. He had been tried, and so far, no one had any luck, and they did not think he could be handled. He was barely halter-broke, wild and on the fight.

The horse was brought in with the small herd next morning and corralled. Come afternoon, there was a big audience around the corrals, word having quickly gotten around. Boulon said he was on the corral fence, where he had a good view. Professor Beery asked some of the boys to put the horse in a separate corral by himself and then leave him be.

When this was accomplished, Professor Beery went into the corral alone with this wild range bronc. In his hand, he carried a small, light stock whip, about five feet long. Looking at the horse, the cowboys figured he was taking a big chance just going into the corral on foot, never mind trying to do anything with him or trying to gentle him.

Professor Beery started talking quietly to the big black, while slowly advancing, and then he would stop and talk quietly and gently flick the little whip. As he got closer, the big black started nodding his head. Very soon, he was up close to the big black and petting him on the neck, still quietly talking. The horse just stood there and eventually let him handle and pet him all over, showing no sign of anxiety or fight. Beery used the little whip to rub the bronc's feet and flicked it gently all over his feet and body. Boulon said, in no more than 30 minutes, that big black, considered to be some kind of an outlaw, was following Beery around the corral.

Before the hour was up, Beery had climbed onto the big black's back and rode him at a slow walk around the corral, without a strap on him. He got off in the middle of the corral, talked and petted the big horse, and when he left the corral, the big black bronc followed him to the gate.

Folks just could not believe their eyes, and Boulon said, "I was watching his every move from the corral fence, and I still can't figure out what he did, so gently and quietly." After what he told me, I could understand more of what I would read in the old book but still could not quite figure how it was done. I have concluded that Beery must have had a special way with horses.

His methods, I think, are very superior, and I have tried to practice what I have been able to learn, to the extent that it definitely works for me. I think the most important thing I have learned is to determine what it is all about from the horse's side of the picture. Eliminate fear and force, give a horse his space and try to put yourself in his place, thereby leading to a greater understanding between horse and trainer.

Most horses are very cooperative if they understand what is wanted and expected of them. Be their friend, and they will usually try to cooperate. I have learned and still say, get a horse to the point that he wants to work with you, rather than feels he is being forced to do something he does not understand and still has to do. When you get to that relationship with a horse, you have it made. From then on, as you work together, you complement each other, to the success and benefit of both.

There are exceptions. Horses have personalities that differ, same as people. It is to be expected that occasionally you will find a horse that's hard to work with, but occasionally, you will find a person that might be difficult, too. Bear in mind, that person could be yourself and you do not realize it. It's tougher for horses to understand all this; their understanding of the English language is somewhat limited.

Getting on this subject of horses, which I am very interested in, seems like maybe I got a little sidetracked and had a small runaway, so back to the haying camp.

The haying was going good. We put up a lot of hay, all loose, no balers them days in those parts. The ranch had 300 or 400 cows to feed. There were big, loose haystacks all over the fields. It was getting close to the first of September, and the Kelowna Rodeo was coming up on Labour Day, in about a week. I was looking forward to getting in the saddle bronc riding, but it was not to be.

I do not know whether bouncing around on the metal mowing machine seat had anything to do with it or not, but I had developed two big boils on my butt. One on each side. To say they were kind of sore was a gross understatement, and maybe some would say I was chicken and could not stand a little hurt. I just couldn't see me climbing onto one of those hard-seated committee saddles, on top of the hurricane deck of one of those rodeo broncs, sitting on those two boils, or carbuncles, or whatever they was. I figured there was no way I could ride a bronc for 10 seconds under those conditions, so I did not enter. Being as I was okay standing up, I went and helped around the chutes.

Same as in Vernon, the bucking horses were run in off the range. There was a lot of good horses in the bunch that was pretty quiet, similar to present-day bucking horses, but there were quite a few wild ones, too.

They used some of the wildies in the bareback. Getting the bareback rigging on them was difficult at times, for some of them fought in the chutes so bad. I remember one of them wild broomtails, in particular. He was a small, slim, light bay with a blaze and black mane and tail and was, I think, as wild as the hills he came from. He kicked, reared and fought in the chute, but we finally got him rigged out. The rider nodded for the gate.

The bay came a-charging, bucking high and wild. About six seconds out, he jumped high, with his head between his knees, hit the ground and sucked back all in one move, it seemed. The rider was looking good and riding high until then. When the horse hit the ground and sucked back so fast, the rider went over his head, and we thought he was in trouble, for his hand was still in the rigging.

The horse kept bucking, and we could see the rigging coming over onto his neck. The rider still had a hold of the rigging, and that little fuzzytail got his head between his front legs and slipped right out of the rigging backing up. This all happened in a matter of seconds. The horse ran off, and the rider got up with a grin on his face, still had the rigging in his hand and held it up, still cinched together and showed the crowd. Nobody got hurt, but sometimes unusual things can happen at rodeos.

After the rodeo was over, we headed back to the motel room a bunch of us shared. I was riding in the back of the pickup truck, and, all of a sudden, the truck started heading for the ditch, gravel spraying from under the right front fender, and we came to a stop. I did not know what happened, when I seen a tire and wheel rolling along the bottom of the ditch and tip over. The spindle had broken suddenly, and thanks to Cog's good driving, he managed to keep us out of a wreck, even with the right front axle ploughing gravel.

The truck was towed to a garage to get fixed, and we got a ride to the motel to clean up for the dance. It was a good dance; a little Johnny Rye livened things up here and there. A couple of women got in a knock-down, drag-out, hair-pulling fight, but otherwise everyone had fun. Hell, we even enjoyed watching them women discuss their differences.

The Kelowna Rodeo was over for another year. Someone had told me a person could make good money picking apples, and so as haying was over, I stayed to try it, being as I was right in the heart of apple-growing country. I was told that anyone should be able to pick 100 boxes a day and, at 12 cents a box, that translated into $12 a day, very good wages for the year 1946.

I had no trouble getting a job and went with another young fella to the apple-growing ranch. We got a small bunkhouse, had to buy our own grub and cook it. That was okay, but as I had never picked apples before, the 100 boxes a day the fella talked about was far beyond me. After a week, I'd only got to about 40 boxes a day, so I decided I'd best quit trying to make a fortune picking apples and stick to what I knew: horses, cows, grass, fences and hay.

One bright spot I remember in that apple-picking week: the other young fella knew some folks who had a small ranch close by and, one night, he said, "Let's walk over for a visit with them; you will like them." When we got there, the only one home was their daughter, a beautiful, blue-eyed, dark-haired girl about 19, who my friend knew quite well. A very nice girl with a wonderful personality, and, believe me, I would have liked to know her better, but them days, I was so shy around girls I did not hardly know what to say.

We sat on the porch and visited for an hour or two, till we had to go back to our apple-picking shack. I never saw that beautiful young lady again but still hope that the world has been treating her real good ever since. I do not remember her name but thought of her off and on in the following years. Fifty years later, she was to be my inspiration for a song called "Memories of You" on my recent country western album, *Cowboy Country*. I left the apple picking to someone else and went back to my home range, to make my living the way I knew how.

CHAPTER 8

BUILDING THE BIGGEST LITTLE RODEO

Back on home range again, after my pro rodeo attempts and being a poor apple picker, I was a bit financially embarrassed. Got some experience and no regrets... well, maybe just one. I wonder if I stayed and got to know that pretty ranch girl better, I might have stayed in that country. Who knows?

One thing I do know: even if I did not know her name, I have never forgotten her. After all these years, I can still see her in my memory, sitting there on the porch visiting with us in the moonlight. Sometimes I think I should have stayed picking apples and got to know her better. Then, why would any girl get too interested in a young cowpuncher who only had a saddle and bedroll to his name? That's one question I will never have the answer to. There has been a lot of water run under the bridge since, but back to my return to home range and what lay ahead.

Being financially embarrassed, as soon as the last of the hay was up, I went back to work in the bush till spring. I would sooner have worked with cattle and horses, but there was no sense looking for ranch work when the pocket was plumb dry, and a paying bush job was right there. It was a good winter, and I came out come spring with some wages saved and jingle money in my pocket.

The Hagens: George, Art, Louise, Henry and Norman, taken in 1948, "the same year that Dad passed away."

Spring was upon us and, as usual, we had the spring work on the farm done and had started looking forward to the up-and-coming stampede on the reservation. It turned out that the folks on the reserve had decided to quit the rodeo and just carry on with a sports day: baseball, football, races, etc. There was about a dozen of us aspiring young cowboys in the valley who were disappointed, but not for long. We would organize our own rodeo!

It was the spring of 1947. There were some natural open river flats right along the road up the valley, about eight miles or so north from the reserve, that was just waiting to have an arena built on them. We all got our heads together and did some figuring. It had to be built with volunteer labour.

We cut the posts out of the bush; Dad supplied the slabs and planks from his little sawmill to build the arena and chutes. First thing you know, the whole community was involved, and things were taking shape. The Farmer's Institute decided to sponsor us, which was very good, for it gave the whole project a sort of official community status. Everyone showed up and, as the saying goes, many hands make light work, and it was headed for success.

My brothers and I hauled the slabs and planks on an old 1929 one-ton Chevrolet truck we had. The cab had been built of light lumber plywood and had no doors but did have a windshield.

About the last load, my brother was driving. We had on a fair decent load, with a 10-gallon drum of coal oil standing upright on top of the load behind the cab and tied there. Halfway to the arena, we came up a small hill that had a sharp turn at the top. We were chugging along at eight or ten miles an hour and something caught in the steering. The damn truck would not make the turn at the top of the hill.

Before my brother could get it stopped, the left front wheel dropped into the ditch and the truck turned over on its back, throwing me out. I was on the outside, and, there being no doors, I sailed over and hit a tree, which saved me from going over the riverbank.

I got up quick and ran to the truck, plumb upside down on its back and one front wheel still turning slow. My two brothers were under that wreck, and I was scared that they might have had it. Much to my relief, George, who was driving, hollered, "Anybody hurt?" and Henry answered from under the wreck, "I am okay."

I got to the truck, and there was my two brothers standing on their head and shoulders, upside down with their legs under the dashboard. The seat of the truck was lying on top of their hindquarters. The wooden cab was all smashed to hell.

Norman, Louise and Henry: "Louise was just a little thing, but us boys used to tease her that all of us against her was just about even."

I pulled the seat off them sideways and proceeded to get them untangled and pulled out from there. It was sure a tight fit, but with them squirming and wiggling to get a little slack, I finally got Henry out of the middle of the truck.

Luckily, George was driving. Him being the smallest of us three boys, he somehow fit around the steering column. It had not hit him, but he was sure jammed in there beside it. Now that Henry was out to help me, we managed to bend George in the right shape and got him clear, too. Lucky that tree caught me from going over the riverbank, so at least I was able to do something to help us all get out of the wreck.

We could not really tell why the steering jammed—badly wore, I guess. What saved the day was the 10-gallon, coal-oil drum tied to the top of the load. It stayed upright when the

George with Rex: "George was the second youngest of us; he lost his battle with Parkinson's a number of years back."

truck turned over, holding the truck and the load high enough off the ground that the boys did not get hurt. Our primitive form of a roll bar.

We just left the damned thing lying there, walked the rest of the way to the arena and went to work. We would need a team or tractor to roll the truck back on its feet.

Next day, one of our neighbours brought his old tractor up and rolled it back on its wheels. The motor started right up; we had reached under and turned off the key before we left it. It sure smoked like hell, getting that extra oil burned out of the upside-down engine. We added more oil and tore the rest of the cab off and finished hauling our load of slabs to the arena, with one of us driving, sitting on an old box we had brought. We drove it that way the rest of the summer—kind of wet when it rained. Come fall, we got a regular cab off an old truck and put it on. It even had doors and windows that worked and put us back in style!

Back to the new arena. Rodeo day was fast approaching, and we had quite a bit to do. Luckily, the Farmer's Institute had gotten things pretty well organized, and with women, kids and anyone able-bodied enough to walk pitching in, we got it done on time. It was a real community enterprise.

The big day was here. Early in the morning, the boys saddled up to go and hunt up some bucking stock. Half went for horses and half went for cattle. Any cow or steer that was away from home and was not being milked and any horse not looking at the scenery through a collar was bucking stock that day. It was all open range around there, so as long as you kept out of people's yards and hayfields finding bucking stock, it was okay.

Me, I had put the sideboards on the cab-less truck and hauled water from the neighbour's for drinking water and for the women to cook wieners with at the rodeo. We had rounded up an old wood cook stove with a piece of stovepipe on it to help the women with their culinary efforts.

By noon, everything was ready to go, but as there were not many contestants in the riding events, we had to dream up extra events to fill in the performance, like a cowhide race, hat and boot race and other events. Someone had a brainwave, probably me, that we hold a novelty softball game to start off the afternoon, between the girls' team and the riders. Hell of a good idea, if the girls were willing. They were. This had been planned ahead of time.

Norman, Rex and Henry clowning around for a picture: "Rex was a part of the family for many years."

Someone said that would not be quite fair, us big guys against them little girls. We better figure out to give them a little edge to keep the score half even. How were we going to do that without being obvious? How about the riders having to play in their batwing chaps and high heels? That should be a novelty and even things up. Hell of a good idea—talk about your noble thoughts!

It was time to get the show on the road. The grass arena was the ball diamond, stepped off to about the right size with the bucking chutes as the backstop, behind the plate. The girls were ready, and I mean ready. The regular girls' softball team, all practiced up and all grew up. Nurses off duty from the hospital, the neighbour girls in running shoes, white shorts and T-shirts and all looking very capable.

The first inning was tough. Seemed like it did not matter where we hit that ball to, whether it was a ground ball or a fly, there was a snow-white beauty right there.

Well, the first inning was over, the score was four to nothing, and the girls had the four. Oh, hell, that was all right, we had six more innings to go. We should easy catch up and beat them by then.

To make a long story short, the ordeal was finally over. I think the crowd loved it. The score was 18 to 2 in the girls' favour, and they had not even worked up a sweat.

They pranced around that field like a bunch of fairies, seemed never to miss a move, while we was grunting and sweating in all that gear and about as graceful handling that ball as a bunch of cub bears wearing boxing gloves. I've often thought since, a damn good thing the girls' ball team didn't change into rider's clothes and enter in the rodeo, the way they polished us off on the ball field.

Well, now for the cowhide race. It was a two-man team, and the track was one end of the arena to the other. One fella was on horseback and got his rope tied to a dry cowhide, with the other end dallied to his saddle horn. His partner was riding the cowhide any way he could hang on.

There was about six or seven teams entered. Everybody was lined up at the bottom of the arena, ready, when someone hollered go. The older horses that had been used to dragging stuff on a rope did not mind and just ran straight to the other end, dragging the hide.

Not so with a couple of them young horses. When they seen that hide following them, they got wild eyed and was leaving the country. One ran off to the side, and when the rider turned him back, somehow the hide turned over on top of the feller riding it. However, it was a race; the rider did not throw his dally, and the hide man never let go and skidded the whole length of the arena under the hide. That was okay, the rules being flexible. When the fence stopped them, the race was over, and, after digging the grass and cow dung out of his shirt collar, he was ready for the next event.

The hat and boot race. Well, this was on foot. All the contestants piled their boots on the boot pile and hats on the hat pile at the bottom of the arena and headed for the bucking chutes, bareheaded and in their sock feet. The idea was that whoever was the fleetest of foot and got down, put his hat and boots on and got back to the bucking chutes was the winner.

Here again, the rules were a mite flexible. The hats were no problem, but if someone with a size-six foot got hold of some number-nine boots, he was away and running, while the guy with the number-nine foot was having a little trouble fitting his running gear into that pint-size footwear. I guess it was fair enough; the guys with the small feet pretty well won. At least the tall guys got to the pile first, and, of course, the only boots they could get into would be in the bottom of the pile. It went over pretty well, seemed as if the crowd enjoyed the friendly confusion.

It was then time for the main rodeo events. We didn't have any roping but had saddle bronc, bareback bronc, cattle saddle riding and ordinary steer or cow riding. You just stood by the

Saddle cow riding at the Kispiox Valley Stampede: "The cow lay down, and the judge told the rider to stay on until the bell so he would get a re-ride."

empty chute, and whatever happened to run in was your critter for that particular event.

I do not much remember who won, except that, with Lady Luck on my side, I won the cow riding in the saddle cow–riding event. A tall, lanky black and white cow run in my chute and bucked high and straight. Not too hard to ride, and I won $8!

Some of the other boys were not that lucky. One cow came out, bucked a little, and lay down before the whistle. Then there was a big, white-faced, two-year-old steer, fresh off the range, that was without a doubt the best bucking cow critter there. To ride these cattle with a saddle, as they do not have any withers, we had to use a soft, big, cotton rope crupper under their tail to keep the saddle from going over their heads. You could not flank them tight, or they would sometimes lie down.

Well, this big two-year-old steer was not too agreeable about having a saddle cinched on. The cotton rope crupper under his tail injured his dignity quite a lot more, and he was about ready to do something about it. When Drew nodded his head and the gate swung open, he started him good and was looking like he would ride him.

The way that steer come out, I figured there went the saddle cow–riding money. The steer got it figured different: he only had four feet but looked like a windmill in a storm and was really pouring it on. I do not think anyone this side of the Rio Grande could have rode him that day. Drew was a good rider, but that day it was a case of, "it takes a damn good bucker to throw me, but it sure doesn't take him long."

We came close to having a bad accident right there. Drew hit the ground on his back; the steer was still pouring it on and jumped on him. Lucky his hoof was off centre on Drew's chest and slipped off to the ground, taking half of his shirt and a strip of hide off his ribs. We ran over to him as he was getting to his feet and asked if he was hurt bad. "No," he said, "that strip of hide will grow back, but I paid $4.95 for that shirt, and I have only wore it since morning."

One thing we did have at that first rodeo was a very good pickup team. A strong, tall rancher was picking up, and his wife was hazing for him. Anyone who made the 10-second whistle was picked up in style. Soon as the whistle blew, Helen would haze the bucking horse, and Ted came in from the other side and picked the rider off, and they never missed. I have seen many hazers and pickup men since and would have to honestly say Ted and Helen were among the good ones.

The sun was sliding down close to the mountains to the west, and our rodeo was over. We took care of the bucking stock by opening the corral gates, and they all headed back to the open range—all except a few good, gentle workhorses that was good

Norman and Henry and other contestants at the First Annual Kispiox Valley Rodeo in 1947: "We really started something—they still hold an annual rodeo to this day."

buckers. They had to go home, for in all likelihood, they had a date next day with a collar and a set of harnesses.

Nobody was in a hurry to leave, and we contestants headed for the old wood stove where the women still had those big pots of coffee and wieners going. Not having eaten since morning, that grub tasted as good as what comes out of a high-class café. It had been a real good and successful day, a good crowd and nobody got hurt. Well, Drew walked a little crooked, trying to keep his pinned-together shirt off his skinned ribs, but still

George with one of his many pets, a calf named Tex: "George had a real fondness for animals."

wore his usual grin. Someone asked, "Does your ribs still hurt?" Drew grinned and said, "Only if I laugh hard."

The very first Kispiox Valley Rodeo was over. Little did we realize, that evening, as we sat by the fire eating hot dogs, drinking coffee and talking about the day's events, that we had started an annual event that would carry on for all these years.

In June 1997, they celebrated their 50th anniversary of the annual rodeo. Someone sent me a copy of the 50th anniversary booklet they made up for the occasion: a bareback bronc and rider on the outside cover and titled The 50th Annual Kispiox Valley Rodeo, The Biggest Little Rodeo in the West.

It has come a long ways since our first community effort. It is still a community project but plumb modern, with good corrals and an arena and a community hall and seats for the spectators.

I was invited to attend and wanted to go but was nursemaid to 950 cow–calf pairs in a community pasture in Alberta, 1500 miles from the rodeo grounds, so couldn't make it, which might have been a good thing. I would have maybe done something dumb, like riding a saddle bronc, just for old time's sake, to celebrate the 50th anniversary.

In 1947, I stayed on home range, as haying was coming up before long, and then on Labour Day, the Bulkley Valley held their annual Telkwa Rodeo and Barbecue. We could not miss that.

My two brothers won first and second in the steer riding. My youngest brother placed in saddle bronc, and I lucked out and won the saddle bronc riding, just by the skin of my teeth, though.

This big black horse was sure testing me, and the whistle blew just before we parted company. As I was going over his head, he let me come down square on top of the saddle horn on the end of my tailbone. Well, it got my attention, but was not too sore till the next morning. I will tell you, I was fairly careful when I sat a-straddle on a corral fence for a few weeks. Come New Year's Day, my tailbone was still a mite tender but, in time, got to be good as new.

Next year, I went to the Telkwa Stampede again but did not do much good, just placed in the wild horse race. That year was pretty routine, looking after our own stock, haying and working on some small outfits as well as back in the bush. Come the spring of 1949, after the spring work at home was done, I headed for the Cariboo cattle country to size up the big outfits.

I got me a job for a couple of months on the Chilko Ranch west of Williams Lake, which at that time ran around, I think, about 5000 head. I went home and helped for a short time, then me and another fella headed for Kamloops, hoping to get a riding job on a big outfit. Every cowboy in that part of the country wanted riding jobs, so we were too late to get on.

Norman and George pictured with a couple of green-broke colts: "There was always some work to do around the ranch."

Haying was still in progress, and as we were walking down the sidewalk in Kamloops, we met a feller with a big hat and asked him if he knew of somebody who could use a couple of hands. He grinned and said, "Yes, if you guys want to go haying." We said sure. He said to have our gear ready; he would pick us up in a couple of hours. We had our job.

We worked for him through haying; he ran around 1000 head, and we were done in time for me to go back to my home range and enter the Telkwa Rodeo on Labour Day. By this time, they had fixed up the grounds by adding more spectator seats, and the rodeo attracted quite a few contestants.

That year, I did better: I won the bronc riding on a big chestnut mare, which fit me good and was not too tough to ride, a real good bucking horse. She was one of the nicest broncs I have ever been on.

At that same rodeo, my brothers done well, too. George, I believe, won the steer riding, and my brother Henry came in third in the saddle bronc and rode feeling terrible. He had eaten something that did not agree with him. I had been out in the first go-around, and Henry was up in the second go-around. When they ran his bronc in the chute, a big, stout, blue roan, Henry was lying down behind the chutes feeling pretty rough.

I went over to him and said, "The way you are feeling you had better not tackle that big bugger and turn him out." He said, "To hell with that; I paid my entry fees, and I am gonna ride him." He asked me to saddle his horse for him and holler when his horse was ready. I rigged up the big roan with someone else helping me and hollered to Henry when his horse was ready to go. He dragged himself over and climbed onto that big bronc, looking about as healthy as something the cat dragged in and forgot to kill.

Luckily, the horse was quiet in the chute. Henry shoved his spurs high on the horse's neck, leaned back and slid the buck shank back in his hand where it felt right, gave his hat a tug and said, "Pour him out." That big blue roan came apart and was plumb serious about laying Henry on the ground.

When the whistle blew, Henry was still there, combing his hide with the spurs. The pickup man took him off, and he went back and lay down. I think that ride must have done him good. Before the day was over, he was feeling better. I think if he had not taken sick, he would have put me out of first into second with that horse. As it was, he won third.

Anything can happen at a rodeo, and something kind of embarrassing happened to one of the saddle bronc riders. A young fella I had never seen before and did not know where he came from drew a big, stout brown horse, a real powerhouse.

Contestants at the Labour Day rodeo in Telkwa, 1947: "I won the saddle bronc that day and earned myself $67."

This fella was wearing just an ordinary pair of new overall pants and had a red hammer strap on one side, I suspect made for carpenters. Nobody thought nothing of it, of course, but them kind of pants is not tight-fitting like Levi's, and the crotch hung pretty low.

He got on the big, stout, brown bronc and nodded for the gate. Out they came, and this old pony came apart with his head between his knees. The rider was sitting up there real pretty, but about halfway to the whistle, that bronc threw one at him that made him come unbalanced, and he pretty near went over the horse's head.

Trying to get straightened up aboard this cyclone, he leaned over the saddle horn about parallel to where that horse's neck should have been. His feet were still in the stirrups, so his legs were straight down, making his body sort of like the letter L, face down. Right there, that big bronc hit him in the ass with the cantle board, and he went out the front door like an arrow out of a bow. As he was going, the saddle horn caught the low-hanging crotch of his pants and tore it plumb out, boxing shorts and all. It happened so fast, he was plumb unaware of it.

He got up and turned toward the grandstand, and the crowd started cheering and clapping. He, in all innocence, stood there waving to the crowd and grinning, pleased they were giving him a good hand for a good effort.

The crowd kept cheering, and as the feller turned a little, I seen how bad his pants were tore. Everything that showed he was a man was in plain sight. I tried to help by taking my hat off and running over to him and holding it in front of his belly. The crowd thought, I guess, that was funny and cheered some more. The poor guy looked down and then said to me plumb quiet, "I did not know; I guess they seen all they need to."

By this time, all the contestants realized what the situation was; they ran out, we all gathered around him and walked him out of the arena. He said, "It's the only pants I got with me. What will I do now?" I said, "What size do you wear?" He said a 34 waist. I said, "Come on, I got a couple of extra pairs at the hotel that'll fit you; I'm 34, too." He said, "Thanks, give me your address, and I will mail them back to you."

Sure enough, a month later, I got a package in the mail. My pants clean and pressed and a note saying thanks a lot for helping to preserve his dignity. I have never seen him since.

We took our winnings and headed back home to stack 20 acres of green feed we had left to dry while we were at the rodeo. We got it up in good shape just in time. It started raining a few hours after we topped off the stack. Summer was again coming to an end.

CHAPTER 9

THE BIG COW OUTFITS

Haying was over, and we spent the rest of the fall odd-jobbing, getting ready for winter, digging spuds and the garden and working out at small jobs here and there. Come about the first of December, my youngest brother and me decided to go to the cattle country in south-central British Columbia and headed for Kamloops to work for a cow outfit for the winter.

By the time we got there, it was getting cold, and there were not enough jobs and too many cowboys. There turned out to be about eight or ten of us looking for winter jobs at the same time. We all had a few dollars, so we were able to hang on for a couple of weeks.

We were lucky, though, in the fact that an older, married cowboy ran a good-sized livery stable in downtown Kamloops. It was set up with the upstairs all fixed up like a hotel with many rooms—a good, clean place. His wife looked after the room part, and we all stayed there. At a dollar and a half a day, it was affordable and warm and comfortable.

We ate at the Chinese café on the main drag and could get a damn good meal, with lots of coffee threw in, for 60 to 80 cents, depending on what you ordered. We were all doing okay and slowly, one or two at a time, would get a job for the winter. Our ranks were being thinned down to just a few people, when I heard that the Douglas Lake Cattle Company, out of Merritt, could use a couple of hands.

I phoned the manager, and he said yes. "Catch the Greyhound tomorrow morning to Merritt. The big ranch truck is going into town for a load of oats. I will tell the driver to pick you up at the bus depot. The wage is 90 bucks a month, a bed in the bunkhouse and meals in the cookhouse." I said, "Thanks, we will be there."

My brother and I had a job for the winter. That left only two or three of the guys in town looking for jobs, and I heard they were hired on with some cow outfits a few days later.

We caught the Greyhound for Merritt early in the morning. It was only about 60 miles from Kamloops, so we did not have far to go. We pulled into Merritt at the Greyhound depot, and the ranch truck was waiting, having already loaded up with oats.

Then we got a shock. The driver had a woman and a couple of kids who had to ride inside, so if we wanted to go with that truck, we had to ride outside on top of that load of oats. It turned cold enough to pop the knots out of the planks on a wooden bridge, and we had 20-some miles to go. The driver said he did not know the lady had to go home that day, back to the ranch, so there was nothing else he could do.

We decided to tackle the trip. We put on all the extra clothes we could, then piled our saddles, which were in gunny sacks, and our bedrolls up front for a windbreak. We laid down flat on our bellies on top of the oats behind them and headed for the ranch. By keeping our heads down, the wind from the speed of the truck pretty well went over us. It was a nice, quiet day, but we were getting to feel the cold pretty bad before arriving at the ranch. It had been one of the longest 20-some-odd-mile trips I had ever travelled on a truck, but after we thawed out in the bunkhouse, we were none the worse for wear.

We hung around the home ranch for a day or two, not doing much and getting acquainted, waiting to be picked up to go to one of the smaller ranches, which was a feeding camp, where we'd be feeding cows the rest of the winter. Those days, they fed on sleighs with big hayracks on them. That was okay: we were both teamsters. They gave us teams and sleighs hauling hay, two men to each sleigh.

That was just one feeding camp; there was three or four feed camps all together. This was a big outfit; their cattle count was well up in the thousands.

The weather moderated fairly well shortly after we arrived and gave us a chance to fix the fence in the bull pasture, and then, right around Christmas, it turned cold again and did not warm up till sometime in February. I mean cold, between −20 and −50°F (between −29 and −46°C), most every day.

One good thing: we had a good, warm bunkhouse, a real good Chinese cook, excellent chuck and a good, warm barn for the horses. Luckily, we did not have much wind that winter. Of course, this was southern British Columbia, and not the southern prairies. I believe it was probably the coldest winter, with more snow than had been seen for some time in that country.

The cowboy crew was cut down fairly small for the winter, to about six or eight cowboys. Most of the rest was running pitchforks, hauling hay. One fella by the name of Blondie was the waterhole rider. It took him all day to cut waterholes in the creeks and lakes for our feed camp and the home ranch four miles away. He worked from the home ranch and had dinner at our cookhouse before working his way back to the home ranch before dark.

One time at our camp, we were feeding close to 4000 head, which kept us a mite busy. Of course, they were split up, so there would not be too big a bunch in one field. In that kind of weather, the winter tends to feel long when you work seven days a week. Seemed like them cows liked eating on Sundays, too, just like the rest of us.

The mobile hay balers were just starting to come into use. The ranch had a few bale stacks we saved for Sundays. As bales were faster to load and unload, we would manage to be done feeding by noon. That way, we had Sunday afternoon off and only had to look after our horses in the evening.

Off, that is, from hauling hay. Sundays were the day we had to heat water on the wood stove and drag out the old washtub and scrub board and wash our socks, long johns and whatever, by hand. It was sure nice in later years, after somebody invented washing machines, to find one in the bunkhouse on a ranch. A fella could sit back and let them long johns wash themselves and listen to the motor run, when the exhaust pipe was going through a hole in the wall and it was barking outside. Modernizing and mechanizing was slowly sneaking up on us, as far as washing goes, for the better.

We put in a good winter, busy, but well fed and warm after work. We had a battery radio in the bunkhouse, so we had some music and news for entertainment. One Sunday, it came over the news that a light airplane had crashed somewhere, killing its pilot. One of the older fellers was sitting on his bunk and, when he heard this news, said, "Them damned airplanes is damn good medicine." I asked him what he meant by that, and he growled, "One drop and you're cured." I guess from that viewpoint, he was plumb right. I thought about his opinion and figured he was about dead on.

To this day, I have never been off the ground in a plane. Course, that isn't the only reason: height gets to me. If I have to go up a yard pole, 12 or 15 feet high, I am getting too high to my liking. The topside of a good cow horse is just fine for me. A fella appreciates a horse's height to keep from wearing his hind legs off from walking.

The cold weather dragged slowly along, but we got a moderating break sometime toward the last of January, and the cowboy crew moved a lot of our cattle to a new feed camp. We had too many for the amount of hay we had to see us through till spring.

That took some pressure off the feeding crew and gave us a chance now and then to catch up on the woodpile for the cook and the bunkhouse.

The cold spell finally broke in late February, and it came with a bang. One day, you would still be humped up, trying to keep from freezing on your way to the feed ground, and the next day the eaves on the buildings were dripping water. Spring was on its way, a very welcome occurrence. One thing about that winter: nobody slacked off on work, leaning on a fork handle. We had to keep working like hell to keep warm so we would not freeze. Even so, a few of the boys that was not used to that business did suffer a little frostbite occasionally.

With the coming of spring, I left the ranch and went back to my home range for a while; I had some important business to tend to for a couple of months. My brother stayed at the big ranch a month longer than I did, and then he showed up back on our home range. The winter feeding at the big ranch was done for another year.

After the usual run of spring work on the farm, crops and the garden planted and cows all calved out, I headed back for Kamloops and got on with a small cow outfit out of town about 15 miles. I think they were running about 800 head at that time. It was a good outfit, and we were caught up on the work fairly quick. It was a short job. I was hired on as an extra hand, as they needed to catch up on fencing and moving cattle out to grass and branding. The short job well petered out in a month or so, but haying was coming up, so I went to work haying for the same outfit I had worked haying for the summer before. That was good, getting back where I knew everybody.

After the first crop of hay was cut, I was sent out to build four miles of fence, kind of as a foreman, having the haying crew as a fence crew. The hay fields were being irrigated for the second crop, so we were kept on the job fencing until it was ready to

Norman, George and Henry preparing to go on a hunting trip to the mountains: "Sounds like they had some fun, but they didn't bring home any game."

cut. After the second crop was cut, haying on the outfit was over. There was a small rodeo coming up further north in the Cariboo Country, so I decided to go.

With a little paper money in my pocket from haying wages, I figured I would invest a little in entry fees and try to double it. It did not quite turn out that way. I did not place in the bronc riding, missed my calf and should have won the wild horse race, but not that day.

Them days, most places required you to ride into the unsaddle chute at the bottom of the arena to determine the winner in the wild horse race. First man in was first, second man in was second and so on. I was on a good team; the ear man went up that rope like a squirrel, with the shank man right behind him. The wild bronc was eared down, and I got my saddle onto him right quick. The boys handed me the buck shank and turned him loose. He bogged his head and went to bucking straight for the catch pen. I was the first man there; the rest were still saddling.

I figured we had the wild horse race won, but the bronc had it figured different. He refused to go in the unsaddling chute. I had to get in first to win. While I was arguing with that bronc, three other contestants rode by me into the chute. Then my bronc followed the others in. That really made my day. I was there first and wound up in fourth place, the crying hole. They only paid three monies—first, second and third—in the wild horse race.

Nevertheless, the trip was worth it. Besides having a good time, I ran into the cow boss from the Circle S and got a riding job for roundup but had to wait for about a month until roundup started. Just about an hour later, I ran into one of the boys I met three years ago and had hayed for after the rodeo at Vernon. He had bought another ranch, was still haying and offered me a dollar a day more than regular wages if I would come and run a horse-powered sweep rake for him for a month. That worked out just right, to take up the slack till roundup started at the Circle S. It made me feel a little more forgiving to that wild horse race bronc that refused to go in the unsaddling chute first.

After the rodeo and dance was over, I let my head heal up a little. It felt big after associating with Johnny Rye off and on during the dance. I headed for my haying job and got there in time to have supper and a good night's rest, which I surely needed. Next morning, I was as good as new.

We just got through with that haying job, and it was time for me to leave for fall roundup. Everything was working out good. I pulled into the yard at the Circle S ranch, and damned if one of the boys working there hadn't worked haying with me the summer before. I was with familiar company.

The cow boss cut me out some horses, and in a couple of days, we were organized for fall roundup. There was a lot of country to cover, mostly bush and timber range. It was a pretty big outfit. I think they ran between 3000 and 4000 head all told, at the time, on a range that would take a damn good travelling horse to go from one end to the other in a day. I had not done too much range riding steady in the last year or two, just for small outfits and rodeos.

The first day I rode for 10 or 12 hours, and my hind legs felt like they were coming loose at the roots. I was plumb willing to get off by the time evening came. I was just soft from the lack of steady riding, and each day got better as we went along. In a week's time, I did not even feel too tired after riding and rounding up, even on long days. There were no short days at roundup.

Along with roundup came time to wean the calves. We put all the cows and calves into the big holding corral and worked together on horseback. There was a small field connected to the corral where the cows were turned out, and we left the calves in the corral.

On this particular day of weaning, watching the gate, I saw one of the best gate horses work. Her owner was about the best gate man I have ever seen. When we were ready to start weaning and take the cows away from them big calves, the cow boss said, "Gilbert, will you watch the gate?" Gilbert said "Okay, but let me go down to the creek and cut a willow first."

He came back with a piece of fresh willow about three feet long and about an inch-and-a quarter thick. He peeled all the bark off, so it was nice and shiny. At the risk of sounding plumb green, I asked him, "What's that for?" He said, "To help my horse; if one of those big calves tries to duck under her neck when the pressure is on and is trying to follow his mother through the gate, I just shove this shiny stick in front of his nose.

The calf sees the stick and stops long enough that my mare has some time to turn him back and let the cow go."

He went and opened a 14-foot gate and tied it back to the fence. He then mounted his grey mare and, with his shiny stick in his hand, positioned his horse and himself in the middle of that wide opening, facing the cows in the corral. With a grin on his face, he said, "We're ready, let them come!"

The rest of us, working in pairs, brought the cows out in small bunches and, of course, the calves wanted to go, too. They were not crazy about the idea of being weaned, but they could not get by Gilbert and that little grey mare. They were beautiful to watch work; sometimes, the cows would come in bunches of maybe six or eight with their calves. That little mare worked off her back feet mostly and just snapped like a whip; she moved so decisively and fast stopping those calves. Gilbert rode her as if he was grown onto her back, and when the rush was over, only the cows got out, and we chased the calves back away from the gate into the remaining cowherd. We would bring more cows, and so it went till we were done.

Remember, Gilbert and his gate horse was watching a 14-foot hole in the fence with the gate tied back. That is the way he wanted it, he said, so he would have room to work. The rest of us would bring the cows as slow as we could, but the cows being cows, it did not always work that way. The ground was froze, and all the horses was sharp shod, and believe you me, the frozen chips of ice and dirt was sure flying off of that little mare's feet as she ducked and dived, forth and back, stopping those calves.

Gilbert was a superb horseman. He had trained that mare himself, and being a top gate man, the two of them done a beautiful job. When the day was done and we finished weaning, that top hand Indian cowboy on his top gate horse only let one single calf get by out of 635 head. At the end of the day, one of the boys rode into the little holding field and roped the lone calf that got by and led him back in the corral.

I told Gilbert that he must have the best gate horse in the Cariboo Country. He just grinned and said, "Yes, she's pretty good, but not as good as old Black Jack, from the Alkali Lake Ranch." I thought to myself, Black Jack must be some horse, if he is better than the grey mare.

I later learned that old Black Jack had a reputation in that part of the cattle country that was not equalled by anyone. I never had the opportunity to watch that mighty old black horse work, but a lot of my friends had; some had rode him and all agreed that they never knew a cow horse that could cope as good as he could. It did not matter whether he was on the range or in the corrals, working cattle or watching the gate.

Weaning was over, but we had to let the cows and calves bawl and beller for about three days, till they got used to being separated, before turning the cows back on the grass. We then put them big 500- and 600-pound calves into the feedlot for the winter, to grow into yearlings.

An amusing thing happened at this weaning. A little bit of cowboy humour, I guess you would call it. A young fella who had never been around cows was hired on at the home ranch to do odd jobs and chores. The night before we weaned, we were all bellied-up to the table for supper in the cookhouse at the home ranch and kind of discussing the upcoming weaning the next day.

One of the boys made a wisecrack that we might have a tough time finding enough bottles around to wean them calves slow. The young fella that was a mite green asked "What's the bottle for?" and one of the boys grinned and replied, "We can't jerk them poor little calves off their mothers sudden-like, we have to taper them off their mother's milk slow. So, I reckon we'll bottle-feed them for three or four days."

By this time, every cowboy there was contributing ideas on how to do this. All of us were just exaggerating to beat hell to make this joke better and better. The young fella said, "Well, I'll sure help with that and find enough bottles." One of the cowboys said all serious-like, "We appreciate your help, but we'll need 635 bottles—that's quite a few." We just left it at that. We finished supper, figuring everybody knew we were joking around and making light talk. Next day, we weaned the calves, and nobody even gave our supper table joke from the night before a second thought. The young fella quit later that fall and went to a better paying job.

About a year and a half later, I was going into a café for dinner one day when I saw him. I sat down with him and visited while we ate dinner. He asked how things were going, and I said, "Fine, how about you?" He said he liked his job and was getting along good. Then all of a sudden, he started grinning and said, "You guys sure pulled the wool over my eyes at the Circle S at weaning time that fall."

I had forgotten about our little bottle discussion long since, so I asked, "How did we do that?" He reminded me, and I said that it was just a joke and we just forgot it. "You didn't believe any of that, did you?" "Well," he said, "I was plumb green and did not have the faintest clue that you guys were anything but serious. The next three days, I gathered every bottle on the home ranch and wondered why one of you did not come and get them. I did not find anywhere's near 635 bottles, but I figured you must have had enough from last year to wean them calves slow."

I felt somewhat bad, him going to all that trouble over just a joke, and said so. He just laughed and said, "A person learns as he goes along, I guess. I know better now, and besides, all those bottles needed gathering up anyway. If I had thought a little practical, I would have known it was just a joke. I figured it out about the fourth day, but damned if I was going to admit you guys had successfully pulled my leg." "Well," I said, "I'm glad you didn't hold it against us. It was all in fun." He just laughed and said, "Hell no, maybe it'll work for me sometime, just for fun."

After weaning, we trimmed the feet and ingrown horns of some of the older cows. We ran them through an old doctoring chute, thereby saving us the trouble of roping and stretching them out on the frozen ground.

One white-faced, pot-bellied ol' girl was stuck in the chute. It was a mite narrow for her big belly. In trying to scratch her way through, her front feet slipped on the frozen ground, and she went down on her knees with her butt end sticking pretty near straight up. Try as we might, we could not move her. I got on my horse in front of the open chute and handed the loop of my rope to one of the boys. They dropped it over her hind end so we could give her a pull. She still did not move, with my sharp-shod horse pulling hard on the rope. We squared up again to give her another pull, and I touched my horse with the spurs to get him to try a little harder.

That was the wrong thing to do. I guess that old brown gelding had given it all he had the first time. He got mad and went to bucking while still hooked to the cow, which was still stuck. I was not expecting it, and the first jump caught me off balance. It threw me ahead enough that my Lee overall jacket hooked over the saddle horn, locking my hand, and I could not throw my dallies. He kept on bucking and turning in circles, winding me in the rope and pinning my arms to my sides.

One of the boys ran up, grabbed his bridle and stopped him. Lucky for me he did not try to run off. That rope could have been a whole lot tighter fit if he had. This old gelding was plumb gentle, and they turned him back in a tight circle to get me unwound and get the rope off the cow then had to unhook my coat off the saddle horn so I could get my hand loose and throw my dallies.

After all this, the old cow must have got rested or mad; she gave a big heave and slimmed that big belly through the chute and got out alone. Good thing: we were looking to tear one side of that old plank chute out to turn her loose. I do not know why she did not try a little harder in the first place. Cows being cows, I guess she had her reasons that we could not understand.

We cleaned up odds and ends and took some of the neighbouring ranches' cattle home, as they had strayed onto our range during the summer.

It had gotten toward the end of October, and we had a few inches of snow and then a good rain, and it froze hard after the rain, turning the yard into a sheet of ice during the night. Next morning, it was like a skating rink.

We had the horses in the barn. The saddle horses were okay. They were sharp shod. The work team was still barefoot. We had to pack water to them in buckets till we got them sharp shod, so we could get them out of the barn to go to the water trough.

The ice lasted about a week. A thaw came and took it away and lasted a few days before it froze again. We got about four inches of snow, and it was back in the saddle again to round up the odd straggler that had been missed at roundup.

In that timber country, we needed the snow for tracking. It made it easier to find a cow critter that had been missed as you could not see very far. When you found a set of tracks, you just followed them. There would be a cow or cattle at the other end of those tracks. When you found them, you brought them home, regardless of whose brand they were wearing. All the outfits done the same and sorted them out later and sent home any critter that belonged to someone else.

It could be a miserable job after a fresh snow, getting wet with snow coming off the tree branches and down your coat collar. That was timber range cowboying, but all in a day's work. Anyone who has rode the range for a living knows it's not all fun and games, even though we would sooner cowboy than do anything else.

On toward Christmas, it snowed close to a foot. We started to move some of the cattle, the old and thin ones, off the winter range and onto the feed grounds. Anyone who had itchy hands soon had that remedied, running them pitchforks.

After New Year's, we stayed home. The ranch was 60 miles from Williams Lake, BC; me and another fella had to go and round up a few hundred head of two-year-old steers off the winter range along the Fraser River. It was mighty cold, about −20 or −30°F (−29 or −34°C) most of the time. We were camped in an old ranch house along the bank of Little Dog Creek. That house was colder than hell froze over, I am sure.

There was one good room that we used like a bunkhouse and done our cooking and sleeping in. We had a big, old wood stove made out of a 45-gallon oil drum. We had lots of wood and sure did need it. In the evenings, we would sit by the big old stove, roasting in front and having to put our coats over our backs to keep from freezing behind. Not exactly the Waldorf Astoria Hotel, but fine if the weather was good. Even so, it looked pretty good when we came in just at dark, when it was −30°F (−34°C), after gathering steers out of the brush along the Fraser River all day.

CHAPTER 10

THE CARIBOO COUNTRY

We finally got all the two-year-old steers on the Fraser River range gathered and had them in a small field with good grass, ready to go to the feed grounds at the Mountain Ranch. The weather was warming up a little, so we made ready to trail them two-year-olds back to the feeding camp along the main road. Someone from the home ranch came to give us a hand and we headed them out.

The weather had warmed up to about 0°F (–18°C), so it felt pretty near like spring, compared to what it had been. We did not mind leaving our cold old house on Little Dog Creek and were glad to be heading back to the warm bunkhouse at the feeding camp.

When we got the steers to their destination, it was getting dark, but a light in the cookhouse said chuck was about ready. We were ready for someone else's cooking by then, too. We put our horses in a warm barn, got our bellies filled and all was right with the world. We were already forgetting the cold week or two we spent at Little Dog.

Next morning, we were introduced to the pitchforks, harnessed the team and went to feeding them hungry steers. That was okay. We had lots of help: three of us counting the foreman. It turned out to be a good winter-feeding job, even if we had a little problem with too much foxtail in the hay.

After a few weeks, we noticed some of the steers slobbering and not eating so well. Why foxtail will slowly collect in a critter's mouth is a good question. It must be the little barbs on the heads of that foxtail grass that is to blame. I do not know of any other grass hay that will do that. Mind you, it takes quite a lot of foxtail content in the hay before it becomes a problem and, for some reason, only affects some of the critters, not all of them. In our case, we had to cut out 18 head and clean out their mouths.

As this was a brand new feeding camp, there were not any corrals built yet. We had to head and heel them big steers and stretch them out on the ground between two horses. Luckily, there was a big old stackyard built of poles that was empty, so we had somewhere to work. It had a foot of snow for protection on the frozen grounds.

We herded them 18 head into the stackyard. Them being confined, we just headed and heeled them. One of the boys from the home ranch came up, and we did the roping. That left the other two people on foot. When Morley and me got one roped and stretched out, the other two would pry open the steer's mouth and take out the wads of foxtail. We did them that way, one at a time. Some of them had raw sores beginning, but they healed up and were eating well in a couple of days.

The winter passed uneventfully otherwise. Spring came, and feeding was over and calving about to start. Branding time came and went.

About the first of June, I got an offer from another ranch for $50 a month more, about 100 miles from there, so I decided to see if the grass was greener on the other side of the hill. Besides, a $50 raise was quite appealing them days.

After drawing my pay, I loaded my bedroll, saddle and rigging into the old car and headed for the 6-3 Jack Pine Ranch and the jack pine country. That outfit was some 40-odd miles from Williams Lake, only the opposite direction. That way, I was still in the country and would run into the boys I knew when we all happened to be in town. It was summertime, so there was no snow to worry about, and we got to town quite often, not like in the winter.

This new job was in a different kind of country, mostly jack pine and poplar, with big, wild, wet meadows here and there. It sure made good grazing. There were two big meadows about a square mile each, which grew good, tall grass. They would dry up by the middle of the summer, so we could cut the hay. They were the ranch's hay supply. All of it was wild grass, and the cattle thrived quite well on it during the winter.

The haying there was all done with horses powering the mowers, rakes, hay sweeps and overshot stackers, just like the old days. I came on the job a couple of months before haying started, so we were busy moving cattle, fencing and getting all the odd jobs done before haying. The odd jobs were getting the mowers and rakes ready and building a new overshot stacker.

One man rode at the cow camp, some 30-odd miles away, where the cows were on a summer range. I missed the riding job, so I had to ride a mowing machine, dump rake and hay sweep for the summer, instead. I was a fair-to-middling teamster, so it all worked out okay.

It was a pretty good job. I liked driving horses, had been doing it since I was a kid. I drove horses on ranches, in logging camps and even did a bit of teamstering on farmland. When we got through the haying, the big meadows had loose haystacks all over them. From a distance, they looked like big bread loaves all over the meadows.

Fall was coming upon us, with the usual "get ready for winter" stuff to do. The fella at the cow camp had to leave and go home, so I went up sometime in September to look after the cows on the summer range till roundup. It was a nice fall, mostly good weather and warm. It was nice to get back a-horseback after haying. It was all bush and timber range, but I was used to that.

"My dad called these hay cocks; each one is about 100 pounds of hay, and would feed one cow for about five days. Everything was very labour intensive in those days."

It was somewhat enjoyable alone at camp, just me and the horses and cattle on the surrounding range. It was a place where you could enjoy solitude for a while. I rode a couple of young horses when things was going good and not much to do, kind of saving the good, broke horses for roundup.

It was a small outfit, and, as I was alone, I started gathering cattle a little early and put them into a field to be ready for the trail home. It took me a week or so, and when I had them all in the field, I sent word back to the home ranch that I had them all. One of those boys came up to help trail them home, but before we left, we rode the range for a day or two to make sure I had not missed anything.

It snowed a little before we pulled out but not enough to amount to much. We left early in the morning; it was going to be a long day. Thirty-odd miles is a long drive, but the calves, being ready to wean, were big enough to travel that far. It was well after dark when we finally got home.

The day of trailing was uneventful. We trailed slowly pretty well all the way, through the bush. The cattle had an old wagon trail to follow.

We only had a hang-up in one place. We had about 200 cows and calves, so the two of us handled them easy. About halfway home, the leaders stopped on the old wagon trail, looking at something, and the rest of them bunched up behind. I rode up to see what it was, and damned if there wasn't a big, old muskrat travelling across country on the snow. He was a big, cranky-looking old fella and was coming right down the middle of the road. There were three or four inches of fresh snow; he showed up real plain and was not figuring on a bunch of cows making him get off the road.

The cattle were bunching up, so I rode up, figuring on running the muskrat off the road into the brush. He was not gonna have no part of that and seemed to be ready to take on both the horse and me. There was a turn in the road right there, and while that big, black muskrat and me were discussing the situation, them lead cows found an old trail going straight ahead from the turn in the road and headed off into the bush.

I left the muskrat to get around the other side of them cows and help my partner turn them back. It was getting dark, and we still had 10 miles to go. The last thing we needed was to have that herd scatter out in the brush that time of day.

The cattle were starting to speed up, heading into the thick brush faster than we could get around them, but they were still bunched together and following the leaders. It looked for a minute or two like we were going to lose them, and then help came from a much-unexpected source.

My partner had a big, rangy-looking part collie dog. He was sort of a "Heinz" dog, 57 different varieties put into one hide. He was not much of a cow dog, as far as know-how goes, but he saved the day.

Right when those cattle were straying off, that dog was off chasing rabbits. We could hear him yelping, and then we saw him coming straight at the cowherd, 30 miles an hour, on the heels of a rabbit. We figured for sure them old cows were going to take to the timber on a high run.

The rabbit seen the cow herd and figured it wouldn't be too good going amongst them cows with that big old dog snapping at his tail feathers. That rabbit turned off to the right, running for his life, that old dog yelping and only about one jump behind. That rabbit ran at them lead cows on an angle just at the right time and place, both him and the dog running under the first lead cow's neck. That done the trick.

The leader bellowed and turned, started to run and damned if she did not run back on the road heading for home. A mangy mutt and a rabbit saved the day! I breathed a sigh of relief, how could we be so lucky? My partner laughed and said, "How do you like that for a cow dog? He knew just what to do." I just grinned; that chase had saved our bacon. I said, "Good thing that rabbit was a little cow shy and didn't run into the middle of them, but sure, I'll admit, they done the right thing."

We could joke about it now—we had been saved from a big mix-up and were on our way home. I tell you, we were not joking when we first seen that rabbit and dog heading for the middle of that cowherd. It had turned out very well for us.

The dog gave up on the rabbit, never did catch him, and was satisfied to follow us quietly home. The cows followed the road from then on, no problems, and we put them into the home field finally, after trailing for three hours in the dark. The new snow helped to see a little, so we never lost any along the way.

We let the herd rest for a couple of days and then brought them in and weaned the calves. After the calves were weaned and were in the corral, they bawled and bellered around for three or four days, till the cows left and went back to grazing. We kept the calves in the corral on feed for about a week before they were taken to the home ranch and eventually sold.

It snowed a little bit more, and we moved the cows to some big meadows back in the bush, where the grass had not been cut and was standing like a hayfield. It made for good grazing. We packed salt to the cows and cut water holes, and they stayed till Christmas. There was not a road to these meadows, so we took salt in with a packhorse. All in a day's work on a bush country, jack pine–covered cow ranch.

After Christmas, we moved the cattle back to the feeding camp from the meadows where they had been all winter, grazing. The grass was getting used up, and the snow was getting somewhat deep. They would stay on feed the rest of the winter until spring. As there were two other men there to feed, I went down to the home place and fed cows at the Onward Ranch.

About the middle of February, one of the boys at the feed camp had to leave, so the boss sent me back to the 6-3 feed camp to take charge of the cows and look after the outfit.

The snow was piling up more every day, it seemed. Before spring, we had about four feet on the ground. You could hardly ride off the trails or the feed grounds. Horses could not go in all that snow, with it pushing against the breast collar.

The hay-hauling trail to the hay meadow was kept open from everyday use, hauling loose hay with the teams pulling sleighs with big hayracks for feeding the cows at the camp. We had about a three-mile haul.

When we cleaned up a stack and had to break a trail to another one, we had to make three or four trips from the road to the new stack with the empty sleigh to get a trail broke before we could put on a load. Even then, we had to load light till we got the trail packed.

The first trip breaking a trail to a new stack was tough. We had to stop and rest the team every hundred feet or so. Luckily, the stacks were not too far apart.

There was a time in March when we were completely snowed in. Good thing we had laid in lots of grub. The road was plumb impassable. Finally, toward the end of March, a fella showed up with a big TD14 Caterpillar with a 3-by-10 plank bolted to the top of the blade so the snow would not boil over the top. He had to make two trips, 15 miles from the main road, to clear our road, so we could get out with the old one-ton truck. The manager at the Onward had sent him in. It was not long till the cows would start calving, and we had to get them out of the high country down to a bare, good calving pasture.

It would be about a six-day drive, so I rounded up some hay bales and left a ton of hay at each stopping place along the road. There were old, empty homestead places along the way with a cabin for us to stay in, old barns for the horses and a place to feed the cows. We would just work our way from one place to the other each day. It was still cold at night, with two or three feet of snow in the high country.

At the home feed camp, we built a closed-in corral on one of the hayracks to haul the little calves that were already born. We partitioned off about four feet on the front of the rack for the teamster and camping equipment. We were all set to hit the trail to the low country.

I had hired a couple of good, extra men to help with the drive, and, on April 4, we headed them down the snow-ploughed road. The snowbanks on each side made the road like a trench, so we took about 50 or 60 head apiece, one bunch ahead of the other, and strung out to keep moving without bunching up. The team and rack led the parade, with the little calves riding in style.

We made the first stopping place just before dark, unloaded the little calves to go with their mamas for the night, fed the cows and horses, then went to an old cabin, lit a fire in the old stove and proceeded to feed and water ourselves. A couple of heifers looked like they were fixing to calve, so we put them in an old barn so they would be handy. Sure as hell, we had to pull two calves about 10:00 PM, and we were thankful for that old barn. So it went, pretty well the same at each stopping place.

In the morning before leaving, we would rope all the little calves and load them onto the hayrack to ride for the day. On about the third day, coming down into the low country where it was getting nice and warm, we ran out of snow. The horses could not drag the sleigh on the mud much farther. We slowly worked our way to the next stopping place.

Some folks lived there on a small ranch by Spoken Lake. We were there early, took care of the stock, and I asked the rancher if he had a rubber-tired wagon we could borrow to hook the team to. He did, so we got all hands together and lifted our calf corral hayrack off the sleigh, and it fit on the wagon perfectly. We were still in business.

Next morning, we were on the trail again. The next stopping place was a good day's drive, so we got going early and made it without any problems. A couple of cows calved that night, but down there it was bare ground and quite warm, so that was okay. We had to pull one calf. A few calves were being born at each stopping place, and they were slowly filling up our hayrack pen, but we only had two more days and so should have had room for any newborns.

Two days later, we pulled into the calving field at the 150 Mile House, and there the grass was starting to green up, ground was all bare and we were all glad to be at the end of the trail. We unloaded the little calves to go to their mothering, took care of the horses, got something to eat and stopped for the day. We had a successful trip, considering everything.

The next day, the other boys took the wagon back to its owner and headed back to the feeding camp, which was also the head-quarters for the 6-3 Jack Pine Ranch. They then headed home for the horses, which still had to be fed till the snow was gone up there in the high country.

Me, I had to get the truck and bring some provisions out from town, for I had to stay with the cows to calve them out. There were no buildings of any kind in the calving field, just an old corral in fair shape and a pole stackyard.

I set up a tent with a wooden floor, close to the corral, to live in and had to haul drinking and cooking water. Luckily, the tent and corral were right beside the main gravel road, so I could get right to them, with my provisions, equipment and horse feed loaded on the truck.

I spent eight weeks in that tent camp, calving those cows, riding every day. There was times when it got a mite cold, but I had many blankets. I had no heat in the tent; my tin camp stove was outside for cooking. I had made the floor for the tent long enough so that about four feet of floor stuck out in the front, kind of like a porch floor, that the stove sat on. A lot of the time, the wind would blow at night and blow my stove down the little hill to the corral. I would have to lug it back to the tent and set it up again before I could make breakfast.

Kind of a nuisance having the stove outside when it was raining. I had a canvas that I would stretch over the stove on a couple of posts to keep the rain out of the frying pan. I only used it when it was raining a lot. Generally, the weather was fair that spring, so it was okay.

The cows were done calving about the middle of May, but we left them in the calving field till about the middle of June, so the calves would grow big enough to trail back to the 6-3, where the cows had wintered. It took only three days for the return trip.

When we got back to the feed camp ranch, we turned them into a hay meadow to feed for three days and let the calves get rested up. We still had another two days' drive from there to the cow camp and the summer range.

When we got to the cow camp, we let them rest in a little field for a day then branded the calves and turned them on the range for the summer. It was nice to be done. I stayed in the cow camp to look after the cows on the timber range. The rest of the boys took the team and wagon and their horses back to the 6-3. One married fella stayed at the ranch for the summer, and all the extra help were paid off and went home.

I rode at the cow camp for a couple more months and was offered a job with the Cariboo Cattleman's Association for more money, so I took it as soon as the owner got another rider. This was the first time I had ever held a job in town. The Cariboo Cattleman's Association office and feed store was right close to the railroad siding. I looked after the feed store and unloaded all the grain, which came in 100-pound burlap sacks, in boxcars, a carload at a time.

That would keep me right busy for a couple of days, but it was fixed up pretty well. I used a two-wheeled rig, special made for the purpose, something very similar to the two-wheeled rigs used nowadays for moving fridges, stoves, washing machines and such.

In between unloading cars, it was pretty easy; we had a steady flow of business in the feed store, but it was spaced out most of the time, so a fella could put his feet up and have a coffee often. All in all, a good job, with good men to work with.

There was three of us, all told: the manager, the cattle sales representative and me. Once in a while, I would go and help Slim, the cattleman, down at the stockyards.

I and another feller, who worked at the western store and saddlery, lived down at the stockyards in a little cabin. It was big enough to walk in but hardly room to turn around, so you pretty near had to back out. It was a good little cabin; warm, as long as we kept the wood cook stove going, even in winter.

It was a real nice winter that year, only a foot of snow after New Year's, and it was gone by the middle of February. Kind of unusual for Williams Lake in the Cariboo Country.

It sure turned out to be a dry spring. We sold a lot of range pellets that spring; it was so dry the ranchers had to help the cattle on the range with feed, waiting for the grass to grow.

No rain in April or May; the situation was getting a little grim.

On the fifth of June, it started to rain. It drizzled heavy for three days and three nights. When the sun came back out, the weather turned nice and warm. You could stand back and pretty near see the grass growing.

In a week or 10 days, the range was plumb green, and the grass was getting tall. It sure brightened up the range folks and put a smile back on everyone's face. The whole countryside, as well as the whole town, depended on the grass on the range to keep the cattle industry going. Everyone's living more or less depended on the cattle business, directly and indirectly, except for a few small logging outfits starting out in the bush, and they needed hay for their horses.

About the first of July, the annual Williams Lake Rodeo was taking place. I decided to enter the bronc riding, as it had only been a year since I was riding steady, so I figured I could still compete. During the spring, Slim had gone and picked up a five-year-old mare he owned from when he worked for the Douglas Lake Ranch at Merritt. He figured she would make a bucking horse. Good reason to think so, too: the mare was a direct niece to the notorious Devil's Dream, which belonged to a top bucking-horse outfit from Washington State.

I think Slim's mare was barely halter-broke. Slim wanted me to try her out before the rodeo, but I did not want any part of her. She looked like she could be tough, and I did not even really want to draw her in the bronc riding.

Well, you guessed it, when they drew the saddle broncs for the first go-around, they drew me horse No. 4. When I went to check out the horse I had drawn, Slim's mare was wearing a big yellow 4 on her hip. I guess I was going to be the first rider to try her out, after all.

When my horse came in the chute, I did not even want to go near her. I got a couple of friends, both bronc riders, to saddle her. One of them asked, "How do you want your saddle set?" I had every confidence in him, so I said, "Wherever you think so I can ride her, same as if you were going to ride." He grinned and said okay. He did a very good job of rigging her out while I was putting my chaps on. I just wanted to concentrate on riding her; as I could see and feel, I would have my hands full.

The chute boss hollered, "Get ready, boys!" I was the first one out. I climbed onto her in the chute and knew right then the 10-second whistle could seem a long way ahead.

My friends belted me down; I nodded my head and swung my spurs over the points of her shoulders as her front feet hit the ground on the first jump. There was no doubt she was following in her aunt's footsteps. That mare was wild and green her first trip out of the chute. She came out like a cyclone, but I was doing okay, building up a decent score, so I thought.

About six or seven seconds out, she threw one at me that I could not ride, and we parted company. It was probably one of the luckiest buck offs I have ever had. I was lying there on the ground watching her go, and it did not take a genius to figure out why I was on the ground. About the third jump after I came off, she went way up in the air, just a-sunfishing. In doing so, all four legs were out sideways, and she hit the ground flat on her side, got up and kept bucking, threw herself again then bucked on down the arena.

That was one time I was glad to be on the ground and contribute my entry fees to the winning riders. Had I been on her when she threw herself on her side the first time, I could have been in bad trouble.

The second go-around, I did not really fare much better. I drew a tall, black horse by the name of John Doe. This was an experienced bucking horse, and he had enough ability that he did not have to take second place to any of them. I figured this was okay. I could ride him, and he was sure as hell the right horse to put me in some day money.

I nodded my head, the gate swung open and damned if he didn't come out nice and easy backwards and turn plumb around the wrong way. It threw me a little wrong, not expecting it. As he straightened out toward the arena, I swung my feet way up and started him so he would not mess around anymore. He got the message, all right. He ducked his head and poured it on.

He bucked around in a small circle right in front of the chute. It was kind of like a tornado that was not going anywhere. Just before the whistle blew, he and I parted company. He did not leave, though; he just kept bucking practically on top of me. I did not dare get up, might get my head kicked off, so I buried my nose into that arena dirt and waited for him to leave.

One of my friends said he seemed to be bucking all over me. He said he heard a sharp crack like a pistol shot, figured I was kicked in the head and had rode my last bronc. John Doe finally bucked away from me, and when I realized he was going, I turned my head with my left cheek still on the ground so as to see him go. I was not about to get up until I knew it was safe.

I got up without a bruise or scratch on me, just as healthy as when I climbed up on him.

I reckon my guardian angel must have stepped in to help somehow, or maybe old John Doe did not step on me on purpose —most horses are that way. They usually do not step on someone, unless by accident. Anyway, a miss is as good as a mile away. I was fine, and it's all a part of bronc riding.

With bronc riding, you win some, you lose some. I did not win any money, but I came out of that close shave with my hide and bones all where they were supposed to be, so I guess I was still a winner. It was a good rodeo; we placed, I think, in the wild horse race and had a whale of a good time for three days and three nights. With all the folks from the surrounding ranches in town, along with contestants from western Canada and the western USA, the town was just a-jumping.

The low hill west of the arena turned into a real tent town, with folks coming in from long distances away and camping for the week to take it all in. Some came from ranches and reservations several days' travel, with horses and wagons. I suppose nowadays that same low hill is probably covered with modern trailers, RVs and new trucks. There have been some changes in the rodeo picture as time has passed.

The rodeo was over, so it was back to work for a while, but not for long. A friend of mine, a good bronc rider, and me decided to load our rope horse onto a covered rack on my pickup and head for Alberta to try our luck. We gave notice at our places of employment, and when they found replacements for us, we made ready to see if the grass was greener on the other side of the mountains. Course, we figured in paying our way at various rodeos along the way.

Looking back, I can understand something about that old saying, whoever wrote it: "The best made plans of mice and men so often go astray."

To start with, we had left our horse in a barn at the stockyards with the saddle on. Going down to pick him up, there was my new saddle, lying on the edge of the road, ready to be picked up by a couple of guys stealing a load of hay with an old truck at the hay shed. They heard us coming and disappeared, so I took the key out of their truck. I told my partner to stay in our truck, lock the doors and watch them. I said if they come looking to go to war, get the hell out of there.

Then I cut across country toward town on foot, flagged a ride, got the Mounties and gave them the keys to the hay stealers' truck. The Mounties and I could not find them, as they had hid well. George and I got our saddle and horse and, as we were ready and could not be of any help, headed out for the prairies.

The Mounties had the key to the hay stealers' truck; from what we heard later, a couple of them just camped in the grass and waited. About three o'clock the next morning, just as it was getting daylight (this was the middle of July), the waiting paid off. Those two guys were plumb absorbed in trying to hot-wire their truck to get the hell out of there before they were caught.

A couple of Mounties tapped them on the shoulders and asked if they needed some help. It was not exactly the kind of help they needed, but the Mounties were nice enough. They invited them to use their beds and have breakfast at the "Crowbar Hotel." That was the last we heard of it.

CHAPTER 11

ALBERTA BOUND

With the Mounties on the job looking to nail those would-be thieves' hides to the wall, and being as George and me were of no more help, we headed down the road, bound for Alberta. It was about three o'clock in the afternoon, but it was the middle of July—the days were long—so we decided to drive for a few hours and find a place to camp for the night.

After a few hours, we saw an old corral in half-decent shape on the side of the road, in the middle of a grassy opening with a little creek trickling through the jack pines. Our first night's stop, with grass and water for our horse, wood for a fire to cook on and a corral to keep our horse from straying while we slept. Pretty first-class accommodations.

About dark, after we'd fed and watered ourselves, we put our horse in the corral after letting him graze for a couple of hours, rolled out our bedrolls and called it a day. We slept like a pair of babies and did not wake up until the warmth of the sun on my bedroll woke me up.

George was still comfortably snoozing away, sounding like a crosscut saw working its way through a jack pine knot. I turned back my sleeping bag and looked out. It was a beautiful, sunny morning, and sitting there looking at us were two of the biggest dogs I had ever seen. One looking at George, the other one at me.

At first, I thought they were wolves. I let out a holler, woke George, and he rared up as if somebody hit him in the butt with a hot branding iron. We were both looking to see if there was a club close by. We did not need one; them two big dogs was plumb friendly, just curious. I guess they had never seen two people sleeping on the ground under the trees.

We cursed at them and hollered, telling them to get the hell out of there. They looked at us as if they were offended and finally left. I think we hurt their feelings, and they most likely figured they did not need anything to do with two guys that were so unsociable. I guess they thought right, but it gave us quite a start. To wake up and see what seemed to be a pair of big timber wolves at first glance, sizing us up and drooling at the mouth just did not make us the friendliest guys. Imagination does play tricks on a person sometimes, before you realize what is real.

It was still early, but we crawled out right away, and, while George was building a breakfast fire, I watered my horse and let him go to grazing for a couple of hours before we headed on down the road. We knew there was a one-day rodeo at a small place called Bridge Lake off the main road, so we figured we would stop there, get entered and maybe make some travelling money.

We camped not far from the turnoff, so we got there early enough to be entered. This was not too far from Williams Lake, so many of our friends were there, too. We did not make any money but stayed for the dance. Sort of a going-away spree before heading for Alberta.

A good friend of ours, Little Joe, from the reservation near Williams Lake, won the bareback bronc riding. We were glad he won it. For a couple of years he had been trying but seemed to always draw tough horses. Little Joe didn't only try to ride them, he came out of the chute spurring like a world champion and just couldn't seem to make the whistle. There were times when us other boys told him he just spurred himself off. Little Joe would just grin and say "One of these times it'll come together. It's got to be pay dirt or eat dirt."

Pay dirt day finally came, and he had drawn a tough horse. He came out spurring like usual. When the whistle blew, Little Joe was still there, hoeing the dollars out of that bronc with his dull spurs. I think he rode good enough that day that the judges could have handed him the book to mark his own ride to win, and it still would have been fair. Needless to say, we all helped him celebrate his win that night. As we hadn't got into our bedrolls till near sun-up, we kind of slept in till near nine o'clock.

We finally got going on a side road heading in the right direction with two other friends who needed a ride to Clinton. On towards suppertime, we came to a wide place along the road with lots of grass, so we decided to camp for the night. Someone had lived there previously; the house was gone, but there was a good little barn there. It even had some hay in it. Being as it looked like rain, we had shelter.

After grazing our horse and putting out our supper fire, it was close to dark. We stabled the horse, fed him some hay and used some more hay to fix a mattress to spread our bedrolls on behind the horse. The barn was wide, with lots of room. It was time to call it a day. We were right about the weather. It rained like hell that night.

Come morning, the sun was shining again, and after making some breakfast, we were on our way. We drove along for a while and heard some clattering and banging under the truck, so we looked. The front universal was shot. The truck would not go. Just what we needed. Lucky we were only about 25 miles from Clinton.

We unloaded the horse, and George caught a ride to Clinton and got a new universal. Our friends and I pulled the truck apart so we would be ready to put things together when George got back. After testing our mechanical skills, we were back on the road, headed to Alberta. We dropped our two friends off in Clinton and kept on going. We went as far as we could before we had to stop for the day and set up camp for another night.

The next day, we got a good start. We had a friend living south of Vernon in the Okanagan Valley, and we wanted to make it to his place before dark. I had put new tires on the truck before we left, so we would not have any tire trouble.

It was hotter than the hobs of hell that afternoon, driving along the lake south of Vernon. We heard a loud bang, like a shotgun had been fired under our butts, and the truck settled to the left and did not drive so well. I stopped right away. That brand-new tire had a hole in the side of it. It was big enough that you could have run a full-grown tomcat through it without disturbing his hair. I looked at George, he just shook his head. So far, Lady Luck did not seem to be on our side.

We put on the spare and made it to our friend's place before dark. After hearing about our trouble, Dave said he would take us to a tire shop in Vernon to get a replacement. Lady Luck made a comeback. The tire shop owner said the best he could do was offer us a new tire for five bucks. I near tore my pocket getting that five bucks out, before he changed his mind! We were ready for the open road again.

After spending the rest of the day and another night with Dave, we headed south through the Okanagan Valley and got to Osoyoos, where we had to hunt up the Mounted Police to brand inspect our horse again, before heading east to Alberta. With that done, we headed east towards Grand Forks. As the afternoon was wearing away, we found a good camping place beside a little creek and stopped for the day. We unloaded our horse; he drank and went to grazing, dragging his halter shank while we rustled up some wood, built a fire and proceeded to get supper.

We were about ready to eat when George looked around and asked, "Where's Billy?" I looked up, and my horse was gone.

We looked up the road where we came from; there went Billy, walking along beside the road with his head turned sideways so he would not step on the halter shank. He had decided he had ridden far enough and was heading for home. We jumped in the truck and passed him. George caught him while I turned around, and we went back and finished supper.

From there to Fort Macleod, Alberta, things went better. We could not travel fast—all gravel roads, them days—but we found good places to camp each night, with feed and water. It was turning into an enjoyable trip.

The rodeo was just over when we got to Fort Macleod, and somebody had gone off and left some good hay bales that needed using up. We put our horse in the rodeo corrals, and, with good hay, we had it made.

We drove down on the cottonwood flat along the river where the old original North West Mounted Police fort had first been built after a trip across the prairies in 1874. The fort was gone, but we found a good camping place among the poplar trees and decided to set up housekeeping for a couple of days to get our bearings.

As we had been problem-free for a few days, it seemed that things were going okay. Well, that was until we had a problem loom up on us when we were not looking. As we had not exactly had the best of luck here and there, upon checking our financial resources, we found out that we were near flat broke, and there was no job to get to tide us over for a while.

After a couple of days, we traded in a brand-new set of tire chains to an understanding gas-station owner for a full tank of gas and a quart of oil. We were on our way to Calgary.

We got some money by putting some of our equipment in a hockshop: my bronc spurs, a new pair of extra boots of George's, a wool blanket and a saddle. Out of all that, we got $35 and headed for Bassano.

Being financially embarrassed, we pulled into the rodeo arena out of town and set up camp, feeding ourselves and grazing our horse. Luckily, we still had a supply of grub. The one-day rodeo was taking place in a couple of days, and, because we had found a haying job the day after we got there, we took part as the entry fees were only $5.

Going back to the day we arrived in Bassano, I must say that camping out in July sounds like fun. Well, not that night. The black clouds came boiling in just as we had finished supper, and it started to rain a little. We found an elevated place on the ground and spread our bedrolls. We both had waterproof canvas covers, so we did not worry too much about a little rain.

One of the worst thunderstorms I have ever seen blew in about 10 o'clock. When the lightning flashed, you could see for miles, and rain came down by the bucketful. We pulled our bedroll tarps over our heads and hoped they would do the trick. They did; we were warm and dry under them, out there on the prairie, beside the corral. Sure lucky we had that little piece of high ground to lie on, as next morning there was little lakes of water in all the low places, glistening in the morning sun.

Next day, the one-day rodeo was on. We were entered in the bronc riding and me in the calf roping. Well, rodeo being rodeo, things happen, and we never made it pay. I bucked off in the bronc riding off a Calgary Stampede horse. I caught my calf fast, but somehow he got halfway through the loop, resulting in a belly catch. The stopwatch kept right on counting the seconds before I got him tied down, fighting and kicking. No money there.

My partner drew a real tough horse and was putting on a winning ride. Just before the whistle, that old bronc threw one at George. He could not quite weather the rest of the storm and hit the ground just as the whistle blew. He was sure enough spurring us up some hamburger money when that happened. It was close, but close only counts in the game of horseshoes.

The boss on our haying job kind of wanted George to stay a little longer, he being a good man riding colts. The rest of us would finish haying and do some fencing while he rode colts. At the end of the three weeks, there were a few rodeos in northern Alberta to go to, so we decided to go. Haying was pretty near done, and the boss, being an old rodeo man himself, understood. We were paid and headed north.

The weather was good, and the south wind, going about 60 miles an hour behind us, gave us some damned good gas mileage. Gas was only about four bits a gallon them days, but then we had been working for regular wages at $4.50 a day and room and board. I guess it averaged out to a certain extent, compared to today's price range.

Next day, we pulled into a town north of Edmonton, called Barrhead, for the first rodeo. We drew well but were not marked good enough to win anything. I mentally had to question the judges' marking for my partner, because, in my opinion, he put on a beautiful spurring ride, never missed a lick on a hell of a good horse. One of the best rides there, I thought. It was not any use saying anything or complaining; the judges' decision was final. I guess they had different ideas than I did, and they were marking the cards.

On the way back, we stopped for another one-day event at a place back in the brush called Sandy Lake. Real nice lake, and everybody had to camp out. That was enjoyable, even if we did not make anything, kind of like a community picnic with all the contestants. There was really no money up: $5 entry fees, and every event was hotly contested. The fellow who won the bull riding made $35 on a bull good enough to win Calgary on.

They were decorating the steers' horns with a ribbon, instead of bull dogging, and that was all real fast times; the first three fastest times were separated by only two-tenths of a second, the fastest being two and two-tenths of a second. There again,

I think the winner made about $30. I am sure those same times could have placed at Calgary. No matter what happened that day, we all had fun.

People were still busy haying around the area and, as luck would have it, we found a rancher who needed a couple of guys. We went home with him, helped him finish his haying and then went haying for one of his rancher neighbours after that.

On this outfit, we done most anything related to a ranch: haying, fencing, working cattle, a little branding. Whatever the ranching job, we were ready to do it. This suited us fine. After all, we were a couple of top hand, British Columbia cowboys. That was how a lot of the prairie folks seen us, only I did not hear the top hand part mentioned as often as the British Columbia cowboys part.

We had been working steady for about three weeks, the weather being favourable, when the time came for the last rodeo of the season for us. We talked it over with the boss and, being as the work was pretty well caught up, he gave us time off to go. He added with a grin, "You'd make more money staying at the ranch!" This was something to consider, but then again, we had come all the way to Alberta to try our hand at riding them prairie rodeo broncs. We figured we had to take a last kick at the cat before the rodeo season was over for the summer.

Bright and early on a sunny morning, we threw our saddles and riggin', camping gear and bedrolls in the truck and headed for Saskatoon, Saskatchewan, a whole day's drive away. We had previously entered in the saddle bronc riding by phone.

Saskatoon was putting on a big two-day rodeo with all the trimmings. When we pulled into the rodeo grounds, there were Ferris wheels, rides and concession booths covering about an acre of ground. People were all over the place, taking in the midway attractions. Sure enough, there was going to be a fun time for all.

We found the rodeo entry office, with a bunch of contestants standing there, passing the time and visiting, and I heard one of them say, "I wonder who's going to be the lucky guy to draw that old Farmer bucking horse?" Being as I knew him a little and as this was a completely strange bucking string to me, I was curious and asked the guy, "Is old Farmer a good draw?" He said that Farmer was one of the best buckers in the string, if you can get out of the chute on him in one piece. He was terrible to fight in the chute if he got upset. "You'll find out when you draw him," he said with a grin.

Of course, I knew he was pulling my leg; the saddle broncs had not even been drawn for yet. Deep down, I was hoping to draw a top horse, gentle in the chute, but did not want to say anything.

The next morning, when the bronc riding draws were posted, we looked at them, and I had drawn a big bronc by the name of Hell to Set. George got Jack Frost, sort of a frosty-coloured roan. We were both happy we got a couple of good horses and missed out on old chute-fighting Farmer.

The rodeo got underway about 1:30, and come the bronc riding section, I eased down onto old Hell to Set. He was standing plumb still; I nodded my head and out we came. I got him started good, and I was still riding high when the whistle blew. So far, so good.

George was getting ready for old Jack Frost and eased down onto his back. Everything was looking good, when, all of a sudden, just like pulling a trigger, Jack Frost reared over backward in the chute and George was under him. I had visions of my partner getting into real trouble, but the day was saved.

When the horse reared over, he did not go all the way down, as his withers caught on the back gate so he was sitting on his ass, kind of like a post leaning against a fence. This created a small, empty space on the ground inside the corner of the chute. That was where George was. How he had managed to get there was anybody's guess.

George was small, strong and wiry, also quick as a cat. It was not the first time he had saved himself on a rearing-over-backwards horse. He was not hurt and hollered out for somebody to open the chute gate a little so he could get out. The accommodations were a mite crowded where he was.

One of the boys opened the gate just a little, very easy so the horse would not try to move. A couple of us reached in and dragged George out. We swung the gate on the back chute around to meet the gate we opened, forming a V to give room to get Jack Frost straightened up and back on his feet. With this accomplished, we reset and cinched George's saddle. He eased down the second time, and the horse stood still long enough until George nodded his head.

He got that old horse started high in the shoulder and went to riding. He spurred from the shoulders to the cantle board until the whistle blew. Jack Frost had bucked just hard enough he could not get a re-ride. We both had marked 70-something, just out of the day money, but in a nice position for a shot at the average if we drew good horses the next day.

We sure did not have anything to complain about the bucking abilities of the horses we drew the second day. All we had to do was ride them.

George drew the best bucking horse in the string, Blue Bill. He was very seldom ridden and had bucked off some of the best riders of the time. He would surely put the man who could ride him in the money. I drew the second best in the string, old Farmer.

When the bronc riding section came up the second day, the chute boss told his helper to run old Farmer in alone and get him out. After he was gone, they would load the chutes with the other broncs. Somebody asked why. The chute boss said, "We have to try to keep him quiet. If he gets upset, he will tear this outfit apart." Talk about music to my ears.

I was standing right by the chute boss, when he asked, "Where's the guy that's going to ride him?" I said I drew him. He told me, "Do as I say and get out as fast as you can. Mark your buck shank where you want to grab it, get down on him and nod for the gate right away. Once you're out, you'll be okay."

I followed his instructions to the letter, nodded for the gate and started him high in the shoulders. He turned the crank, and I was riding him good. My ability was sure being tested. I figured that I was building up points toward the average good, when I lost my right stirrup.

This calls for an automatic disqualification. It pretty near brought tears to my eyes. Farmer did not care, he had a job to finish, and it did not take him long. With that stirrup missing, he ironed me out in a hell of a hurry. There was damn little satisfaction in hearing the announcer say, "Don't feel bad about bucking off that fella; there is a mighty good bucking horse."

No money for me, but we still had an ace in the hole. George had to ride yet, and he drew to win. George was a real good rider, with a very good spurring lick. With any luck, he was going to make the whistle. Blue Bill had other ideas. Along with being a top bucking horse, he had a trick or two he could use. We were told if you took a short shank on him, he would drive his head right down between his knees and jerk the rider over his head. If you took a long shank on him, he would throw his head up toward your face, thereby giving too much slack, and put his rider out the back door, over the cantle.

Well, George figured he would just take a medium shank, so he would be ready for him either way. He nodded his head, started him good and high and was looking good. Blue Bill must have done some figuring of his own. He was just getting going, and George was riding real pretty, when Blue Bill threw his head way up, giving George way too much slack. The next jump, he drove his head down between his knees, catching George off balance, jerking him over his left shoulder. Blue Bill had just put another notch on his six-gun handle, so to speak. There went our last hope of doing ourselves some good, but we still had a job to go back to.

That was not quite the end of our fun, if you could call it that. At this rodeo, the amateur bronc riding event was after supper, after the evening performance. There were seven contestants in this event, and I guess the stock contractor did not pick amateur horses for those young fellas. Five of those young fellers drew some tough horses on the first day and were ironed out something unmerciful. They did not want any part of it in the second go-around.

The rodeo was basically over, just the amateur bronc riding left. The stock contractor was in a bit of a bind, with only two contestants showing and the grandstand full of people to see the event. He wanted to keep his image and put on a good show, so he was trying to talk any one of us who would listen to ride a horse out for him for a $5 mounting fee.

Nobody wanted to, as we had all rode our stock during the afternoon and had put our rigging away. I finally gave in, along with a couple other fellers, and told him I would take one out if he would give me an easy horse that showed good. "No problem," he said, "throw your rig on that bald-faced sorrel." Then he changed his mind. "Wait, take old Brownie; he's practically a re-ride in the bareback, but he sure as hell done a lot better in the saddle event."

Brownie poured it on good. I was in a storm, and I do not know how long I rode him. I do not recall hearing the whistle. He bucked me off on that hard ground in the corner of the arena where it is not worked up. At this rodeo, they had portable chutes and just cultivated a baseball field for the arena; they fenced it in the right size with steel posts and a snow fence.

I was lying on the ground, watching old Brownie buck crosswise in the arena, his head down low, mouth open, bellowing like a bull. He did not see the snow fence coming at him, since his head was between his knees. He hit the snow fence with enough momentum that he turned over on his back, landing on the hard ground outside of the fence. Like one of my friends said, "That was one of the luckiest buck-offs you ever made." My neck was saved again, and I have never ridden another horse for mounting money to this day.

CHAPTER 12

THE PRAIRIES

Another dry run. We had to go back to the ranch next day. We decided to go to the dance that night, though, and maybe swing a good-looking girl or two in a two-step or foxtrot and have us a little fun. We did have fun, but when I crawled out of my bedroll next morning, my left wrist was complaining something awful.

I had reached out for the ground to break my fall, when Brownie bucked me off the night before, and sprained it very bad. The joys of trying to ride bucking horses. That wrist was so hard to live with; no doubt, that is what woke me up. It hurt so bad that George had to drive home. We made it back to the ranch by sundown.

After soaking my wrist in hot water for a couple of hours, I hit the sack after being fed and watered. Luck was with me, as I had to drive a tractor with my good hand, so I did not lose any working time. It was somewhat rough for the first week, with that wrist throbbing steady. It did not do anything for me, except to keep me informed that my heart was still working. I could feel every beat in my wrist.

I was too tough to go to a doctor. I was kind of scared, too, as he might want me to lay off work. I could not afford that, with a truck payment coming up at the end of the month. The wrist finally healed up, but I think I probably broke a bone in there, not just a sprain, as I wear a little bump where it healed. Oh well; all is well that ends well.

The outfit I was working for was not that big, but they had three carloads of fat, two-year-old steers to ship to Winnipeg. They were running with some other critters, so we saddled up one day, rounded them up and proceeded to cut them off by themselves and trail them home.

There was an old, fenced-off road allowance right alongside the field they were in. We used that as a sort of makeshift corral. We were pretty good on horseback. I was riding Billy, my rope horse, and George and the boss' wife, who was helping us, were also mounted good. Everything went well. We got them sorted out in time. We should be home for supper.

They were range steers but seemed halfways gentle. Gentle, that is, until we just had them started for home. A gust of wind came up and blew a big old paper bag that was stuck on a sagebrush right over the back end of the bunch.

It seemed like a ripple went through the whole herd. They were off and running like the devil was on their tails. We just had to let them run, me trying to steer them for home on one side, George on the other and the boss' wife bringing up the tail end. Those steers kind of ran out of steam after a mile or two and settled down to a walk. We had them in the home corral in plenty of time for supper.

Next morning, we headed them out to the stockyards in town by the railroad tracks. The weather was still warm, so it took us near all day to trail them the 15 miles to town. It was on toward early evening, but the days were getting shorter, and we still had to sort them over and grade them before loading.

We cut them into three groups: one carload of top steers, one of second cut and one of tail-enders. They would be leaving for Winnipeg early the next day. It did not give us much time, as there were only the two of us, and it was getting dark fast. No electric lights at the yards and not even a flashlight, but there was a big yellow moon in the sky to sort by.

We kept on working and got finished about 10 o'clock. Thank goodness for that moon. They were loaded and headed for Winnipeg, and the boss and his wife went with them for the sale.

When they got back, we cautiously asked the boss what the sales ring and people thought of our moonlight sorting. He grinned and said, "I don't know how you did it, but they only switched two steers around in all three car loads." We just looked at each other and said with a grin, "Good men, and good horses." The British Columbia cowboys had not done too badly, after all.

Shortly after that, maybe a week or two, the weather cooled off considerably. We were still cutting green feed with an old tractor hooked onto an old horse binder. As we never brought any long johns, we were shivering hard enough in the mornings that our teeth were chattering hard enough to chip the enamel off our choppers.

We had been working for a month, or so, since that last rodeo, so we were back in the chips enough that we could go buy ourselves some long johns. The boss said to try the general store. It was a small town, so it was hard to say if we would find a store with long johns for sale.

We got in the truck, after quitting a little early for the day to make the store. We sure hoped that the store would have something. The thought of riding them steel implement seats the next morning in just overall pants was enough to make us shiver right in the truck.

We made it to the store just before closing time. I said to the storekeeper, "Would you happen to handle long johns?" He said, "I've ordered some, but they aren't in yet." My jaw dropped, and I could feel a glassy look come into my eyes at the thought of another day of freezing.

"Come to think of it," the storekeeper said," I've got two pair of blue label Stanfields woollen long johns left from last winter, but they'll be too warm this early in the year."

When I heard that, I was so happy I could have climbed over the counter and kissed his whiskery mug. I told him that they would be just fine, we would take them. Those woollies were a little prickly for a day or two, but it was sure nice to feel warm again. Nice and warm.

We finally got the winter feed all cut and stacked. The fall season was coming to an end. We still had some cattle work to do before my partner went back to British Columbia, and I stayed on for the winter. I had to keep my truck payments up and figured I would just winter there at the ranch in Alberta and maybe go back to British Columbia in the spring.

We rounded up the cattle and were working the yearlings. As we were putting them in the corral, one made a runaway break past the gate. Billy was on the job, and we went to pass her on the high run to bring her back. It looked like this one was heading for parts unknown.

There was an old wagon rut going past the corral. It had been worn quite deep many years before and was now grassed in, and the heifer was following that old road. There was about three or four inches of soft, wet snow on the ground covering the old wagon track, which was round at the bottom. As we were to find out right quick, it was slipperier than a fresh-caught salmon.

My horse was running wide open to pass that yearling, when he planted his front feet on the edge of that round track. With the wet snow on the ground, down we went. Having that much momentum, my horse slid on his side for nine paces with my leg under him. I guess the snow saved us. My horse did not get hurt at all. I was not quite as lucky. My leg never got broke, but it was not much good for walking for a week or so. We were lucky. My horse was okay, and by the grace of the good Lord, I never got hurt too bad.

I hobbled down to a patch of willows and cut myself a forked willow, about an inch and a half through, long enough to make a crutch. I used a gunnysack to pad the fork up, so it was a bit more comfortable under my arm. I managed quite nicely on my makeshift wooden leg until my own leg was usable again. After everything that happened, that heifer, she came back on her own that evening.

By working horseback, I was able to help sort the heifers from the steers. The steers were going to the feedlot to finish out for next summer's trip to the Winnipeg auction market. After about a week, I was able to throw away my willow crutch. George was on his way back home, and there I stayed at the place, just for the winter or so.

Well, planned intentions do not always turn out the way they are meant to, so here I am, 45 years later, still in Alberta. I have been back home to British Columbia a great many times since then but not to stay. I go back and spend a week or so, visiting my old partner once in a while. I also go back to my home range where I was raised and see my brothers now and then. I guess this windy, rolling range must have just got in my system. I am still a cowpuncher, among other things.

Winter was coming on, the ground wasn't froze yet, so me and another feller dug in a bunch of fence posts to enlarge the feedlot and give them steers more room as they grew bigger. By the time we planted them fenceposts and cut and hauled enough green poplar rails, it turned really cold. It froze them fence posts in solid.

I was nailing those frozen poplar rails on one morning in −10 or −15°F (−23 or −26°C) weather. There was snow on the ground, a little wind and it was plumb uncomfortable. A spike deflected off the hammer and hit my thumbnail, full power against that frozen pole. I will not mention any of the words I used to explain to that hammer it had done the wrong thing. One thing or other made me figure that this cowboy business did have some drawbacks, but as usual with such things, you get over it.

It turned right cold that winter for quite a spell, down to −40°F (−40°C) but not much wind. We were hauling hay to the cowherd about two miles from home with a team and sleigh. That kind of weather made them two miles long, and you were damn glad to get to forking hay just to get warmed up. The cows had good shelter in a small field surrounded by a real dense growth of big willows where we fed. At least those cows had a bit of comfort for the winter.

Winter hung on almost till calving time, and the whole outfit, including the stock, was awful glad to see the snow melt. Through it all, we had a good, warm place to live and a good, warm barn for the horses.

With calving time upon us, I was on horseback fairly steady. The weather was getting nice, snow was gone, birds were back and flowers were starting to bloom. The cowboy business was looking good again. Not much money, but being well fed and watered, a fella tends to feel contented. We had some bad days, of course, having troubles calving them heifers, but then that, and other things you run into in the ranching world, is all in a day's work.

The steers in the feedlot were putting on weight, growing big and getting fat, but would not be ready to trail to the stockyards for a while. They were on heavy feed and doing well. It would be about another 60 days before they would be on their way to Winnipeg.

In the meantime, we kept busy with a little bit of farming for green feed for the cattle. Branding, fencing and the general run of the ranch work kept us going. There were always those last few cows to calve out and, of course, feeding those steers in the feedlot.

Branding time went smooth, with some neighbours' help, and in one day, all the calves were decorated with the ranch brand. The last critter we had to brand was a small yearling heifer with short, very sharp horns sticking straight up out of her head. She was also a mite unfriendly, so we were being a little careful.

We cut her out with a couple of half-gentle cows into the branding corral. It was fenced in with a solid board fence about eight feet high. The boss' wife was on horseback, so I said, "I'll heel her on foot and give you the rope so you can dally up and stretch the heifer out for branding." We manoeuvred around a little, and I made a clean double-hock catch. I handed the rope to the boss' wife, and in less time than it takes to tell about it, the heifer was stretched out on her side.

After tailing her down, I quick-like held her head down, while Stan got the hot iron to decorate her hide. With me on her head and the horse sitting back on the rope holding both legs, we got her done, neat as you please. In doing so, although we did not realize to what extent, we rather wrecked any good disposition she might have had left.

Stan came over, and we told the boss' wife to ride ahead. I got off the heifer's head, so she could get up and kick the rope off. The heifer jumped up, and there Stan and I stood, the main objects of her recent discomfort. She just lowered her head, aiming them sharp little horns at us. She let out a beller and came a-charging, intending, I guess, to ram us into that eight-foot, solid board fence.

We both took off as if someone hit us with the business end of a hot branding iron. There was no place to go. We could not go over that fence; it was solid, with no cracks in it.

We both spotted a hole halfways up, about six inches square, that a piece of machinery had knocked out years before, and made a jump for it. When everything stopped, Stan had the toe of his right boot in the hole, I had my left boot toe in the same hole and we were both holding onto the top of the fence. The heifer was right under us, just shaking her head, madder than ever that we got away.

The boss' wife rode in and worked the cow away, out through the gate, and we jumped down. Stan looked at that hole in the fence, four feet off the ground, and said, "How in the hell did we both manage to get up that high and get a toe hold?" I said, "Just jumped, I guess, just like this." I tried to get there by myself and could not make it. I asked Stan to try it, but he could not make it, either.

Goes to show you, in the spur of the moment, that adrenalin gives you that much-needed boost to do the impossible and save your hide. The heifer's disposition and needle-sharp horns, no doubt, gave us the needed incentive to make our escape. It was the only way out, without thinking. No time for that.

The rest of the crew allowed as to our agility, said Stan and me sure never looked so acrobatic. One stout feller grinned and said, "With them needle-sharp horns scratching the ass of my pants, I most likely would have made it, too."

After turning the cattle out and taking care of the horses, we were done. The boss brought a couple of cases of beer out of his truck, and we proceeded to have a couple of "barley sandwiches" and relax while we were waiting for supper. The neighbour women had come over for branding and were helping with the culinary efforts.

Once supper was ready, we were ready to belly up to the table. It was a regular feast. Cowboying can have its gratifying moments. That after-branding feed was one of them, along with those barley sandwiches.

It was getting on toward haying time, so we got things ready for that. After all the haying equipment was in shape and ready to go, we took time to trail them fat steers to the stockyards and ship them off to Winnipeg. While the boss and his wife went with the cattle to get them sold, Stan and I got a start on haying.

This outfit had good-quality cattle, and the boss and his wife were wearing nice smiles when they got home. They were happy with the sales results, as the steers hit the top of the market. I was a little pleased myself. I had the satisfaction of knowing that I had helped feed and look after them in the feedlot and finished them to the top of the market.

An amusing thing happened during haying. We were cutting wild hay along a mud-bottom creek that divided the meadow. To get to the other side with the machinery was a long way to the nearest crossing. The mud-bottom creek had been dried up for quite some time and felt solid to walk on.

The boss figured, if it was dry enough, we could cross over on that solid clay bottom and save many miles. It made sense. Stan said, "Let's get a shovel and dig a hole to see if it's solid enough underneath so it'll carry the weight of the machinery." We decided we would bring a shovel down the next day and give it a go.

The boss got a little impatient. He said he was sure if we went fast and did not stop, we could drive the old Ford half-ton across and see if the creek bottom was solid enough to carry the weight. The meadow was smooth, and the creek was shallow. The dry creek bed had a gentle slope, both going in and coming out the other side, and was about 30 feet wide. The boss got in the truck and backed up about 100 yards from the creek bank. He grinned and said, "Boys, I'm going to blow right over that creek!"

He started in low and right quick shifted into second and climbed onto the foot throttle. Stan and I were standing there, watching. The boss headed for the creek with the gas pedal on the floorboards and actually got airborne as he left the grassy bank and flew halfways across.

The truck didn't have quite enough momentum to make the other side and landed on that mud bottom, driving all four wheels through the surface to the soft mud underneath. He dove in clear to the frame. We thought he might have got hurt, but he looked out the window and growled, "I guess we'll have to go around, it's purty soft under here."

It took us most of the next morning to get the old Ford back on solid ground. We had to use a big John Deere tractor and a long cable to pull it out. Sometimes, I guess, a man can get in too big a hurry. Good thing no harm was done.

Haying was about over, so I left that little cow outfit and took a little time off. I went to a couple of rodeos and just odd-jobbed for a spell. About the first part of September, due to financial embarrassment, I was in need of employment right quick. I hit it lucky.

I was leaning against a corner of a hotel, in a big town about 20 miles north of where I worked on that little cow outfit, when along came Roy, a feller I knew well. He was a neighbour of the folks I had been working for. We visited some, standing on the street corner, under the eves of the hotel, out of the rain. He asked where I was working, having heard that I had left the little cow outfit. I told him I was not and was looking for another job. He grinned and said, "Good! I am looking for a good man for harvest. You're hired, if you'll go harvesting." Harvest wages were better than regular ranch wages, so I said, "You've got your man." He wanted me to come as soon as I could, that day or the next would be good. I told him that I would be on the job the next day, for sure.

We were going into the hotel café for a coffee, when an elderly feller stopped across the intersection and looked both ways to see if all was clear before crossing. It was raining very hard. He stepped off the sidewalk to the street, and down he went, as if he had been shot.

Roy ran into the hotel to tell the lady at the desk to phone the doctor, and I ran across the street to help him. He was out cold, lying on the wet street.

I spotted one of the town police a little ways off and hollered to him to come and help. A couple other people came running, and the cop, the other two guys and me made a cradle with our arms underneath the elderly feller to carry him to the hotel. Roy came running back out and grabbed his feet, and we got him into the lobby just before the doctor showed up.

The lady at the desk had already pulled the cushions off the chairs in the lobby to make a bed on the floor for him. The doctor came right away and, upon examining, announced that there was nothing to be done, he had gone "over the hill." The doctor suspected a fatal heart attack. Goes to show that one day at a time is the way we all live.

I went down to Roy's next morning and got lined up for harvest. It was still wet from the rain the day before, so we got things ready to start cutting the crop when it dried. This was at the time when the threshing machines in that part of the country was just starting to give way to combines. Some of the threshing outfits still managed to go strong. In addition, tractors had taken the place of horses for a lot of work, and we used a tractor to pull the horse binder for cutting the crop.

After the grain was stooked and dry, the threshing outfit would move in with six or eight teams of horses and wagons to thresh it for storage in granaries. It took us a good three or four weeks to cut and stook all the grain.

Roy had a good-sized operation. It went well, no breakdowns. I drove the tractor, and Roy rode and operated the horse binder. After the grain was cut and stooked, we had to let it dry for a couple of weeks.

We were just about done with the odd jobs to get ready for winter, when Roy said to me, "Why don't you get a job on the threshing outfit? You'll get a month's work, and they're paying pretty good. Ten dollars a day for a man and team." I said, "Sure, I would, if I had a team and wagon." Roy told me to take his. He told me he would let me use his horses and wagon. The horses would cost a dollar each a day, and the wagon went with them.

That sounded like a good deal, so I went to work on the threshing crew. It paid very well. I cleared $8 a day, room and board. We worked a 12-hour day, with a coffee and lunch break at midmorning and mid-afternoon.

Come the appointed time to go to work on the threshing crew, I hooked up Roy's big team of greys early in the morning and headed down the road, about six miles to the first farmer's place, where we were going to start.

I got there just as they were having their morning lunch and coffee break. I was not exactly a neat-looking sight, with my beat-up, old cowboy hat, a week's growth of whiskers, needing a haircut and wearing well-worn, half-clean work clothes.

The threshing machine boss said, "Have a sandwich and coffee up before you go to hauling bundles." Roy actually had got me the job, so none of the crew had ever seen me before. I rather thought, good thing Roy had recommended me, looking as scruffy as I did.

Most all of the crew were of Scandinavian descent, so they talked Norwegian and Swede among themselves a good deal of the time. A few days passed, and we got acquainted. What they did not know was that I was also of Norwegian descent and, at that time, understood everything they said.

I heard many harmless remarks, wondering were I came from, how old I was, and one guy grinned and said, "He looks almost like an old-time outlaw." Another guy said he did not think so, but you never could tell, me wearing all them whiskers and old clothes. So it went; I was getting along well and making friends, outlaw or not.

I was actually enjoying myself, listening to various opinions, which were voiced quite frequently in my presence. They were always harmless and in good humour. Everybody felt quite comfortable; this guy only talked English, never smiled too much and did not have much to say, only grinned when spoken to in English.

The third or fourth day after I arrived, we stopped for a mid-morning lunch and coffee break. No one was paying attention to me, and one of the guys was telling a joke in Scandinavian. It was building into a real good joke. I was making an effort to keep a straight face and look indifferent, since I supposedly could not understand a word.

I had just taken a mouthful of coffee when he got to the punch line. I busted out laughing, spraying coffee all over the ground. The rest quit laughing, as if you had turned off a switch. Their jaws fell near down to their chests. You could have heard a pin drop, and then the person who told the joke said, real quiet, "You understand us? Why didn't you tell us?" I said, "You never asked."

For the next couple of days, each one, when he had a chance, apologized to me in private and said he hoped he did not offend me in any way. I said, "Hell no, I enjoyed every minute of it. Don't even think about it." By the time threshing was done, we were all the best of friends and had a whoopdee-do of a party to finish the job.

With threshing finished that year, all the farmers who had their grain threshed by our outfit were happy. The weather was still very nice, and I had to think about getting a winter's job. I took Roy's team and wagon home and paid him what I owed him for using his outfit.

I stayed with Roy and his sister for a day, then loaded my gear into my pickup, thanked them for the use of a good harvest wagon and headed for town. It was now the latter part of October, and with my threshing wages jingling in my jeans, I was off to find a job for the winter to keep body and soul together and a roof over my head.

CHAPTER 13

TRUCK DRIVING AND TOWN LIVING

It was a beautiful fall, warm and sunny. I headed for a good-sized town about 30 miles north of Roy's. I figured the cow outfits should be hiring for the oncoming winter, so I did not anticipate any difficulty getting a job. I was looking forward to a few days off to rest up. Them 12-hour days, seven days a week, for the last month on that threshing outfit had worn me down a mite.

When I got to town, the first thing I did was open a bank account and deposit about two-thirds of my harvest money. I did not want to pack all of it on me. I figured I could afford a hotel room for a few days at five bucks a day and rest a little, while nosing around for a job. I slept, read and ate in the hotel café for three days. I had a beer now and then and did absolutely nothing, except kept my eyes and ears open for a job the whole time.

I heard about a job, but it was not cowboying. One of the garages in town got a big truck for hauling water for an oil rig, and they needed a driver. I thought, why not, I am not a truck driver, but the gearshift is practically the same on the three-ton as on a pickup. It had a floor shift, and it had a heater in it, so it did not sound so bad. I thought it might be better for the winter than feeding cows with a team of horses. I would have the shelter of the truck, instead of feeding in the freezing, windy, winter weather. I talked myself into giving it a whirl, went down and talked to the garage owner about the job.

The job was still open. He asked if I had any experience. Well, my folks brought me up to always tell the truth, but I figured this could be an emergency. There might not be any other jobs to get. I was quite confident that I could handle the job, so I said, "Yes, I've driven a three-ton truck before." "Fine," he said, "this ain't much different. The job is yours, but you need a class three driver's licence." I told him it was not a problem.

What I had failed to mention was that the grain trucks I drove were empty. I had occasionally had to move one around somebody's yard when it was in the way. I had a valid driver's licence already, but I had to also get a class three licence so I could drive that truck.

I went to the Mounted Police station, which was also the licence office, and told the Mountie that I needed a class three licence to get this truck-driving job. I had a spotless driving record, if he was at all concerned. He said okay and gave me a 10-question written test. I had 10 minutes to complete it, and I needed seven right to pass.

He was a pretty decent person. I think he realized that I was a mite green, so he said, "I'll give you a little tip. Go through the whole test right quick and answer any questions you know well first. Then answer the hard ones last. It will save you time, and maybe you will get seven correct right away. Then you will have time to argue with the tough ones with the time you have left."

He saved my bacon. I done as he said and finished just as he said, "Time's up." When he finished marking, he looked up and grinned. I had passed the test with seven right answers. He fixed me up with a class three badge to put on my belt. I was now a truck driver. Back in those days, being able to get a driver's licence in that part of the country was somewhat easier than it is now.

I had worked with the licensing department once since I was in Alberta. When George and I had come from British Columbia and was working on that little ranch, someone brought it to my attention that I had to get an Alberta driver's licence after being in the province about eight months. I was considered a resident of Alberta then.

This was news to me, and I was unsure, so I asked the boss where the provincial building was at, so I could go and ask some questions. He thought there might be one in Calgary or Edmonton and wanted to know why I had to go there. I told him that I needed to get an Alberta driver's licence. "Hell," he said, "you don't need to go there to get a licence. You just go to the John Deere dealer in town; he will fix you up! He is open till nine o'clock on Saturday night."

Come Saturday night, I walked into the John Deere dealer to make an appointment for a driving test. I figured the Mounties or government had authorized him to make the necessary road tests to pass a driver's test.

He stood behind the counter with a grin across his face. He said in a strong Scandinavian accent, "Good evening, vat can I do for you?" I told him I wanted to make an appointment for a test so I could get my Alberta driver's licence. He said, "You don't need an appointment. I got time to fix you up right now. Can you drive?" I said, "Sure, been driving for 10 years."

I showed him my British Columbia licence, and he asked how far I had driven. I did not really know; I did not keep track. Many of those old cars did not have odometers that worked, so they were not any help to my guess.

"Oh vell," he said, "you been driving for 10 years, ve'll put down tirty or forty tousand miles. Dat will be fine." He dug an application form and a driver's card out of a desk drawer. He filled it out with all the required information and got me to sign it. "Dat will be one dollar, please." I could not believe it. In less than a half an hour, I had my Alberta licence. Talk about fast service.

Now here I was, less than a year later. I had passed my written test at the Mounted Police office, got my class three, and I was a truck driver. Them days, seems like everyone was driving real slowly on those gravel roads. As far as I know, serious accidents were few and far between. That probably explains a little why getting a driver's licence was simple.

How things have changed. Driving restrictions and road policy sure toughened up in a hurry, fairly soon after. The public decided they were all in a hell of a hurry. Good thing the relaxed attitude toward driving and road policy changed from what we enjoyed those days. Otherwise, it would be a disaster nowadays, the way people drive.

My restful little holiday was over. I got me a job driving a water truck for an oil rig starting Monday morning. An elderly couple in the residential district had a room for rent, so I made a deal with them and checked out of the hotel.

Come Saturday afternoon, I went down to the garage and got the keys to the water truck so I would be ready early Monday morning. The owner took me out and introduced me to my rig, a three-ton Dodge special. He said to make sure to pack some extra oil, as it burnt a little. He had already put some extra oil on the floor of the cab, so I was okay for Monday. I looked in, and he had six quarts rolling on the floorboards! He told me to check the oil often and to not ever leave home with any less. "Like I said, it burns a little oil, especially when it's pulling hard."

I looked at the water tank. It had been pulled onto the truck with the winch behind the cab. I asked, "How much does the tank hold?" He said, "Only 1500 gallons." He added, "By the way, when you're hauling water, always fill the tank to the brim, or you can hardly go. That tank does not have any splash baffles in it." Whatever that meant.

When I got going, I did as he said and ran it over before I screwed the cover back on. I also got to thinking, 1500 gallons of water translates into seven and a half tons on a three-ton truck. No wonder that old Dodge inhaled a little oil.

She was a faithful old girl; everything worked, even the lights and the brakes. There were times, though, when climbing a hill with a full load of water, she would be pretty winded before she got to the top. Even in bull low.

The oil rig was moving to a new location when I started. While they were setting up, I was busy filling the mud pits with water. The first few loads disappeared into the ground till the soil got soaked up. Then it finally looked like I was starting to gain and got them filled before they started to drill. Everything was going good. After three or four days, I had gotten everything that needed water plumb full.

One evening, after everything had been filled, I was left with about a half load of water on the truck. I asked the tool push, "Where do you want this last half load, in the mud pit?" He said, "No, just open your drain top and run it onto the gravel road on your way back to town." That is the night I figured out what splash baffles were.

Down the road I went, that half load was surging ahead and back something fierce. Every time that water would surge ahead, away we would go. When it splashed back, it would about stop that truck. I finally had enough of it, pulled off onto the prairie and let it all drain out so I could drive home.

When I had left, the tool push told me I did not need to be in a hurry the next morning, as they had lots of water ahead. I got home, parked the Dodge, had something to eat and headed for my room. I slept like a baby, till I heard someone trying to bust the door down. It was about 5:30 in the morning.

It was someone from the owner's garage. "Get up! Get that tank truck going! They lost circulation in the hole last night."

All my reserve water had disappeared into the ground. I jumped into my clothes, drove back to the garage, got my six quarts of oil and headed for the oil rig. That poor Dodge had not even had enough time to cool off.

I thought, I could be in for a long haul. After having heard horror stories from other water truck drivers about going steady, I was a little apprehensive. This could last for two or three weeks, going steady day and night, catching a little sleep in the truck until the rig got circulation back in the hole. Luckily, they had another truck with a smaller tank they put on to help me, and we gained some ground. We were plain lucky; they got circulation back in the hole about four o'clock in the afternoon.

About that time, one of the guys from the garage brought out some sandwiches, which I was plumb ready for. Not having eaten since 10 o'clock the night before, I was feeling a little gaunt.

We hauled enough water that evening with both trucks to keep them going till the next day. From then on, all went well, and in due time, they finished drilling and had to move to another location.

The tool push told me to unload my water tank, as they needed the old Dodge and me to help move. That winch in the back of the truck looked good to them, so they pulled the tank off with the other truck. About that time, I was starting to question my decision to be a truck driver. I'd never loaded anything like that before onto a truck, and I did not really know how to operate the winch. The oil rig crew was very good, realizing that this was not my game. They helped me get used to the loading procedure and were very patient.

My main concern was not to activate the winch at the wrong time, so no one would get hurt. One of the boys gave me some advice. He told me to take my time, and I would get the hang of it. I did okay, but it was sure different from punching cows. I took my time, as he told me, and I guess I held up the parade a little. I was slower than an outlaw going to his own hanging, but we got the rig moved, and nobody got hurt. Truck driving was sure a hell of a lot different than driving a four-horse team.

The next two drilling sites went plumb smooth. Hauling water for an oil rig is not hard work, but that water truck runs on workday hours that would give any union leader a nightmare.

One thing I never could figure. When the rig was done with the hole, the cement truck would come and cement the well casing in. They always did it at midnight or two in the morning. Why could they not do it in the light of the day? The reason for my concern is that I had to be there for the thrilling event. I had to be there with a full load of water because the cement would not mix without it.

The fall was still bare and dry but cold at night. We were on to the third site, when we started hitting our troubles. We were getting along into December, and the water pump for filling the tank wanted to freeze up. To get around that, we got a flexible metal hose and extended the tail pipe on the exhaust. By bending it to fit, the exhaust blew directly on the water pump and kept it warm. It worked real well. I had to pack an axe to open the sloughs where the water came from, but that was not such a big deal.

It started to snow a little, and just before Christmas, the oil rig broke down. They still needed a little water to keep the steam boiler going, so things would not freeze up while the rig was worked on.

Now I had it easy. I drove the old Dodge out 18 miles every day, hauled one load of water to the steam boiler and went home. Regular hours at last. This went on through Christmas. They finally got it fixed just a couple of days past New Year's. There was still no snow to speak of and nice, sunny weather, but it was still cold. All was well.

The drilling routine was back on track—for two days, that is. The big rig broke down again, worse than before. The company said to hell with it and shut her down till spring.

My truck-driving job came to an abrupt end. I was thinking this was not too good, being the middle of winter and no job. My guardian angel was not far away. He steered me down to the garage to turn in the key to the old Dodge, and the boss said to me, "Seeing as you don't need to drive the water truck no more, how about going to work on the grease rack and tire repair? Same wages, and we need a man. You can handle that with no problem."

That was music to my ears. There was good heat in the garage and, by this time, not much of a chance of a feeding job on any cow outfit. They most likely had their crews, by now. I said, "Sure!" I never missed a day's work. It was a tiresome kind of job for a cowpuncher, but this was one cowboy who appreciated an inside job for the rest of the winter.

It was a good winter. Some cold weather, but that was no problem, now that I had an inside job. I learned a little about maintaining motor vehicles, which was okay, as we sure were entering the mechanical world fast. For better or worse, we were obliged to keep up with the times and to keep ourselves fed and watered.

Straight riding jobs and cowboying were getting scarcer than hen's teeth in that part of the country. When you did get one, it was usually part-time riding and big-time doing other stuff. I often found myself driving tractors and trucks along with horse work.

Spring finally came and with it, a new calf crop. The only way I saw any new calves was driving around a little in the evenings and on weekends to get out of town. Even though the crew in the garage were real good people and good to work with, I was getting a terrible craving to get back on the range again. The flowers were blooming in the green grass, new calves running and playing, and old cows were bawling, looking after the little ones. When I drove around on my time off, it was harder than ever to stay working at the garage. So far, no other jobs had showed up, so I hung tough.

June came with beautiful weather outside. In the garage, it was the same as wintertime, except the big doors were open, and time dragged.

About the end of June, I was working on a flat tire when a familiar voice said, "Hello, how ya doin'?" It was a fella from the south area where I had worked on the threshing outfit the fall before. He had a cow outfit that he ran with his brother. After shaking hands and visiting a little, he asked if I was going to stay at the garage permanent. I said that I figured so till a ranch job turned up, then I was getting the hell out of there. Well, he said, grinning, "One has showed up; I'm looking for a man right now as haying is about to start. You can start tomorrow if you want to work for me."

I stuck out my hand and we shook to cinch the deal, after telling him that I needed to give the garage a couple of weeks' notice before I left. I would not just leave them cold without time to get another grease monkey. That was fine with the rancher.

The next two weeks went slow, but in due time, I said so long to the owners and crew of the garage. What surprised me was they said they were very sorry to see me go, even though they would find another grease monkey. I never thought that I had been a good enough hand at that kind of work to even be missed. They were all a good bunch, management as well as mechanics. We had a lot of fun times during the winter. I missed them, too, after I left. Goes to show that everybody can be good friends, whether or not they are wearing bowlegs and high heels behind.

I loaded my gear in the truck and headed south. It did not take long to pack. Those days, I travelled light, with about as much gear as a bear travelling across country. I had a saddle, a bedroll and a bag for my extra possibles, shirts, overall pants and an extra pair of boots and a truck. I guess, truthfully, I did not travel quite as light as a bear.

I showed up at the ranch about noon. It sure was nice to get back on a ranch again, out of the noise and bustle of town. No cars and no trucks roaring by there, and the stink of their exhaust pipes.

After we had eaten dinner, I threw my rig onto the old wrangle horse and brought in a herd of horses. Most was broke to harness. We needed horse power for haying and put our teams together.

The brothers told me to catch two big bay mares for my team, Jeanie and Queen. They said Jeanie was a very good, honest mare, and Queen was good after being worked some. She was sometimes a little balky to start with, as she had not been worked for two or three years.

They were both gentle, so I gathered up a couple of halters and went into the corral to catch them. Jeanie was good; I got a halter on her easy. Old Queen, though, did not want any part of me. After running loose and doing nothing for more than two years, she was not about to come up and stick her head in that halter.

I could not get near her, so one of the brothers said, "Let's cut her off by herself into another corral, then she'll probably stand and let me catch her." It did not turn out that way. Neither of the two brothers could catch her. Finally, Bev, one of the brothers, asked me if I could rope her. I said yes and went to get my good rope off my saddle.

When I went to the corral dragging a horse loop, she went to running around that small corral like a bronc. I was trying to go easy and keep her as quiet as possible, so she would not hit the side of that old corral. She was going around, hell a-hoppin', and reared up to jump the fence. I was ready for her.

As she reared up, the loop settled over her head just as she jumped. Her momentum carried her half over the fence and down she went. The whole fence panel broke and hit the ground with her falling on top of it. The rope was on; she was not hurt, so she got on her feet and faced me with no sign of fight left in her. I had won, and she accepted the fact with grace.

She had good manners and was not even scared. She turned out to be very gentle. One of the brothers said they could not figure out why she acted that way. He thought maybe she was testing me. I put her and Jeanie in the barn, and we spent most of the afternoon putting the corral back up.

We were done with the corral about 4:30. I thought that maybe I should harness and hook my team to the wagon and take them for a little drive.

The mares were plumb gentle to harness. Old Queen acted as if she had been worked the day before. I was careful, though. I did not altogether trust her after the episode in the corral.

I led them to the wagon, one on each side of the wagon tongue, Jeanie on the left and Queen on the right. The boys told me those were the positions the horses liked to work in when they were hooked up. All was ready.

I gathered up the lines and climbed into the wagon box. I evened up the lines and said, "Okay girls, let's go!" I clucked at them as a signal for them to start. Jeanie started moving out, but not old Queen. To say she might be a little balky turned out to be an understatement. She would not move.

I had been driving horses since I was 10 years old and had about 22 years of experience under my belt. My dad had taught me well. Good thing. He was a wonderfully good teacher. One thing he told me was, "If you're driving a horse that is apt to balk now and then, don't ever let him get the notion he is stuck, or he won't tighten a trace. If you are hauling a load, the team needs to rest before getting to the top of the hill. Never wait till the team stops of their own accord. Tell them to stop first, otherwise the balky one will think he is stuck, if he stopped on his own to get his wind. Once he's got the notion that he's stuck, he won't tighten the traces, even though he's a good puller otherwise."

All of this went through my mind. I told Jeanie to stop right away. There I was on level ground, with two 1600-pound horses hooked to an empty wagon, and one of them would not go. I did some figuring. I had never had a horse that would not move an empty wagon before. I could have almost pulled it myself, and I am sure a long ways from weighing what those horses do.

I waited for a while, both horses standing quietly. I got to thinking, if Jeanie was willing, I would just get her going, as she was big and strong. Queen would have to come along whether she wanted to or not. That wagon box pushing up against her butt would convince her to come along.

That is exactly what happened. We kind of turned in a circle as Jeanie took the wagon by herself. As Jeanie pulled, there was not much else that Queen could do but go along with her. Once Queen got going, it did not take long till she was up even with Jeanie and going good. I drove around till it was time to unhook for supper. By that time, Queen was doing her share of the work.

Next day, I hooked them up again on the empty wagon and, after driving around for a little bit, loaded a small bunch of fence posts and tools and drove down along a fence and did some repair work. Queen worked perfect alongside Jeanie that day. After another day or so of light work, Queen was getting to act as a good workhorse should. She was starting to act like a horse that had been working straight through, instead of how she first acted after being turned out for a couple of years.

It was time to start haying, and I hooked onto the horse mower. Mowing hay steady can be hard work for a team of horses, but this mowing machine was relatively easy to pull. Between those two bay mares and me, we cut a lot of hay that summer.

Queen was worked back into shape, carefully and gradually. By the time haying was over, she seemed solid as a rock. I was careful, though. I did not want to come close to overloading them. The mowing machine, the dump rake, the hay sweep and hauling good-sized loads to the stack was all taken in stride. No offer to balk anymore. I was slowly building Queen's confidence, with Jeanie's help. Before the following winter was over, that confidence would be put to the test.

CHAPTER 14

A COLD WINTER

Haying operations were still in full swing. We had to put up enough hay to feed 600 or 700 head of cattle and some horses. We would be at it for some time yet. We were averaging about a stack of loose hay a day. The weather was good, and everything was working well.

One thing about horse equipment: it does not often break down, and when some little thing did break, we could fix it quickly ourselves. Not like nowadays. You have to drive miles to town for expensive parts and then maybe have to wait for days if they have to be ordered in. Ranching business then, as now, did have its ups and downs, when sometimes things did not go as planned.

A smaller rancher was located north of the outfit I was working on, and one of his main wild hay meadows was along the creek, just a few miles from our outfit. This hay meadow would be under water after the spring flood and then dry up by haying time, allowing the rancher to harvest the wild hay crop for his cows.

It was a very good hay meadow, producing a crop of wild hay each year that grew three or four feet tall and thicker than hair on a hibernating bear. Although only about 70 or 80 acres in size, it was the main source of winter feed for this small outfit. It would ensure the rancher's cows would have winter groceries.

Shortly before haying time, the rancher drove down to see about how long it would be before the meadow would be dry enough to get started. When he got out of the truck, he could not believe his eyes. The meadow still was under water, where other years it was usually fairly dry by this time.

He soon found the reason. The flowing creek cut through the high ground at the lower end of the meadow, and an enterprising family of beavers had come along and constructed a dam at the narrow outlet. The rancher had no choice: he had to get rid of that dam. The hay on the meadow was a lifeline; his cows depended on it. "Mr. Jack Beaver" and his family and all his flat-tailed cousins were going to have to move camp.

On his way home to pick up some dynamite to open the dam and let the water out, the rancher met a friend and stopped to visit a little. After telling his friend what happened, he was told to hang a lighted kerosene lantern at the edge of the hole and leave an old coat there after he blew a hole in the dam. When the beavers caught his scent off the old coat and saw that lantern burning, they would not go near there and would most likely go down the creek, find another place for a dam and set up camp. That sounded like a fine idea, and he decided that was just what he would do.

Upon returning to the meadow, he tied two or three sticks of dynamite together, put a cap and fuse in the bundle and shoved it under the lower side of the dam, right in the creek bed. He lit the fuse, went back to the truck and waited. In a couple of minutes, there was a big boom! Mud, rocks, sticks and water flew up in the air. The water started running through the hole with a roar, and the meadow started to drain.

He pounded an old post into the dam on the edge of the break and hammered a nail in the top to hang the lit lantern, but damned if he forgot to bring an old coat. The good coat he was wearing would have to do; it would be fine just for one night. He would remember to bring that old coat tomorrow.

The next morning, he came back to see how the hay meadow was draining. All was peaceful; he could not hear any water roaring, and there was still a lot of water on the meadow. First place he went to check was where he blew up the beaver dam. That hole in the dam was repaired like new. The lantern was still burning, but he could not find his good coat.

Looking along the top of the new repair job, he saw what seemed like something bright coloured. There was one sleeve of his good coat, sticking out of the repair job a couple of inches. The rest of the coat was buried in the construction repair site.

That was too much. He stood there and voiced his opinion about those beavers—in a loud and colourfully profane manner. There was not a beaver in sight. They had gone to their lodges in the creek bank to get some rest after working all night.

If old "Jack Beaver" was listening, he must have had some puzzling thoughts on how those human critters' minds really worked. This fella had blown a hole in his dam and then hung a lantern on a post to give his crew light to work by after dark. Now he was plumb mad and blowing off steam. "Jack Beaver" and his crew had done a good job. The dam looked like new. What was this person mad about? Humans are sometimes tough critters to figure out.

The rancher went back to his truck and left in a shower of dust and grass. He was not gone for long. He came back with a box of dynamite, a roll of fuse and some blasting caps. He put a stick of powder about every two or three feet under the entire length of the beaver dam. He lit the fuses and went back to his truck. In a few minutes, there was a mighty explosion and the whole dam lifted into the air in a shower of water and rubble. This time, the hay meadow would be drained.

The truck left, and "Jack Beaver" and his crew came out to size up the situation. The water was flowing off the meadow in a wide, fast stream—the entire width of where the dam had been.

That was just about enough for "Jack Beaver." He and his crew must have decided there was no way a civilized beaver colony could put up with things as unsociable as they were here. They would move camp.

They followed the creek downstream a little over a half mile or so and came upon a wide willow- and poplar-covered flat. Exploring further, they must have discovered that the high ground on the lower end came close together, the creek flowing through a depression. An ideal place for a dam.

They went right to work, and, before long, they had a new dam, and the water was backing up over the willow flat. This was a much better location than the hay meadow, I am sure. Lots of feed and building material and early enough in the season, so there was plenty of time to get ready for winter. Best of all, there would be no human critters to bother them. "Jack Beaver" and his colony were home to stay.

There was a good possibility that they had come upon the location of an old beaver dam from the dim, distant past. Through the passage of time, any part of an old dam would have decayed into soil and grown over with grass and brush. No matter, the beavers were happy and so was the rancher. It seems that, as with so many things on the range, one way or another, Mother Nature had a way of making things work out.

We were still haying; the weather staying good. We finally were done, with no problems to speak of. Very soon, the threshing outfit would again make the rounds, threshing each farmer's grain. They were already starting to organize, hiring men, teams and wagons.

I had traded the half-ton pickup I brought from British Columbia for a one-ton Dodge with a flat deck. The threshing machine owner figured it would be the "real McCoy" to use for moving tools, gas barrels and whatever else was necessary from farm to farm. He offered me a job helping with the threshing machine, if I would use my truck. He paid me the same as he paid for a man and team hauling bundles. He also supplied the gas for the truck.

Fair job: greasing and oiling machinery, spelling off pitching bundles into the machine when the teamsters ate lunch, shovelling a little grain back in the granaries as they were filling up. Things were well organized.

From six in the morning till seven at night, the machine never stopped, except for one hour at noon, so horses and men could eat dinner. I was making money, $10 a day, for the truck and myself. That was about 85 cents an hour, all the grub I could eat and a place to sleep. Not bad, considering the way the women folks helped each other with the cooking. When the threshing crews showed up, most of the time them meals was feasts fit for a king.

One of the brothers was on the outfit with his team, hauling bundles. The other brother stayed home and took care of the ranch while we were away.

We had another good fall; everybody got their grain threshed in good shape. Before you knew it, it was time for our annual party to celebrate when the threshing, and all the work that went with it, was all done.

After the old head quit aching and shrunk back down to normal size, it was back to the ranch to get ready for winter. Roundup was coming up. We had a few other chores to tend to, such as seeing that harnesses, sleighs and feeding equipment were in shape when we needed them.

The youngest brother and I, both being the same age, managed to find time for some important stuff, like hunting ducks. After all, the ranch could use the duck meat. Turned out well. Their mother was doing the cooking, and the way she fixed them ducks would make you drool at the mouth when you came in and smelled dinner. I think we should have spent more time at that tough duck-hunting job and bagged more of them.

It was still a good fall, sunny and bare ground until the day before Halloween. It was cold in the morning, −30°F (−34°C) on the thermometer. With the change in temperature coming that quick overnight, it felt colder than it was.

That day, we hooked the team up to a rubber-tired wagon and fed some cows that were close to home. They were feeling plumb sorry for themselves, with good reason. Their pasture was somewhat wore down, and the weather was not the best.

We was some thankful when the weather moderated a little after a few days. We had to start gathering and sorting cattle, and we could not put roundup off any longer. It warmed up to about 15 or 20 below (−26 or −29°C) at night. Not too warm, but a hell of a lot better than 30 or 35 below (−34 or −37°C). It must have got up to 0°F (−18°C) during the day. Cold enough—we did not exactly race out to see who could get his butt into that cold saddle first.

One day, we were sorting cattle. I was watching the gate and riding a half-green mare. She was doing okay, but once in a while she would get a little confused when I reined her too fast to stop a cow. A cow was trying to dodge past us, and the mare was resisting the rein, so I reached out with my hand and slapped her on the side of the neck.

I happened to see my finger hit the big head buckle on the side of the bridle but had not felt a thing. I pulled my glove off, and my finger was plumb white and felt about as limber as a six-inch spike. It was in the process of being frozen, and I had to thaw it out. But how? I was stuck at the gate and could not leave.

I figured out one solution and did not have much of a choice. I shoved that finger in my mouth as far as it would go without gagging me. We kept on working, and the oldest brother who was doing the sorting kept looking at me. I suppose it looked bad, and I should have been old enough to have gotten over sucking my finger.

He asked me what the hell I was doing, and I told him. He just grinned and asked if it was working at all. "You bet," I said, "and didn't even miss a cow."

We finally got all the cows home, and the weather was getting more reasonable, now that we were about done. It snowed a few inches and was starting to look a little Christmas-y.

A fella living a few miles east sent word over that we had a two-year-old steer at his place. A few days later, the weather had cleared up enough to 10°F (–12°C) in the morning with the sun shining down. The youngest brother said, "Let's saddle up and get that steer home before it turns cold again. We should be back by noon, if we leave now." Away we went.

We got to the neighbour's place and he was not home, but his wife said the steer left a couple of days ago and, last she heard, had gone further east, to their neighbour's.

We got on his trail, and upon reaching the next fella's place, we found the steer had moved on again. This happened two more times. I guess he thought he was a bull looking for a little company. By this time, it was getting well past noon. Of course, we did not bring lunch, as we were figuring on being home by then. Both the horses and us were feeling a bit gaunt around the middle. Following the local people's directions, we kept on the steer's trail and, as the day was getting short, were trying to hurry, to find him before dark.

About 2:30 in the afternoon, we rode up to a ranch house with a long front porch occupied by three noisy, unfriendly-looking dogs. We stayed on our horses, as it seemed like them dogs were a little unwilling to invite us in.

The door jerked open, and an old cowboy stepped out and yelled, "Shut your traps, you sons of bitches!" Then he looked at us and asked, "Have you boys ate yet?" We told him that we had not, and he directed us to the barn, where there was water in the trough, oats in the bin and hay in the loft. As we were taking care of our horses, he said he would get some dinner for us, since the wife was not home.

What a prince of a man. No doubt this fella had ridden a few cold miles himself in the past. His heart was sure in the right place. Now we would warm up, feed and rest the horses, and our bellies would be filled.

That steer was still on the move. The ol' cowboy said the steer was just down the road a half mile at two Polish brothers' bachelor outfit. While we were filling our faces and being warmed up, he poured himself a cup of coffee and passed the time of day.

We would have liked to visit a little, but as it was getting close to dark, we were going to have to eat and run. We thanked him very kindly for his hospitality. He grinned and said, "You're welcome, anytime," and off we went. He was a man after my own heart; too bad I never got back to visit him again.

We caught up to the steer at the Polish brothers' place just as it was getting dark. Their cows were all close to the yard and gentle. The steer was quiet, too, till he realized he was alone, with two cowboys after him. My partner thought, "Just point him in the right direction, hope for the best and keep him going."

There were a few inches of snow, so we could see a little in the dark, 'cause he made us ride to stay with him. Every time we heard barbed wire squeal, we slowed down so we would not hurt our horses in the dark. That steer never stopped, but we had to take the fence down or find a gate. By now, he was headed for home on his own, so we did not need to steer him. He finally got into the right field with the ranch cows.

How far we rode or where we went, I do not really know. I was on completely unfamiliar range. It was a good thing the fella I was riding with was on his home range and knew the country.

We got back to the ranch and stabled our horses about nine o'clock that night. After we got in the warm house and were fed and watered, it was not too hard to go to sleep for the night.

Now that the cows were all rounded up and the calves weaned, we could look forward to a few months of hauling hay. It snowed some more and turned colder, so the rustling was just about done. We would have to feed the whole herd and got organized right away. They hired a young fella from Saskatchewan to help.

We had three sleighs with hayracks to haul enough hay, as we had a four-mile haul in one direction and a seven-mile haul the other way. Most days we had time for only one load apiece. The young fella and I had a two-horse outfit each; the older brother was using a four-horse team on a very large rack. By loading all the horses could handle, we managed to keep the cattle all fed.

Things went quite well, even though the weather stayed cold. We worked seven days a week. Them cows eat the same amount on Saturdays and Sundays as they do on other days of the week, so days off were something we would just dream about.

About the middle of December, a blizzard hit and, for two days, we could not haul hay at all. Luckily, we had a half load on to feed the calves a little at the home corrals. Those poor old cows were holed up in a big poplar thicket, waiting out the storm.

When it was over, it warmed up a little. Those cows were awful hungry, and the first load disappeared as fast as Bev unloaded it. I was right behind with another load, so the edge was took off their hunger pretty good. The young fella took his load to the calf feedlot.

The storm had left huge drifts in some places, hard enough so you could walk on them and hardly leave a track. I believe you could have ridden a horse right over most of them. If one happened to be on the road, you just had to make a road around through the field, even if you had to take a fence down. A grader or snowplough had not been made that could move the big ones, some of which were 12 or 15 feet deep.

One day after the storm, the young fella got word he had to go back to Saskatchewan. He was needed back home. This left us with no driver for his team. There was no one to fill in, and we still had just as many hungry cows to feed and just as far to haul the hay.

I said to the two brothers, "Why don't I put his team in front of mine and use two four-horse outfits? I have a big rack, and that way I could just haul a much bigger load." They agreed that would solve the problem, but the little team the young fella was driving had never been used for a lead team. I said, "No matter; they are a good, well-broke team, they'll do the job."

I think the brothers were a little apprehensive at first, about whether the two teams would work together right off. There was no time for a break-in period; those cows needed all the hay we could haul, so the first trip had to be loaded. I was plumb confident. I had been driving horses all my life, and those two little mares were honest as the day was long.

Next morning, I hooked Dolly and Goldie in front of Jeanie and Queen. I had a half load on the rack to unload, so the very first pull was easy. I gathered up the four ribbons and talked to them all, told them to go, and away we went as smooth as silk. I could see right then I would be driving a damn good four-horse outfit. That was their break-in load, if you want to call it that.

After that, their loads were pretty big and gradually got even bigger as the weather got colder. The more those mares worked, the more they muscled up. They were fed and grained well and were taken care of the best I knew how.

We were working well together. I had a lot of confidence in their ability and cooperation, and they in turn had confidence in my teamstering. The two have to work hand in hand to have a really good four-horse outfit, or even a two-horse outfit, for that matter. There came a time before the winter feeding was over where that mutual confidence and respect really paid off.

The winter months were upon us, and we hauled hay every day, as usual. On Christmas Day, we hauled on the short haul to get finished for the day and had a late Christmas dinner. That was okay as the weather had moderated just a little, and there wasn't any wind.

The only break in the cold weather all winter came with a bob-tailed chinook on the Sunday between Christmas and New Year's. It warmed up to 45°F (7°C) during the afternoon, and we figured it might last for a few days. Nice to see the water dripping from the snow-covered eves on the buildings and not feel the bite of the cold on our faces. The warm weather was short-lived, however. It was back to −30°F (−34°C) when we went to the barn to feed and harness our teams on Monday morning.

It stayed cold, dropped clear down to −45°F (−42°C) for a few days in the middle of January. After that, it moderated just enough that we got quite a bit of new snow. No more chinooks. The freezing cold was there to stay.

When we went on the long, seven-mile haul, it took all day, including the travelling time and loading two four-horse loads of loose hay. Of course, we packed a lunch those days and, by noon, we would usually have one sleigh loaded.

Once the hay was loaded, one of us would take the scoop shovel hanging on the back of one of the hayracks and dig down to the ground through two and a half feet of snow for a place to build a fire and eat lunch before the long haul. The other one would take the axe and hunt up some dry diamond willows for firewood.

We dug a hole in the snow big enough so we could both get down by the fire and sit on the snowbank for lunch. With the snow shovelled out of the hole, it formed a high enough bank that we were quite comfortable out of the breeze and warmed by the fire.

We melted snow in an old gallon can over the fire for tea and, with a green, forked, frozen willow for a fork, thawed our sandwiches so we could eat them. Our lunches would be harder than a cast iron sleigh shoe after travelling seven miles to the haystacks in a paper box.

We were finally done with the seven-mile haul around the middle of February. We broke trail to another meadow about three and a half or four miles from home. This was much better, except for the fact that we had to pull our loads up a long, fairly steep hill.

One thing that helped: there was a level break in the hill about halfways up, with room enough for both four-horse outfits to stop. One would stop behind the other, so the horses could rest a little and get their wind before pulling up over the top part. That was a much-needed rest, as the horses were usually well-winded after pulling the bottom part, which was the steepest and hardest pull.

One afternoon, around the end of February, we went down to the meadow for a couple of loads. By then, the road was broke out good so we could haul a fair load. As we always worked together, we would pull a sleigh up beside both sides of the stack and help each other load, one sleigh at a time.

We loaded Bev's sleigh first and then mine. By the time we loaded the first sleigh, there was only about half a load left in that stack for me. We had already hauled quite a few loads out of that same stack earlier.

The hay in the bottom of the stack was good to feed but tough and heavy from sitting close to the ground. When we got it cleaned up, we needed more for a load, so we moved over to another stack to top it off. Since we had not touched it yet, we had to take the scoop shovel and get as much snow as we could off the top.

We decided we had better load light, as the tough bottom hay of the stack we had just finished, combined with topping the load off with the snow-saturated hay off top of the new stack, would consist of a lot of weight. We did not want to overload my team pulling that hill. We forked on what we thought would be the equivalent weight of a load of dry hay, as we had been hauling.

With cleaning up the last of one stack and topping the load off the new one, we made a mistake. I did not know it till starting up that hill.

Bev had gone on ahead and was pulling up on the level place to rest his horses. We were just starting up the hill. The way my horses were laying into those collars and pulling, I quickly realized I was badly overloaded. It was almost dark by this time, and by the time we were halfways up to the resting place, the horses' breathing was coming in a steady roar. I knew they did not have a chance to get to the top without getting their wind.

I hollered "Whoa, girls," right on that steep slope. They stopped and braced themselves against the back pull of the load, hung on the face of that hill and held the load still. It was dark enough; I could not really see how much they were heaving for air. I could see the traces of the wheel team against the white snow, and they were moving in and out, like an accordion being played. The horses' breath was still loud, but I could hear that they were starting to get their wind.

We stood there and waited till I couldn't hear them breathing hard. All the time they stood with braced feet, holding that heavy load. We stood there for what seemed like a long while; I could not hear their breath, and I could just see the traces against the white snow. I made sure they had all their wind back and were breathing normal. They would need every breath they could muster before getting to the top at the resting place, where Bev was still waiting.

We were ready to try it. I said, I suppose almost like a prayer, "Queen, don't fail me now." Queen cocked one ear back when I spoke to her and still stood quiet. I gathered up my ribbons, all four horses came to attention and I said, "Take it easy, girls, till I get these lines even." I braced both feet on the top wooden crossbar of the hayrack, tightened the lines a little and said, "Come on girls, lets try it!" and whistled to them.

They took hold perfectly at the same time and went to pulling. The sleigh started up the hill. It was all they could do and all I could do to hold their noses off the ground. Their feet were churning the snow with tremendous effort. Queen and Jeanie, the wheel team, were tall horses, and they were pulling so hard their bellies were within a couple of feet off the ground. Dolly and Goldie, the leaders, went up to their knees in snow but kept right on trying.

I was only 160 pounds. With both feet braced against the cross member of the hayrack, I was trying my best to keep their noses off the ground. They were depending on me. With four big horses laying on their bits and trying to keep their feet under them, pulling with every ounce of muscle they possessed, it was all I could do.

I kept talking to them all the time. "Come on, girls, you can do it"—and do it they did. Dolly and Goldie got their front feet on the level resting place and got their footing and helped Queen and Jeanie get theirs, too. We had made it.

We pulled up behind Bev's load where he was still waiting and stopped. My horses' heavy breathing came in a steady roar from the four of them. I have never before or since seen horses pull like that.

Never in my life have I been more proud of anything than I was of those four mares standing there, getting their wind back on the level that night. I had asked them to do the impossible, and they had come through with excellence. The thought came to me. Maybe I had achieved the point where I was as good a teamster as my dad had been. One thing I knew for sure: if not for his teaching, we would never have made it. It was as if Dad was on that load with me, helping us get to the top of that hill.

For a mare that would not move an empty wagon when I first hooked her up the summer before, Queen had come a long ways. She had passed a gruelling test of ability, honesty and endurance, along with her teammates, to the point of absolute excellence.

When my team had their wind back, Bev spoke to his team; we both pulled over the top with relative ease, as it was a much easier slope than the one we had just come up.

When we got home to the yard, Bev called to me to unhook, and he would feed his load to the cattle. After pulling my sleigh runners up on a couple of old boards so they would not freeze down during the night, I unhooked. I took the mares' bridles off and hung their halter shanks up in the harness, and they went for water.

I went to the barn, leaving the door open, and filled the manger full of hay. They came in, going to their own stalls, where I tied them up and unharnessed them. I then filled the manger for Bev's horses, bedded all the stalls, fed my team their grain and put grain in for Bev's team.

By the time he was back, I helped him put away his team after they had watered. We unharnessed his horses, took the lantern and headed for the house. We just got outside, and I said to Bev, "Go on to the house, I got to go back to the barn. I forgot something." He went, and I turned back to the barn. I hung the lantern back on the wire, went in the stalls to all four mares and gave them each as good a hug as any man can give a horse. I just had to let them know how much I appreciated their efforts. I could tell by then that they knew what I meant.

I like to think that they made that supreme, successful effort for me. That kind of relationship between a man and his horses is what every good equestrian dreams about and very few of us achieve. For my part, I guess I will never really know if I was the real motivation behind their successful, very honest effort. I do believe I was a part of the team. I took the lantern off the wire, closed the barn door and went for supper. It had been a long day.

CHAPTER 15

HOMEWARD BOUND

As had been the case all winter, morning came early. We crawled out of the sack at five in the morning. We went out, fed, harnessed our horses before breakfast and would be hooking up by 7:30 AM. As February was on the downhill slope toward the end of the month, the days were getting longer. We had daylight, instead of the dusky dawn, to hook up in.

It was a nice day coming up; no wind, little cold and the four mares were well rested after their tough pull of the previous evening. We took that heavy load, fed it to the cattle first thing and then, with both outfits, headed for the closest meadow to load up. We needed to make two trips that day, to get the cattle caught up on their feed. As it was only a two- or three-mile haul, we were back by noon and made the second trip after dinner.

So it went. Spring was surely coming. Around the end of March, the weather warmed up and the snow started to go. We still had a few weeks of feeding, but with longer days and warm weather, it did not seem too long before the ground turned bare and the cattle were turned out. With lots of prairie wool left over from last year and the new grass starting to come, we had for sure made the winter.

It was nice to know the feeding season was over for another year. The long, cold winter we had just come through had rather dragged both horses and men down some; however, everyone had put up a good show. One thing for sure: both the horses and us were all in top working shape. No need for any muscle-building exercises, and with spring and summer work coming up, we would likely stay in shape.

We turned the horses out to pasture for a well-earned rest, slowed down ourselves and, with spring here, our dispositions improved somewhat. Winter was over. I decided I needed some time off, too. The boys were going to have to do the calving themselves.

I still had only the flat deck on my truck, so I needed to build a horse rack to carry my saddle horse wherever I went. I asked the boys if it was okay for me to borrow their tools and fix up my truck before I left. They said sure, so for a week I worked on my horse rack after I was done chores.

I built a good one, with iron bows like a covered wagon to stretch the canvas cover over, and put a window in the front in the bull board so my horse could see out when we were travelling and watch the road. I put a false bottom in the manger about eight inches down, leaving the space underneath for saddles, a bedroll and travelling possibles. Rigging the false, shallow bottom in the manger with loose plywood resting on each side made it easy to get to. It was just like opening the lid on a trunk.

I built a cleated loading ramp that slid under the box, between the box and the truck frame. That was as handy as a pocket on your shirt, because you could load or unload a horse anywhere. I did not need a loading chute or a side hill.

The truck deck was six-by-nine feet, so a horse could turn around to come out. That way, he could see where he was going when he come down the ramp face first. No danger of backing over the side of the ramp. It worked like a well-oiled clock, and when I was at a rodeo, I would just get a bale of straw, make myself a mattress, unroll my sleeping bag and my bedroom was ready.

There are not too many RVs today that can accommodate both a man and his horse in the same room. Of course, we had to take turns; it belonged to the horse when we travelled and was mine for sleeping. If the weather was bad, I would get a room, so my horse had a dry, warm place to sleep in the truck. I would just unload him for a little exercise, water him and feed him, then put him right back in the truck.

A friend said, years later, "I think that outfit of yours must have been a forerunner to the modern RVs, except they are not built to share with a horse." That pony and me travelled a whole bunch in relative comfort that summer. Course, we'd stop and work for a spell here and there, to keep the hamburgers and oats coming.

I finally went back to work for a cow outfit that was located six or eight miles from where I spent the cold winter. The owner needed help for haying, harvest and roundup, as well as summer riding. That was okay, as I wanted to go back after freeze-up to British Columbia and spend the winter with my mother. It would be nice to go back to the old home range, after being in Alberta for the last 12 years.

I was still in familiar surroundings, as he also worked with horses for haying and feeding. Mind you, modernization was slowly creeping in. He had a tractor for farming, big enough to pull a 14-foot cultivator or seed drill, and a smaller one for mowing. That was okay. Farming and mowing was hard work for horses, especially farming. Mowing is not too bad. Actually, I mowed hay with the horses while Allen ran the tractor mower to get a bunch of hay down to get started.

With just the two of us, we kind of traded around, cut a bunch, then raked and stacked it and cut some more. We were still working with loose hay with horses, buck rakes and over-shot stackers. It was a much smaller outfit, so the two of us worked away at it, the weather being plumb favourable that summer.

We had to take some time off to go riding for a couple of days, as a bunch of calves came down with pink eye. As we both were ropers, we caught them and treated their eyes right out on the range. It was at the end of July, so they were getting big and could run just as fast with one eye as they could with two.

Pink eye usually seems to start in one eye, so even if it was sore and they kept it closed, it did not slow them down. Of course, with a horse thundering behind them, carrying what must have seemed to them as some crazy cowboy swinging a rope, it did not give them any urge to slow down. They just got into overdrive, cranked up to as many miles per hour as was possible and never worried about badger holes, rocks or rough ground.

I was hot on the tail of a big heifer calf that had one bad eye. I did not know how she could watch where she was going and watch me at the same time with her one good eye, but she did.

We were coming across a tame grass flat, and I was about close enough to hang the rope on her, when she suddenly ducked sideways. My old pony was a damn good rope horse, and he ducked right with her. In doing so, he stuck both front feet in the middle of a big, green cow pie, his feet slipped out from under him and down we went at 35 miles an hour. We slid for about 15 feet, with my right foot stirrup behind his armpit, my spur digging a furrow in the grass sod, and the calf never even stopped to see if we were okay!

I thought my horse was hurt, as he would not get up right away—he just lay there. My right foot was stuck under him with the toe of my boot in his armpit and my spur dug into the ground. Allen came riding over right quick as I was wiggling around, and I finally got my foot out from under him.

Soon as I got loose, my horse got right up. He was not hurt at all. That wide breast collar had protected his shoulder as he slid. He must have thought I was stuck and did not move till I got loose.

I was not quite as lucky. My leg was twisted some, and my right knee was not working too good after sliding under the horse for them 15 feet. It was nothing too serious, nothing broke, and I could still ride.

My leg had stiffened up during the night and was pretty useless the next morning, so I crippled down behind the barn to a diamond willow patch, cut myself a crutch, padded the forked end with a gunny sack to fit my armpit and went mowing hay for a couple of days, where I didn't have to walk much. When my horse fell, we were luckily done treating pink eyes, except for the one that got away from me—but Allen got her not far from our mishap.

When we were done haying, we went to cutting crops, as this outfit done a little farming on the side.

After threshing was over, it was nearly roundup time. The cattle had summered in a community grazing lease, so we got in with all different kinds of riders, from good hands to a small operator with a half dozen head, who came riding bareback with a work horse bridle with blinders on it.

When they went to sorting in the big page wire pen, with all the diversified talent on horseback, it was quite an experience to be part of. We finally got the hell out of the way, until those bareback boys on their unique cutting horses got their few head out and were gone. After that, there was more room; the cattlemen worked in an orderly fashion, and the cattle were sorted quickly and smoothly.

Later in the fall, I arranged with Allen to leave my truck and horse with him at the ranch for the winter. I did not need to worry about my horse and outfit for the winter. The truck was parked safely at the ranch, and my horse would be well cared for till I came back from British Columbia in the spring.

Allan took me to town, and I boarded the CNR passenger train for British Columbia and my home range. I was going to

Norman on Mike and Henry on Dusty: "I will always remember Mike—he stayed calm and didn't drag me to death the day I got hung up. It's a lesson I never forgot."

spend the winter with my mother and brothers and do a little logging again, for a change.

In due time, the old CNR train rattled into the depot at New Hazelton at 5:30 AM, if I remember right. That worked out okay, as I knew the mail truck driver, and he gave me a ride down to Old Hazelton, by the Skeena River, where my mother lived. As he had to deliver the mail to the post office in Old Hazelton, he did not have to go out of his way for me.

My mother and brothers were somewhat surprised to see me, as I showed up unexpected. I received a warm welcome from all, and my brother grinned and said, "Can you still remember how to use an axe? I just might put you to work in the bush."

That is the way it went. I fell right back into the logging work quite easily but must admit it was some different from arguing with cows, riding, haying and feeding.

It was a good winter, never had to work too hard. My brother put me in charge of a small logging operation he had, some miles from the main camp. Some Indian friends and I were there, and we worked leisurely, as everything was paid by piecework. We were paid for what we produced, so we did not need to worry about putting in an honest day's work, like on hourly wages.

We did not make a hell of a lot of money, but on piecework, we did not cost my brother's company any extra either and, after all, I was on my winter holidays. At least, that is what I told myself, I guess to justify me dragging my ass. My brother was satisfied, as we finished that particular operation by spring and had spent a pleasant and cold winter constructively.

It was sure nice to spend Christmas again with Mother and the family. Mother was a wonderful cook, and I do not believe I have had as good a Christmas dinner since the last time I spent Christmas with her, 12 years previous.

Spring was not far off. I could feel it in the air, and before long, the snow went to melting. I was starting to think of flowers blooming, new calves and new, wild little critters showing up on the cattle ranges. It would not be long now till I would park my butt in the saddle with a good horse between my knees.

That cowboy instinct, considering cowboy wages, has contributed to me being more or less financially embarrassed every now and then. Like a fella said once, "If you like what you're doing, money isn't everything." Of course, a friend of mine in later years made the observation, "If money ain't all that important, show me what's in first place, ahead of money, to make a living. I'm sure willing to look at it and learn." I guess, when you think of it, they both had good opinions.

The water was running all over from the snowmelt in the bush country on my old home range. The logging outfits were all shut down for the spring breakup, and it was time for me to head back to the Alberta cattle ranges. I said goodbye to Mother and the boys, and one of them drove me to the railroad station, where I got on the CNR, a rattling cannonball heading east.

The conductor collected the tickets after hollering "All aboard!" The whistle blew, the old steam engine went to snorting, the wheels turned, the couplings jerked and the train shuddered and clanked and slowly clattered along the rails. The steam whistle blew again, we gained speed and were on our way to whatever adventures might lie ahead.

I was leaving with mixed feelings. I had spent a good winter with family and friends. At the same time, I was looking forward to getting my butt back in the saddle and a good horse between my knees. It would be nice to get back on the range among the cows and brand-new calves, grass growing up, flowers blooming and all the brand-new, little wild critters on the range.

I was looking forward to Alberta—still reluctant to leave British Columbia, but I would be back every now and then. Someone once said, "Once you've had a drink of water out of a British Columbia river, be it the Fraser, Skeena, Kispiox, Thomson, Stikine or Columbia, you'll always, sooner or later, want to come back for another drink."

In due time, the whistle blew and the big old steam engine slowed down and pulled into the railroad station at Wainwright. Allen was there waiting for me as I had contacted him, and he knew I was coming. He was busy calving, so I pitched in and helped wherever it was needed.

I still had the rodeo bug riding under my hatband, so I said to Allen, "How about us fixing up a roping arena, where we can get some real practice roping your calves, and I'll help you put in all your crops for just my board and room?" He said okay, and we proceeded to get the arena put together and worked.

We would rope calves for practice for about an hour each morning and then farm for the rest of the day. This went on till the crop was in, and we were becoming quite handy at making time calf roping.

After spring work, we went to some rodeos, but the rest of the boys had been practicing, too, so we still had to draw good calves and tie them fast to have a chance at making it to the pay window. I took to the road, heading south, and have not seen Allen since.

I headed for Medicine Hat country in southern Alberta and cowboyed in the south end of Alberta until I retired a from the pasture a few years ago. Some years after I came south, I heard that Allen had continued roping and rodeoing and was the Canadian Cow Milking Champion at least once. I just kept on working and cowboying, rodeoing a little and making a living. I am going to try to take a trip back there and see him and a lot of other folks while we are still all around.

I hit Medicine Hat in early September and, of course, I had to find a job, which I did fair quickly. I went harvesting for a fella up in that Schuler country north of the Hat for a couple or three weeks. I turned my rope horse in with his cows, while I was busy helping him clean his crops.

I was told on a previous occasion that some fella had been drowned in a bin full of flax seed, and although I thought at the time it was just a story, I would be careful if I had to work with flax.

I got my chance. This feller grew flax, and I had to go in and shovel when the granary was filling up. He said to be careful, flax had poor footing. Remembering the story, I soon found out that flax was about as stable as quicksand. I did my shovelling lying on my belly, close as I could to the wall, so I would have the studding to grab onto.

I did not sink down, because I was lying full length on my belly, but I can assure you that running a scoop shovel from that position is not exactly a pleasure. For that matter, running a scoop shovel from any position is not my idea of a pleasurable pastime.

One day, it had rained a little at night, so he asked me if I would go down to the main pasture and pump water for his cows. He said it was just a hand pump, but it was not bad. Away I went and found about 60 head of cattle that was fixing to slake their thirst.

In British Columbia, there were many hand pumps on shallow wells, and the water would come gushing out in a big stream. Not so here. I knew nothing about deep wells. I pumped and pumped, could feel the suction of the pump through the handle, but no water came. Just about when I was about ready to give up, go home and tell the man his pump was haywire, a little dribble of water came.

I worked the handle a little faster. It kept coming but just a small stream. It is an experience that, luckily, most people have missed, watering 60 head of thirsty cows with a stream of water not much bigger than peeing on a prickly pear cactus. I was sure glad that he would usually water the cows himself, so he could keep me busy on the swather. I was plumb glad we did not have any more wet nights while I was there.

Harvest was over; I got paid, loaded my horse and headed back to Medicine Hat. I was again unemployed, but not for long. I had a friend who was an auctioneer and rodeo clown, who had a second hand store in Medicine Hat. After putting my horse in a corral on water and feed in the stockyards, I stopped in to see him. He informed me that he knew a rancher who had bought a small, additional cow outfit in the Cypress Hills and was looking for a man with experience to run it. That sounded like just what I was looking for, and Tex offered to run me out to negotiate some employment for the winter.

We saw eye to eye, and I got the job. Look after the ranch and about 200 head of cattle, and keep things in shape. It turned out I was the only one there to do my own cooking, be my own boss and do all the work, which I could handle quite well. I was set for the winter.

I was the chief cook and bottle washer, foreman and crew all rolled into one. The only way I could give anyone hell for not doing things right was to stand in front of the looking glass and berate the guy looking back. Never had to; he was just too good a man for me to find fault with!

Winter was coming on, so I was getting ready, checking rigging, corrals, feed bunks and so on. The haying and stacking were all done when I came, so it gave me time to put things in shape before the snow came.

I would be feeding with a big team, which was sure okay with me. The grey horse was only green broke, but the old black horse was plumb solid and gentle, so by spring the grey was also broke good. I did have the odd bit of difficulty with him during the winter, mostly because of small, bad habits he had acquired somewhere along the way. By spring, he had turned into a very good horse.

It got somewhat lonely, working and living by myself. I had to be on the ball, take care of myself and not get hurt. There was no telephone on the place, and someone only showed up every couple of weeks. Mind you, I was okay. In a pinch, I had my truck.

Come spring, I had the cows to calve out. That could be a little touchy in spots, as some of those mama cows did not take kindly to anyone getting too close to junior. After that, I had seven two- and three-year-old colts to break out, but by that time I was well experienced in these things and had figured

Art handling the team at the Brown Ranch in the Cypress Hills: "The winter of 1967, I was feeding over 200 pairs with a fork and wagon."

out working alone. I looked after yours truly first. First, I did not want to get hurt; second, I needed the job (being as it was a good one); and third, the outfit depended on me to keep going.

During the early summer, I got things in good shape, so the boss said it was okay to take a week off and go to the Calgary Stampede, which I did and got in the roping. I had a good week there, camping along the river with some friends and taking in all the activity of the "Greatest Outdoor Show on Earth." It was a nice break. On returning home, it was back to riding, haying and ranch work, till the Medicine Hat Stampede at the end of July, then more riding and haying.

This ranch was close to the little town of Elkwater, where the offices for the Cypress Hills Provincial Park were located. While on the ranch, I had become friends with the assistant park ranger in charge of logging and thinning operations in the bush. He was in need of a timber hacker for thinning the small jack pine timber by piecework.

Upon telling me the prices paid for cutting the different sizes of pine rails, I got plumb interested. I had learned the bush work trade years ago, and on a contract timber cutting I figured I could make roughly twice the money I was making on the ranch.

I got the job. I needed the extra money. I did not like to leave the little ranch, as the owner and I got along very well, but he understood. I went to Medicine Hat, bought some good tools and for the next four years would be working for the provincial park with timber and running their sawmill.

CHAPTER 16

THE CYPRESS HILLS

I had never expected to be back working in the bush out on the open prairie. The Cypress Hills stick out of the prairie in southern Alberta, just a few miles north of the Alberta–Montana line.

It is really something; those hills with all that timber are pretty much like the British Columbia bush, once you get into the forested area. They are just a timbered line of hills that run east and west from Alberta into Saskatchewan, 40 or 50 miles in length, I suppose, about five or six miles wide and very scenic and picturesque. They are pretty much all provincial park. I was going to work for the Alberta side.

The local storekeeper told me I was crazy to quit my ranch job, said cowboys do not know nothing about bush work. He said that, after a couple of weeks, I would be wishing I were back on the ranch. He told me the men already working there were busting their asses to make $10 or $12 a day, so I would have to work a hell of a lot harder here for a few dollars than I did on the ranch.

Well, this cowboy knew the bush, and I was going to prove it. I would not have to quit the ranch—I liked it there—but I intended to make twice as much as he said.

Every day after I had made $20, I would go home. The storekeeper just laughed, wished me good luck and told me to hope for a lot of moonlit evenings as I walked out the door. I just kept going.

I did not tell him that I had my own axe by the time I was eight years old and that my dad and those British Columbia loggers had taught me well. I knew how to use those logger's hand tools, such as saws, axes, peaveys and cant hooks. Knowing the tricks of the trade and the use of hand tools, especially an axe, made the work much easier and faster.

Come Monday morning, the park ranger met me at about 7:30, and we went to the bush to the work site. He showed me the way he marked the trees he wanted cut, mostly fence rail–size, and that they had to be dragged out to the road and piled in separate piles according to size, as each size was a different price range. They had put in roads at various intervals, so we had to drag those green trees no more than 100 or so feet to the road after they were limbed and the tops cut off.

I got to cutting timber about 8:30, and that first day went real good. I had 21 dollars' worth cut by 4:00. I stopped for the day and went home.

I was driving past the general store at 4:30, so I decided I would stop and have a ginger ale and chocolate bar. I was also curious to see if the storekeeper might crow a little. He did.

I walked through the door and heard, "You played out already son? It's only 4:30." I told him that I had made my $20 and decided to call it a day. He thought I was pulling his leg, but I informed him that I had actually made $21 that day. I was ready to prove it. "Jump in my truck, we'll go count them poles up."

His eyes got big, and he said, "You're serious, aren't you? How the hell did you do it, when no one else can?" I had to tell the poor man the truth. Growing up in a logging camp, you learn the tricks of the trade from some very experienced men. There are tricks in every trade to make the work easier and quicker. Bush work is very hard work, and if you can make it easier on yourself, you do it.

Branding at the Brown Ranch: "We would head out to gather the cattle at 2:30 AM so we could get the branding done in one day."

I worked in the bush cutting timber for a couple of years. By then, the thinning operations were pretty well done, as there were quite a few men working at it.

I went to a few rodeos the second summer I was there, as I still had my horse. I was lucky to be able to board and room at a small ranch right close by the park and was able to keep my rope horse there. They were real good people, did not charge me for my horse, so I helped them with their livestock on weekends or after hours. It was a treat to do a little cowboying on weekends, and they lived only a couple of miles from the ranch I had just left.

There was also a rodeo arena and roping club in the vicinity, with a pasture for the roping stock. An interesting thing came out of that. A rancher living some miles from the roping arena supplied 10 cows and calves for the summer, which he pastured in the roping club pasture. He told me that he had done very well on the deal. Besides the money he was paid per pair, he said the calves we chased and roped every Sunday weighed a lot more than the calves he had at home on the range at weaning time. Nobody seemed to figure that out.

We did look after them, though. We put a limit of three runs on the calves each Sunday, two if the weather was very hot. Maybe the extra weight gain came from being muscled up from beating them horses to the ketch pen, where the gate was always left open. If the calf was not caught before he made his straight run to the catch pen, he was home free.

It was an interesting pastime and good practice, too. The ladies and kids barrel raced, and at the end of the season, there were belt buckles and trophies for the ones who had done the best, whether due to good luck, good management or both. It did not matter, it was just good fun. I believe the roping club is still going, but it's mostly team roping and barrel racing now, I think. They still have a rodeo on the first of July that has been running for 40 years or more.

As the timber thinning process was over, when I came back from them rodeos, I went to work for the Parks Department by day. When I got back, my old friend the forest ranger told me that the truck that hauled in a sawmill had just dumped everything in a pile. They had tried without any luck to find someone to put it together and set it up ready to go to work. Being prairie country, sawmill men in them parts was harder to find than hair on an egg.

Well, I told the ranger I would set it up for him if he would give me a man to help. I would even train the crew and run it for him when it was set up. He looked at me in surprise and said, "You? I didn't think you'd know anything about sawmills."

Art on Danny at the Elkwater roping club: "This picture was given to me by a friend, Morley Shaw."

I suppose I surprised him a couple of years ago when I said I could run an axe. I had to tell him that I had set up and run quite a few of these very same mills in the British Columbia bush. He went and talked to the chief ranger, and next morning they had a man waiting to help me set up the mill.

We took great care to keep the whole setup perfectly level both ways, from the ground up—from the square cement blocks on the ground for the upright posts, to hold the mill deck, right to laying the tracks for the carriage to run on and the circular saw frame itself. That way, we never had any problem of anything getting out of line and were able to saw very good, evenly-cut lumber.

We installed the edger that came with it, built rollers to roll the lumber and slabs on and set up the cut-off saw to trim the bad ends of the lumber and cut most of the slabs into wood for the camp kitchens.

As most of our timber was relatively small, we did not cut our 15,000 a day. It did not matter; the logs came from an area of the park in which the lake area was being extended. A dam would be built and a creek turned in to fill the lakebed, which would be stocked with trout for tourists and fishermen.

Hauling all the usable spruce and pine to the mill for lumber saved some expense, as the park had their own building material. Later, after the first winter of sawing lumber, they acquired a small planer that I set up, and we planed a lot of the lumber for the park building projects.

The last two years I worked for the Cypress Hills Provincial Park, I took the middle of the summer off to run my own little business. I had acquired the necessary permits and leased some land toward the west end of the lake, where I set up a small trail-riding outfit. I acquired about a dozen head of gentle horses, bought a bunch of economically priced riding saddles from Hutchins & Sharp Western Wear and Saddlery in Medicine Hat, hired me a couple of young cowboys for trail guides and called the outfit Cypress Trail Rides. I was in business.

For a small outfit and not too many tourists, them days, we did okay. Didn't get rich, but it was interesting, to say the least, and a nice break to get out of the bush and away from the timber operations for three months.

We had some interesting little things happen. We had a woman on old Sonny, one of my gentlest horses, who backed him into a deep ditch. He turned over flat on his side. A bad moment, but Sonny and the lady both got up unhurt, none the worse for wear. The lady was a little shook up. Sonny took it all in a day's work.

Leo, the cowboy guide, explained to the lady that you could only stop a horse by pulling on the lines if you are going forward. Pulling on the lines going backward did not mean "whoa" to the horse, it meant "back up." The horse backs away from the pressure on the bit.

Well, it never happened again, as the boys got to watching those urban riders pretty close. We did not need any accidents. That had been close enough and, luckily, all was well.

I had bought a nice little bay horse we called Shorty for a guide horse. Shorty was a good little horse and well-broke most of the time. He had one bad habit that just did not seem to want to get corrected. He would buck once in a while, downright serious, and did not want to quit till his rider was on the ground.

He was ridden till he would quit numerous times but would always give it another go when he felt like it, and you never knew when it was going to happen. He could be going along, at peace with the world, it seemed, when, for no reason at all, down went his head and the rodeo was on. It was sort of a 50–50 deal. Half the time, Shorty bucked his rider off, and the other times he got rode till he quit. He was never given to a customer to ride. He was strictly a guide horse.

The boys and I were getting a little tired of his actions. It was not a good situation to be in, on the verge of getting bucked off, especially when you have others to look out for.

One day, Stormy had to ride, by himself, up to the top bench of the Cypress Hills for something. He took Shorty, as that was the horse he usually rode, and Shorty had been very good lately. Had not bucked for damned near a month. We all figured he had made up his mind to turn over a new leaf and had quit bucking. He was such a good little horse, and we were all pleased to think that he would be plumb dependable.

Come about two o'clock, Leo and me were just getting up from the table after a late dinner, when Leo looked out the window. There was Stormy, walking up the driveway, packing his ear bridle. We went out to meet him and asked, "What happened, Shorty take to you again?" "Yeah," Stormy said, "right along the jack pines. I do not know what set him off. I was riding him good and hanging onto his head, when somehow he threw his head sideways and flipped the ear bridle off." It did not have a throatlatch on it, so there was nothing to secure it.

"Well," he said, "the bit came out of Shorty's mouth. I pulled up on the reins, but now the bit was under his neck, against his chest." Shorty had a plumb free head, and it did not take him long to iron Stormy out. Stormy got up, picked up the bridle and tried to catch him to ride him back home, but he took off.

"Have you got any idea where he went? And how the hell did you get home? It's got to be six miles from where you hit the sagebrush," I asked. As Stormy was mumbling under his breath about what a little son of a bitch Shorty was, we got out of him that Shorty was probably still running around somewhere in those jack pines; one of the park wardens had come along and given Stormy a ride home.

Well, Leo and me got him filled up with a belly full of dinner and a pot of black coffee. After he ate, he sat and glared at the wall. Finally, he grinned and said, "I guess I should get my saddle back. Let us take the truck and some oats. I think between the three of us we can catch the little bugger. I'll take my bridle with the throat latch, and we'll see if he's so smart next time."

We went up to where Stormy got bucked off. Shorty had pretty well stayed put. We caught him, Stormy checked the saddle and climbed aboard, Shorty's ears pointed toward home and away they went. When they got home, they were back to being good friends. Shorty had been the true gentleman he was capable of, and Stormy said, "He's such a good little horse. Sure hope this is the last time it happens."

One day, the boys came in with a trip of riders late. It was hotter than the hub of a dry wagon wheel, but I had supper ready, so I hollered to them. "Throw the saddles on the fence and feed the horses, then come in and eat while it's still hot. We'll put the riggin' away after we eat."

After supper, one of the boys had said what a good meal it was, but it needed a little ice cream to top it off. That sounded like a great idea, so we jumped in the truck and drove to the restaurant, figuring we would only be gone for about 30 minutes.

When we got back, we went to putting the riggin' away in the saddle shed. There was one saddle short. It was my new roping saddle. A saddle does not disappear into thin air. Someone had driven in while we were gone and swiped it off the fence. The Mounties had a couple of men stationed at the park during the busy season, so we headed back to town and reported the theft.

Come about next February, I was at a Saturday-night dance in Medicine Hat, when a friend came to me and told me where my saddle might be. All the boys I knew were keeping their ears and eyes open, watching for my saddle. So I climbed on the phone and called Constable Purdy in Medicine Hat. He said he had heard the same thing. He would come by the next day and pick me up, and we would go look.

We went to this rancher's place, and he said did not have any stolen saddle. The Mounties asked if he had bought a saddle lately. The rancher said that he had bought a saddle for his daughter a while back, but he was sure that could not be it. "I got it from a person in the bar who gave me a good deal on it. Let's go to the barn and I'll show it to you," he said.

We went to the saddle room in the barn and, sure as water runs downhill, there sat my saddle on the rack. The rancher said, "I can't let you have it, I paid good money for that rig!" I said, "Yeah, but I paid twice as much good money for it last summer, and it's still mine!"

We finally convinced him that he could not keep stolen property, even if he paid for it. In due time, all the odds and ends were cleared up, and thanks to Constable Purdy for a good job well done, I had my roping saddle back.

The business in the park was slowing down, so I decided to sell it to a couple of brothers who were interested. I went back to work on a small ranch on the south slope of the Cypress Hills. I worked for that ranch for three and a half years. It was a good place to work; the owner was very good to work for. It was good to get back to the cows and ranch horses again.

While there, I traded Shorty off to a friend who was starting a bucking string. Shorty did not make a bucking horse; he would only buck when the mood hit him. He finally wound up as a pickup and hazing horse, which he was good at. He practically got over his bucking spells.

I was still interested in calf roping and acquired a good sorrel horse, but it turned out he did not have enough speed for the fast, longhorn-cross calves they were starting to use. This sorrel, Casey, was a wonderful ranch horse, and I kept him for as long as I was on that little Cypress Hills ranch.

I finally bought a bay gelding, half quarter horse, half thoroughbred, which those calves could not outrun. He turned out to be the best all-around horse I have ever sat on. I bought him as a three-year-old and used him on the ranch.

We built a small roping arena, where I trained him to become a top rope horse. The rancher's son liked to rope, too, so I helped him get started and trained a horse for him. Through it all, he learned to rope, and I got my bay horse working in both the arena and the range, to the point of complete satisfaction on my part.

I had him for 16 years before the sad day he passed away. In all that time, working mostly alone, never once did I go after something with him—cattle or horses—that we could not bring back. He was fast and strong and knew what he was doing. I do not think a cow lived that he could not handle.

Art on Danny: "Danny was the best horse I ever rode; I had him for 16 years, and I wish it could have been longer."

He would get mad and buck me off every once in a while, just to smarten me up. There were times I wondered if he was smarter than I was. Daniel, or Danny, as we all called him, was one hell of a horse. I hope he is in a good place, where the

Feeding cattle in the Cypress Hills: "This is Mrs. Brown's team, Queen and Julia, and my dog, Jimmy, is in the foreground."

sun is always shining, the grass is always green and all the creeks have running water, clear and sweet.

I worked on that small ranch on the south slope of the Cypress Hills then decided it was time to move on. I gave my good boss two weeks' notice and got ready to move. I had a haying job to go to. He didn't want to see me go very bad, as we were getting along real well, but when you're young and single, seems like there's an urge every once in a while to see what's on the other side of the hill.

When the two weeks were up, I loaded my possibles and Daniel into the covered horse rack on my truck and took off for the west end of the Cypress Hills, to help a young fellow who had a ranch about the same size as the one I just left. I stayed with him until haying and roundup was over.

After that, I was offered a job driving a Cat, doing dirt work for a friend and soon to be brother-in-law. Now I sure am not a Cat-skinner, but he said it was all level ground and all I needed was practice. The weather was good, but it was getting late in the fall, so he wanted to run the Cat two shifts a day, to get the project done before freeze-up.

That big old Cat was pretty well worn. It had a lot of slack in the controls, but by the time we were done, I handled it quite respectfully and must say, I moved a lot of dirt.

We were living in a little camper trailer and batching, just getting along on our own cooking. We worked within driving distance of where his folks lived on a small ranch. Every once in a while, he would say we should run over to his folks' for something. It was just natural to go over in the evening, so we would not waste daylight hours, and we always managed to make it in time for supper. It sure beat our cooking!

I had made a run north to where a friend was living and, while there, made arrangements for a winter job west of Sundre, looking after about 70 head of cows and, I hate to admit this, also 53 head of woollies. I did not know a damn thing about them bleating old ewes that I had to calve out come spring. I still do not. They are the only bunch of sheep I have ever had anything to do with. Nothing against people who raise sheep, but from a cowboy's point of view, that one winter's experience was enough.

When I was working on the Cat, I got to know that fella's sister well enough that we got married. When I took the job at the ranch west of Sundre, I had a brand-new wife. She was the main reason I got through the winter with them woollies as she had had a little experience helping a neighbour of her dad's with his sheep once in a while. The feller who owned the ranch I was looking after was a car dealer in town, quite a ways away, so we were on our own.

The cows were easy, even at calving time, compared to them woollies. Every night before dark, I would go out and try to figure out which ewe was going to calve that night. I would rope her and drag her into a big shed, bucking and bleating, and then go get another one. About the second night, I dragged three or four into the shed. I was sure they would lamb by morning.

Next morning, I came out, none of them had any young ones, but outside by a poplar tree was two newborns, near froze to death. It was 20 below (–29°C), and I could not figure out who was the mother.

I gathered them up in a sack and headed for the house. We put them in a box on the oven door, and it did not take long till they were bleating and screaming for something to eat. Luckily, we had a big Holstein milk cow in the barn, so we were able to fill their faces.

As luck would have it, we found the ewe that had them; she was looking for them. We put them all in a pen in the shed and, thank the good Lord, she mothered them.

After that, we ran the whole bunch of them into the shed at night. It was crowded but warm, and I would go out before bedtime in case there was something in trouble. We built some more mothering-up pens along one wall and managed to have good success from then on.

I learned something that winter. If someone offered me a job tending woollies again, I would ride the other way and make myself scarce. No one ever has.

Spring came, and the cows and sheep were all calved out and ready to go on grass. We got an offer to go back south to a big cow outfit south of the Cypress Hills. Again, we loaded Daniel and the rigging up and headed south to the ranch.

I learned something else. When I went north and took the job the previous fall, everything I owned, including Daniel, fit on the truck. Now, after being married about six months, considering everything a woman needs, I had to make three trips altogether to get moved back. Why does a woman need so much more household stuff than a man?

When we got to the ranch south of the Cypress Hills, the calving was done, but they were not branded yet. Then I got a pleasant surprise, just about as bad as that bunch of sheep. It was a very stressed and on-the-go type of place, and they were eager to get to farming, and quite a lot of it.

It was a cold spring. I put on all the clothes I owned, including my sheepskin coat, and still pretty near froze. It was also dusty. We came in the evenings with our eyeballs shining white out of a plumb dust-blackened face. Seemed like the cowboy business was going to hell fast, with no way to stop the runaway on a flat track.

The weather warmed up, and we were done that cussed farming, but it was still highball. Five o'clock in the morning, we had to get all them miles of fence fixed. Haying came along, still highball, but we were getting used to it. Now, instead of freezing, it was hotter than a rapid-firing, three-dollar pistol.

We were stacking square bales by hand, although we had a farmhand to lift them up in the stack. All them cows ate a hell of a lot of hay come winter, and there were only three of us haying. We were there all summer, and during that time, I do not think I rode half a dozen times.

A cow died, and I had to ride out 10 miles to rope a calf and tie it down. One of the boys picked it up with the truck to take it home and bucket-feed it. It sure was wild. I saw it lying beside its dead mother from a quarter of a mile away. I stopped and put my neck rope on and tied hard and fast to the horn, and I said to Daniel, "We'll get one shot, and it better fit."

This was not the first time the bay horse and I had done this. We came up on the side where the cow was lying; the calf was behind her and did not see us. Daniel was walking quietly in the grass. I got my piggin' string in my belt and my rope ready. When we got to within about 50 feet, the calf heard us, jumped up and started to run.

We loped after him a little ways to get him running straight, then I dropped the reins slack and Daniel knew it had to be right now. With a mighty surge of power, he pulled up behind the calf. Before the calf expected it, Danny gave me a perfect shot, the loop fit like a hat and he was down and tied before the truck got there. About 30 seconds to get the job done and a 10-mile ride there and back. Sure beat farming and haying for something to do, though.

One Sunday, we were sitting around the house, resting and drinking coffee and, as usual with ranch hands, we got to talking about horses, good, bad and indifferent. There was a buckskin horse on the ranch that had been there for 12 years. He was a good horse, knew every foot of the ranch, but had one bad habit. You could never drop your reins on the ground when you were closing a gate. You would be on foot, because Buck would head for home holding his head sideways, so he would not step on the reins, and no way could you catch him on foot.

A few guys had found out the hard way over the past 12 years. Walking home maybe six or eight miles, with your horse staying ahead of you, didn't exactly put a fella in a good humour, never mind the high-heeled boots being hard on his undercarriage. Somebody said something to the effect that the boss should get another horse and sell old Buck for fox feed, since he had left a few guys on foot whenever he got the chance.

A big, husky cowboy called Bill finally spoke up. "Don't knock old Buck, he saved my life once." All of us wondering, he went on. "A couple of years ago, there was just me and a young German couple here, feeding. That is, the husband helped me feed, and his wife looked after the house and done the cooking. It was around the middle of January. The weather had been nice for a long while. It was a Sunday. It was mild, no wind and plumb beautiful.

"I was in the process of breaking out and training a big three-year-old colt. We were done feeding early, and I asked the German fella if he would like to go for a ride with me. He was eager, as long as he could ride a gentle horse. I told him to ride Buck. He was plumb gentle, and I would open all the gates so he would not have to get off.

"We decided we would ride down south about eight miles to the Willow Creek Valley, where most of the cows were winter grazing. We thought we would go over there and look at them, make sure they were all okay. Right after an early lunch."

Bill continued, "We headed south; it was such a nice day, we were really going to enjoy this trip, and my colt was going real good. We got down to Willow Creek, passed by an old vacant cow camp that was not used anymore and rode up the valley, checking all the cows. The cows were all doing good, all healthy, no cripples and all in good shape. We were done, so we headed for home.

"We went past the old cow camp, and at the lower end of the valley, I seen the snow and black-looking clouds up on the north side. I figured it was just a squall, so I told the other fella to put the horses in the old shed out of the wind, build a fire in the old stove and wait till the weather had passed.

"The squall was a good one. I figured we may have to wait till morning, but we could not find an axe or saw to cut any wood, and there was not a whole lot left in the old cabin. It was getting colder, and the cracks in the walls where the chinking had fallen out was big enough to run a full-grown cat through. There was no way we could make it till morning with no fire. We were in a bad spot. I kept going out and looking for the weather to clear up."

Bill had our attention. How was Buck going to save his life? Bill's voice lowered as he went on. "Come about four o'clock, I went and looked, and the north side of the valley toward home was all cleared up. The German fella and I decided to get the hell out of there while we could.

"We rode up out of the valley toward home, and it looked good, even up on top. A little hazy, but the wind had died down some as we came to high ground. It was looking like we were going to get home okay, and we broke into a trot.

"We had gone about a quarter of a mile, it was all open country, when the storm hit us with all it had. The wind and snow were so thick you could hardly see your horse's ears. I knew we were in bad trouble. I did not even know which way to go to get back to the old cow camp in the valley.

"I rode up to old Buck and grabbed his rein, stopping him. I got off my colt and told the young German that I was going to tie Buck's reins to the saddle horn, with lots of slack, and no matter where that old horse went or did, do not touch them. That young fellow thought I was plumb out of my mind. He near wanted to cry, saying "We'll die out here; I'll never see my wife and little boy again!" He had never seen or heard of a situation like this before in the old country, and here he was, right in the middle of it.

"My wife and boy, what will they do without me?" he went on. I finally had to tell him to shut up and do what I said. I told him to hang on tight. Buck was our only chance. Trust him, he'll bring you back to your wife and son."

Bill's voice was raspy. "I stepped up on my colt and let Buck go, and he loped off into the storm. I stayed right on his tail. I did not dare lose him. I hoped he knew where he was going, because I sure as hell did not.

"That old horse went down ravines, crossed coulees, went over level country—I have no idea where we went, as it got dark along with that storm.

"Finally, after about an hour of what seemed like wandering around plumb lost, old Buck stopped. I rode up beside him and got his rein. He was standing beside a barbed wire fence. I felt along the top wire and recognized the gate latch by feel. I could not see anything. I threw the gate open, holding onto both horses, got on my colt and let Buck go.

"Buck loped off into the storm again, with me right behind. I still made sure I did not lose him. Mind you, the colt did not want to lose him, either.

"I felt a lot better. The gate we just went through was halfways home. Only four more miles to go, I knew then that we were going to make it." Bill sighed with relief, as if he were there in that storm again.

"It was darker than the inside of a black cow, and the storm was still hammering us, but after a while, Buck stopped again. I got off and felt my way along the wire; we were at the gate to the hayfield, less than a mile to go. I flung that gate back, got on my colt and let Buck go.

"After what seemed like a short while, Buck stopped again. I wondered why. I did not think we had gone far enough to be home. I rode up beside him and felt my chaps brush up against something. I reached my hand out and felt the barn wall. We were home, alive and well, thanks to an old buckskin horse.

"He might have a disagreeable habit or two, but that night he was the best horse alive. He had just saved two men from freezing to death, lost in a blizzard that night. The young German fellow got to see his wife and son, after all. Thanks to old Buck, he's why I'm sitting here telling you all this."

Now, that had to be one of the best, real-life stories I had heard for a long time about a man and his trusty steed.

Haying was about over, and I ran into a rancher friend I had known for years. He said there was a widow lady on the north slope of the Cypress Hills who had a good, little ranch with about 200 cows. He said he had told her he would try to find somebody to help her.

He asked me if I wanted the job. It was closer to town, and he thought it would be a good job. "You got the experience, how about it?" I said sure, but I had better discuss it with my wife first. I would let him know. After talking with her, it turned out that her, Daniel and me were going to move camp again.

CHAPTER 17

FAMILY MAN

We did not have far to move this time, maybe 40 miles, just from the south side of the Cypress Hills to the north side. The ranch we were going to was only about 10 miles from where I worked in the bush and lived at the park, so we were on familiar ground.

We arrived at the ranch about the first of September. The haying was contracted out, so it was all done, but there was still a lot to do getting ready for winter. I do not think the widow lady who owned the ranch had any steady help for the summer, so things were backed up a bit.

Mother Nature smiled on us that fall, and it was just what we needed. One of the most beautiful Indian summers I have seen. I was ready for winter when it came, and even then, that first winter was not too tough.

We had an added bonus at the end of October: a healthy baby boy. Life was good. We had a healthy youngster, a good place to live, a good ranch to work on, a familiar country and good neighbours. As so often happens, a dark cloud loomed on the horizon.

We had no telephone on the ranch, and going for the mail at the park one day, I found that some folks I knew there had been trying to contact me for a day or so. They had a phone call from British Columbia that my mother was very ill and in the hospital. I immediately phoned home to talk to my brother.

We had to go to British Columbia to see my mother. We were in a tight spot with a two-month-old baby, too small to make the trip. Sometimes when you do not expect it, the good hearts of people seem to be there for you. A couple in Medicine Hat we both had known for years offered to take care of our boy, so we could go and see Mother.

These folks were absolutely reliable, a little past middle age and had raised their own kids well. We were so thankful and accepted their offer, knowing our boy would be looked after as well as or better than we could ourselves.

We made it to the hospital in Terrace, British Columbia, from Medicine Hat in record time. We had good connections all the way, using the bus, train and my brother-in-law's car to get there. We got to spend two days with Mother before she passed away.

She had taken ill suddenly, after being very healthy and active. The doctors and nurses did their best. My sister and sister-in-law were with her, to spell off the nurses, all the time. Something went unavoidably wrong, and, just five months short of her 80th birthday, our mother went off into the sunset.

We got back to the prairies to find everything fine. Our boy had done beautifully well, although I think the woman who was so good to look after him for us was glad to see us back. She took such good care of him and was so concerned that he was okay that I believe it was quite a strain on her. We certainly did appreciate what they done for us.

The cows had been rustling in the winter field till then, but it was time they had a little help. I got the big team of bay mares in, trimmed their feet, kept them in the barn on hay and oats and the winter feed hauling began.

The hay was all baled, and feeding was quite a bit easier than when I fed further north, 10 years previous, when Bev and I fed those 600 head with four-horse teams through the long, hard winter of '55 and '56.

As usual, spring got in the air, and this might sound a little unusual, but we had to get the cows in and wean the calves that were still on the cows. At that time, and all through previous years, this outfit let the calves run with the cows all winter. They had a very good winter field, and, come about the end of February, we would get them all in and wean the calves that the cows had not already weaned and then separate them. Usually, about two-thirds of the cows would have their calves weaned by spring.

Some people did not exactly agree with this method, but for this cow outfit, it worked very well. The cows came out of the winter in damn good shape on the good winter grass, and at shipping time, their two-year-olds were as good as any of those of the neighbours, who used more traditional methods, like fall weaning and corral feeding all winter.

As it was around the end of February, it was only about six weeks till the new calves started showing up. I hauled lots of hay, helping in the winter field to keep the cows in good shape for spring calving. We were hoping for good calving weather in the spring, and that was what we got. Things went well. If only we could predict accurately what the weather would be like a year ahead.

After the cows were all calved out, we had to check and fix fences in the summer field and brand. We turned the cows out in the summer field to raise their calves, and I did a little farming. We had to do some breaking and re-seeding to hay, as some of the old hayfields were getting sod-bound from growing hay for the last 20 years.

I ploughed them up and seeded them to oats for green feed. The next year they would be seeded to green feed again. It had to be done two years in a row to get the old sod cultivated for a good seedbed for the new grass seed, with the oats hay as a protective cover crop.

It was only about 80 acres, but back then, it took me a while. Not like nowadays. There was not any big machinery and overgrown four-wheel drive tractors. I had a John Deere D tractor that handled a double-bottom breaking plough, and in that tough sod, that old John Deere would dig and snort, so we had to go pretty slow to do a good job. Considering that the two 14-inch ploughs only turned over 28 inches on each side of the field every round, you can see where even 80 acres took a little time to plough.

After the ploughing was done, it had to be disked several times then harrowed and seeded.

There was a real good wild hay meadow that never would dry up enough to cut for hay, unless it was an exceptionally good year and real dry. The ranch owner had a drainage ditch put in to control the water drainage, but the machines couldn't dig far enough into the meadow, being too wet, so with the low level of the meadow, the water would only drain into the ditch down to the last two feet.

There was actually about 150 feet of ground about two feet too high, between the low level of the meadow and the big, deep ditch that reached in as far as the machines could go. That lady rancher was feeling a little blue over that. She had spent a lot of money on the ditch, and there was still two feet of water in the meadow and too wet on that stretch for even horses to work, so we could not finish it off the old-fashioned way, either. She asked me "What will we do?" "Let me think about it," I said, "I'll figure something out."

I had a little riding to do, checking on the cows and calves. That was a good time to think about it. When I was a kid, most things like that were dug by hand. We still could get some help and finish it off that way, but we'd lose this year's hay crop because the meadow wouldn't dry up till late fall, and there was no way a ditch could be dug under two feet of water, even by hand.

Then the solution hit me. Year before, Dad had told me how to use ditching powder for blowing ditches in wet ground. When I got home at suppertime, I told the ranch lady I could solve the problem with dynamite. She looked shocked and said she did not think it would work. After explaining that I knew it would work, I had seen my dad do it on occasion, all she could say was, "You're serious, aren't you?"

I went to town the next day. Although she did not want to be picking up pieces of me all over the hayfield, she realized it might be the only way. I picked up some ditching powder, blasting caps and a small role of fuse.

The next day, the rancher lady's brother-in-law came with me to the meadow to watch the fireworks. On the two-mile trip from the ranch to the field, he was as nervous as a long-tailed cat in a roomful of rocking chairs. The idea of all that dynamite in the back of the truck and that tin box of blasting caps between us on the seat made little drops of sweat come out on his bald head like raindrops on a window. 'Course, it was a damn hot day—I suppose it could have been the summer heat.

The reason I kept the blasting caps on the seat was to have them ride as smooth as possible. A sharp jolt could set them off—we wanted to be as safe as possible. Considering that there were probably 50 blasting caps carefully packed in that little tin box, and each blasting cap had about 80 pounds of lifting power—well, you do the math.

The blasting caps were touchy; anybody with half the brains God gave a jackass treated blasting caps with the utmost respect. Good idea to treat dynamite with the same respect. A fella lived longer that way, when he knew what he was doing.

We got to the meadow, and I said to Mac, "Take your boots and socks off if you want to help me, I'll show you what to do."

His boots stayed on. There was no way that he was going to touch them explosives, so he went up on a little hill a short distance away and watched from there.

I took off my boots and socks and rolled up my pant legs. I pried open the two cases of dynamite. I took armfuls of dynamite sticks and headed for the meadow. I shoved a stick of dynamite end first into the mud under the water about every two feet. When I had used them all up, I had a string of dynamite sticks all in a row, close to 200 feet long.

The last two I saved for the caps and fuses. I cut one fuse five feet long and the other one four feet, the longest one for the far end of the line and the shorter one for the middle. Being as fuses burn a foot to the minute, it gave me lots of time to get the hell out of the water before they went off.

I very carefully inserted the fuses into the blasting caps all the way and crimped the open end tight around the fuse. I had some wagon grease along that I sealed the crimped ends with to make them waterproof.

I got a six-inch spike and dug a hole in the ends of both sticks of dynamite, slid the caps and fuses into the hole and sealed it up with grease. All was ready, so I waded out and shoved one stick at the end of the line, lit it and hurried back to the middle where I shoved the other stick with the shortest fuse into the mud and lit it. Then I got the hell out of there and went to sit with Mac up on the little hill to wait.

One loaded stick would set the whole string off in the water, but I put in two in case of a misfire. We sat and waited for about three minutes, as my shortest fuse was still fairly long. I was starting to think they might have both misfired; it seemed to take forever.

BOOM! BOOM! BOOM!

The chain reaction in the water set them all off. As we sat and watched, the mud and water flew everywhere. When the "smoke" cleared, there was a new ditch about two feet wide and two-and-a-half feet deep. The water in the hay meadow was draining into the big ditch. "Well, I'll be damned!" Mac said. "I've never seen anything like that before!" The two cases of ditching powder had been a good investment for the ranch.

The haying operations went well. We hired all the baling out to a neighbour, and we had some help for stacking. There were 14 head of dry cows fattening up in the summer field with the cows and calves.

Sometime in the first part of September, the boss lady wanted to ship them, as dry cow prices were good. She didn't want to bring in the whole herd to get those 14 dry cows. "Art, can you cut them out somehow and bring them in by themselves?" she asked." I'll give it a try," I said, "but it might take a while. I'll have to put them in the horse pasture a few at a time to get it done, though." "You've only got a day, so I hope it won't take too long."

Well, I would give it a shot. She wanted those cows to go through a sale three days away. That meant I had one day to gather and sort them and one day to haul them to town to have them ready to go through the sale ring on the third day. Old Daniel, my faithful horse, and me had our work cut out for us. If we could not get them in, they would have to wait for the next sale, next week, and the prices might go down in the meantime.

The summer field must have had eight or ten square miles of grass, so I knew it might take a while. Finding needles in a haystack—that was what this was going to be like.

Come early morning, I rode around over to the gate on the very east side on the field. The cows had to be brought west, so I figured I would start right behind them and with a little luck, find them and work them through the cows and calves. I knew after I found them, those dries were not going to be anxious to leave the rest of the herd.

Daniel and I rather lucked out. The weather was hot, so the cattle were going to water early and were congregating around the numerous water holes and dugouts that held runoff water.

We found a couple of head and headed for the nearest water hole, where we found a few more. It was a slow business. We had to work them slow enough that they would drink, and then we would ease them out of the herd toward the next water hole. We just rode around and slowly moved the dry ones away in a manner where they thought it was their own idea.

Once in a while, one might have broken out, but they could not beat ol' Daniel. He was big, strong and fast, and soon as the critter would head back for the other dries, he would slow down and we let her go back, quiet-like. That bay horse knew what he was doing. Although it was a huge job, when we went into the horse pasture gate just before supper, we had all 14 of those dries. Lady Luck was smiling on us.

We took them down to the ranch yard, and the boss lady had the gates open into a small five-acre pasture. We would leave them on feed and water until just before dark, so they would be in the corral just overnight. They had to go on the truck first thing in the morning in good shape.

It was suppertime; the bay horse and I were both kind of looking forward to wrapping ourselves around a bunch of groceries. It had been a long, slow, successful day, but the corral gate going into the loading pen was not shut quite yet. When supper was over, we waited for a while, and just before dark we headed for the barn, got on our horses and proceeded to put those cows into the pole corral by the loading chute. The boss lady and I thought that, between the two of us, this should take about a half hour. The field was only five acres, and the barnyard corral was connected to it. It was just a matter of pushing them through a couple of gates inside the enclosure. After that, they would be ready to load in the morning. Sounded easier that it was.

We had them going good; some were already through the gate in the barn corral, when one on the tail end broke away and ran right through the fence surrounding the little pasture. We put the others into the barn corral. While the boss lady watched the gate to the corral, I would open the gate out of the little pasture and bring the wild one back.

This cow was on more familiar territory than I realized. I found later that this was not the first time she had been a renegade. She had pulled this trick before and was on her way back to the cowherd in the summer field.

When she saw me and Daniel coming, she took off as if her tail was on fire. We overtook her, but she would not turn. Daniel laid his ears back and ran into her, hitting her shoulder with his, and damn near knocked her down. That made her gain a little respect for the bay horse, but she was still determined to go back. We wound up in a furious cutting contest out there on the prairie grass. She lost that battle.

She finally turned and headed for the corral on the trot. It was not over yet. As we got close to the corral, she took off like a dogging steer out of a rodeo chute, heading east past the corral toward the winter field.

It was getting darker than the inside of a black cow. Daniel was going wide open to pass her and bring her back. In his line of thinking, there was no such thing as letting her get away. I was getting a little nervous. There were badger holes all over the field, it was plumb dark out and Daniel was trying to head off a renegade cow that thought she was trying to win the Kentucky Derby.

As we flew through over the prairie, I remembered the wire gate going into the winter field was closed. We were heading right for it; I figured less than 60 yards away. I pulled back on the reins to stop, but Daniel had a hard mouth and a strong determination to win this battle.

All I could think about was that cow hitting the fence and us being tangled up in those broken wires behind her. In the dark, Daniel and I could be in for some pretty bad trouble: Daniel would be cut up badly from that barbed wire, and we could go end over end and break both our necks.

"WHOA! Let that son of a bitch go," I hollered, hoping he would hear my voice and listen to me. Nothing. I was desperate. I think I must have prayed for some help that night.

The good Lord came through for us. The cow hit the gate at the end, where the latch was. The latch broke and the gate was flung wide open. Do not ask me why, but the sparks flew off that barbed-wire gate like sparks off an emery wheel. That was the only way I could see the gate had been flung open, it was that dark. When I seen that, I just let Daniel go and hung on to the horn.

About 50 yards past the gate, the road went up a short, steep hill. Coming in from the south was a small, shallow creek that ran into the hill and turned back on itself toward the east. Right at the bottom was a 20- or 30-foot dirt slide coming down from the top of the hill.

The cow headed for the creek crossing at the foot of the slide. Daniel passed her like a shot; crossed the dirt slide, which was as steep as a Blackfoot teepee; turned toward the creek and came down on the run, pretty well sitting on his hindquarters. When the cow came out of the creek crossing, there we were, waiting for her.

She stopped right there. Daniel locked onto her. When she moved, he moved right in front of her. The old renegade had met her match. Daniel had won this battle, hands down. How Daniel managed in the dark, at that speed, with that agility—all I can say is that he was the best horse I ever had the pleasure of riding. The cow in front of us was just a dark shadow with a white face.

Breaking the silence, we heard the boss lady holler, "Art, where are you?" I told her where we were at and asked her to follow the road over the hill, to come in behind me so the cow would not be spooked. Once she rode up beside me, we sat and waited for everyone to get their breath back. Daniel and that cow had to be ready for a break.

We sat there in the dark for a while, and finally the cow turned and headed for home. I figured she would just head for the corral and the other cows.

One thing I had to give that cow credit for: she did not give up easy. She had escaped before, and she was determined she was going to get away again. The old cow had to give it one more try.

About halfway to the corral, she took off in high gear again. I sure did not expect it. I thought, "My gosh, I hope we don't lose her now, after all we've been through." It was so dark, I could not even make out where the gate was from where I was.

Again, Daniel saved the day. Somehow, he knew where the gate was. He ran up beside her and hit her with a hell of a thump with his shoulder, knocking her in the direction of the gate. That was it. The battle and the war were over. She gave up and headed for the other cows in the corral.

I closed the gate in the barn corral, just in case. The boss lady had locked the other cows in the loading pen. When I opened the gate to put the renegade in with the rest, she was waiting to get in. She had concluded that she did not want any more to do with the bay horse.

We put the horses in the barn, fed them, bedded them down with straw and headed for the house for some much-needed black coffee. It had been quite a day. The boss lady was happy she had all 14 dry cows heading for the sale and more pleased after the sale. The dry cows hit the top of the market.

Fall time was there before we knew it, and it was time to gather the bulls. The bull pasture was only a couple of miles from the summer field where the cowherd was, and there were only 10 bulls to bring in. It was a job that should not take too long.

Eight of the bulls were good to handle. I gathered them one or two at a time, taking them as I came across them hanging with the cows. Bulls, being bulls, came away reluctantly, so one or two were easier to handle. There was not that big of a distance to travel from the cow to the bull pasture, so moving them from one to the other was smooth.

There were still two out there that kept evading me. One was half on the fight and ran like a bull elk, and the other one would hit for the poplar tree and brush patch and hide.

I figured that we should tackle the ornery one first. We picked him up in the middle of the field, got him headed for home and he took off running. That was okay, at least he was headed in the right direction and the gate was open at the other end. Daniel just followed at a distance, and the bull slowed down, still heading for the fence.

He hit the fenceline right at the gate, but he refused to go through it. He turned left and ran up along the inside of the fence. We loped on up past him and turned him back to the gate. I figured that he would surely go through this time. He just went right on past; no way was he going to leave those cows and go to batching in the bull pasture. We passed him and turned him back again, about a quarter-mile past the gate.

I decided to leave him and try to figure out some way to make that bull a little more cooperative. I rode down the fenceline as the bull headed back to the cows, and, by luck, I found what I was looking for: a broken-off, two-inch fence post that was about four and a half feet long. I did not know if I really needed it, but when you start arguing with about 2000 pounds of fighting beefsteaks, you had better try to be ready.

He had not gone far, maybe a quarter of a mile. When we picked him up again, he started running and we managed to head him back for the gate without much difficulty. He got to the fence but refused to go through the open gate. He headed past the gate along the fence and we overtook him, but this time, he would not turn back. He was getting mad.

I rode up to the front of him, running along the fence and went to gently caressing the top of his curly head with the fence post. That got his attention, and he turned back on the run. When we got to the gate, Daniel crowded into him and, with me caressing the topknot with the little post, we popped him through the gate into the horse pasture. So far, so good.

We were halfways to the corrals, and he was heading in more or less the right direction. I shut the gate and followed him; although he was in a bad humour, by now he had developed a little respect for the bay horse and me.

When we finally got to the open corral gate, he got it in his mind that he did not like them corrals either, and did not want to turn. I was not about to lose him now, if I could help it, so the argument was on again. After a few subtle hints to the top of his curly dome, he finally entered the corral under protest. He was mad, and I do not mean maybe.

He ran across the corral, which gave me time to get off and shut the gate. Just as he saw me on foot, he started back. It did not seem as if he was too mad at the bay horse, but he sure wanted me when he seen me on foot. Needless to say, I got that big plank gate shut in a hell of a hurry.

Next morning, after he had cooled down somewhat, I brought two gentle bulls in from the bull pasture nearby and put them in with him. That evening, he went with the gentle bulls to the bull pasture without any arguments. I just thought, "One left to go." That one was gentle and okay to handle, as long as I could keep him from hiding in the thick poplar and brush patches.

Next morning, before breakfast, I went to the barn and saddled up and fed Daniel his hay and oats. After breakfast, we headed out to pick up the last bull. It was a real nice day in September, nice and warm, no wind and nice enough that I hoped that last bull would cooperate. He was gentle, so I did not anticipate any trouble. I just wanted a nice, leisurely ride on this beautiful, peaceful, sunny day. Obviously, I was looking forward to my ride filled with pleasant thoughts.

We found the bull on the east side of the field with a few cows, right close to the gate leading into the winter field. As there were no cattle in the winter field to interfere, I put him through the gate. He handled like a milk cow. This was going to be easy.

We headed for home and, on the way, we ran into a patch of small poplars and brush. Of course, he pulled his usual disappearing act. The brush and small poplars were thick enough a jackrabbit near needed a machete to get through.

He pushed his way into the thicket and just stood there, and I could not ride in to get him out. He just moved around very peaceful-like, watching me. I could just about figure out what he was thinking—something like, "I am not going home, and now you can't make me." I rode around that brush patch hoping to find an opening. There was none to be found. I could damn near see a grin on his face. He had me out-foxed, but I had an ace in the hole.

That day, I had Jimmie, my border collie dog, with me. The bull moved toward the outer edge of the thicket, but we had lots of time and I was going to wait him out. I rode along on the outside to keep track of him, and he made a mistake. He was standing in the thicket facing toward home, and damned if there wasn't an open lane under the brush leading right up to his ass. I could not ride in there, the willows and brush were too low to the ground, but there was lots of room for Jimmie.

I said, "Put him out, Jim." Jimmie was a good cow dog. We had been in similar circumstances before. Jim did not hesitate, now that I had given him the go-ahead. He went down that lane on the run, grabbed that bull's heels hard with his teeth and between the surprise and hair flying off his heels, that bull let out a loud beller and jumped out into the open.

Daniel and I got behind him quick-like, to keep him from trying to go back and, of course, Jimmie came out right behind him. The bull had no choice but to head west across the winter field for home.

We had been taking our time, and by this time, it was getting on toward noon and getting quite hot. Up ahead about a mile was a small, hard-bottom, rocky lake covered with lily pads, and it was fairly deep. I think it was spring fed because it had nice water. The bull headed for this little lake, which was okay; we had time to get a drink and cool off if he wanted to.

When we got there, he took a little drink and then walked into the water. I rode up to the water's edge so Daniel could drink and Jimmie could get in the water for a little swim and a drink.

As I was sitting there watching, the bull just kept on walking out into the lake till just his head was sticking out of the lily pads. His back was even under water, and that was where he stopped. He had me beat, for I was not about to try to ride into that deep water to flush him out. It was early in the day, so I figured I would just wait him out. He had to come out sooner or later. The lake only covered maybe a quarter of an acre, so he was not far from shore.

I rode over along the side of the lake to a nice patch of grass, loosened the cinch and Daniel went to grazing. We might be there for a while. I lay down on the grass and relaxed so I could still see the bull's white facing sticking out through the lily pads but in a comfortable position. He was not moving, so I pulled my hat over my face to keep the sun out of my eyes. I did not need to watch that sucker. I would hear the water splashing when he was ready to come out.

It was so warm and comfortable in the grass; it was turning out to be a leisurely day. The dog and I were resting in the grass, my horse grazing contentedly, like the bull soaking in the water. I went from relaxing to sleeping.

Two or three hours later, according to the sun, I woke up. When I woke, Daniel had quit grazing and was standing there dozing, resting one back leg. The dog was still sleeping beside me.

I sat up and looked at the water in the lake. The bull was gone and nowhere in sight. I got up and went around the shoreline to look for tracks so I would know which way he had gone. There were no tracks coming out, just the tracks going in. Surely, I thought, he would not have drowned. He was plumb healthy and could easily have come out, even if he had to swim. However, there were no tracks. He still had to be in there.

I stood and tried to spot his head among all those lily pads. Nothing—not even a ripple on the water. I concluded that, somehow, he must have drowned and was on the bottom. I went back to make sure that I had not missed any tracks—nothing. I tightened up my cinch and got on my horse. Now I did not want to go home very bad. I did not exactly relish the idea of riding in and telling the boss lady, "I drowned your registered bull in the lake."

I was sitting there, looking toward home, when I thought I heard a little splash behind me. Now that I was higher up on horseback, I saw a little ripple among the lily pads, and damned if he didn't have the end of his nose sticking out of the water so he could breathe.

He must have gotten a kink in his neck from holding his nose straight up, because while I was sitting there, hardly believing my eyes, he started coming out onto dry land. When he seen me on my horse with the dog beside me, he just started for home and went straight to the bull pasture gate.

It had been a good day, the way it turned out. I had a restful afternoon; I was done gathering the bulls and plumb relieved that I did not have any bad new for the boss lady. When I got home, all was well and supper was ready.

CHAPTER 18

MILK RIVER CATTLE COMPANY

Indian summer was still with us and lasted for most of October. Even when it was over, the weather was still good but getting frosty in the mornings. A little snow now and then that did not stay all through November. The weather was sure cooperating for me to get ready for winter.

As there was only a barbed-wire fence separating the summer field from the winter field, it was easy to move the cowherd to winter grazing. Working alone with just my horse and dog, we just picked up the cows and calves in small bunches and put them through the gate—this way there was no argument, the cows handled easy and never got riled up.

Occasionally, a bunch of cows would take exception to Jimmie the dog getting too close to their calves and would turn back, protective-like, and go on the prod. At times like that, when they started milling back and fighting the dog, I would just say, "Jim, you can't help me now, you'd better stay back." He'd just go back 50 or 100 yards and sit on a little hill, if there was one, or else stay out of sight behind a sage brush, till I got them cows convinced there was nothing to worry about and got them moving again.

When the cows strung out on the trail, Jim would just follow at a distance until I needed help, and usually there would be no more difficulty. Once the cows realized they were heading for the good, tall grass in the winter field, they would pretty well go themselves.

About 1970, taken at Breed Creek: "I don't remember the name of this mare; I just know she was one of our horses."

Before moving the cows into the winter field, I had fixed all the fences around the numerous stacks of wild hay I'd cut during the summer for winter feed if the snow got deep enough to make grazing tough going. This way, the cows winter grazed, and when it got cold and snowy, I would go out with the team and feed them every day. By helping the cows out this way, they stayed in damn good shape and were always full and contented.

By feeding the wild hay first, I could save the good, tame haystacks for spring, when calving time was drawing near and the cows needed better nutrition.

December and January were quite wintry. It got down to 20 or 30 below (–20°C or –34°C) at times, and there was over a foot of snow. I kept the horses in the barn on grain and hay. Every day we had to haul wild hay to the cows in the winter field, about two miles away. Luckily, we did not have much wind that winter, so it was good going.

About the end of January, the wild haystacks were fast disappearing, and I figured I would have to move the cows to the feed ground on tame hay. A chinook wind blew in, and the snow started to get soft and went to melting.

In a couple of weeks' time, the ground was purty well bare, except for a few snowdrifts. The ground, of course, was still froze and icy, which presented a little problem when I had to bring in a water belly steer calf to treat. Water belly is when the steer's urinary tract is blocked. Luckily, there was not too many.

Sometimes I would have a wild ride, as those big calves did not want to leave the cows. If it happened that a water belly was not weaned, then you could bring the cow to get the calf and then turn the cow back out. If a water belly steer calf that was already weaned showed up, then he had to be brought in alone, which could end up in a fair argument on that frozen, icy ground.

I rode steady after the snow went, to watch for water bellies and whatever. Anything that needed treating had to be brought in before it got serious or else it could result in a critter cashing in its chips. I lost very few.

By the middle of February, it was getting just like spring; I had to hook onto the rubber-tired wagon to feed a little tame hay to the cows, as by now the winter field was getting worn down somewhat. There was lots of grass still, but it was getting on toward the time to bring the calves in and wean them and put them all on feed. In addition, we wanted to keep the cows in good shape for calving time.

It was nice enough toward the end of February that, a lot of the time, I worked without a coat. Rather unusual for Cypress Hills country for that time of year.

March was nice, and the rest of the snowbanks and ice were gone before the end of the month. The cows were all back in the winter field after the calves were sorted off and put on feed. It was not long before I would have to move the cows into the calving field. I had done feeding, as the weather was definitely favourable and you could smell spring in the air.

I turned the big team out with the horse herd for the summer, into a big field along the hills where there was plenty of grass and lots of timber for shelter. I just kept Daniel and a couple of good saddle horses home to move the cows and look after them during calving.

The cows were due to start calving about the middle of April, so just before that blessed event was about to take place, I moved them to the calving field. The horse pasture, about a section or so, lay between the winter field and calving field. I decided I would just take my time, work them all into the horse pasture and, when I had them all, just turn them in to the calving field.

The way it turned out, it was a damn good thing I did: there were many good, deep coulees in the horse pasture for shelter. I had just moved everything out of the winter field and had them in the horse pasture all done. Just before dark, I headed for the barn. I would move them the rest of the way out of the horse pasture the next day. I could easily do that in one day, as the horse pasture was only a square mile. I was all set for calving season, or so I thought. There are times when a fella feels it sure is nice to be well organized.

To make a long story short, it started to snow come nightfall. In the morning, there was nearly a foot on the ground and it was still coming down, real strong. Snowflakes as big as silver dollars. It just kept on snowing, despite the fact that the weather forecast on the TV kept assuring us that there was good weather coming. They were right, but they did not say when.

Well, it snowed like that for three nights and two days. When it finally quit, there was between three and four feet on the level. It was not cold, around 20 to 25 above 0°F (−7 to −4°C). Hardly any wind, until it quit snowing, and then enough to drift in some small bunches of cattle in some coulees. As soon as it was over, I saddled up a big, strong, gentle mare to check on the cows that were due to start dropping calves any time.

I did not realize how much snow there was, until I rode out of the corrals. The breast collar was pushing snow as the mare struggled along, having to stop every 100 feet or so to get a rest. I was sure glad I had the cows in that small horse pasture with all them coulees. At least they were as close to home as they could get. The buildings and corrals were inside the horse pasture along the north fence.

They started calving, and unless I was right there to help, that newborn could not even get on his feet in all that snow. Some of the young cows got confused and would, at times, lose the little one. Nothing else to do but boost the baby onto the horse's back, get on myself and head for the house porch, where it was warm, and try to look after him till I could find mama.

One thing about it: there was no trouble to bring the cow back to the corral, just get her into the deep ditch in the snow made by my horse. She could not really go anywhere else. The other end of the snow ditch went into the corral gate.

There was times when we practically had the porch full of calves, me packing them in there on old Star. When I would finally get the cows in the corral, the fun of mothering-up began. Bring out one calf at a time and hope someone would claim him. Luckily, not too many cows were calving, but in them conditions, one was too many.

Then there was several small bunches snowed in, in some coulees. There was a brand-new Polaris snowmobile in the shed, with a small sleigh to pull behind it. That really saved my bacon after a couple of days, when the wind and cold at night had hardened the snow enough that I could drive over it. With that little outfit, I was able to haul a few bales out to the cattle in the coulees and roll the bales down to them from the top. Some of them were trapped for more than a week, but I managed to keep them fed.

One bunch I shovelled out with the scoop shovel, but when I got a trail open through the drift that confined them, they were afraid to come out. They had pretty well given up. I had a bale on the snowmobile sleigh, so I broke it and scattered hay all along the bottom of the deep trench I had dug and went away and left them. Hunger got the best of them, and the next morning they had followed the hay trail out.

I was lucky enough that there was a small stack of tame hay right next to the corrals and a gate from the yard into the horse pasture. The wind had blown the snow off through the gate and cleared a small area outside. There, I fed the main bunch of cows with a Ford tractor equipped with a snow track on the hind wheels, pulling the stoneboat.

The cows all finally struggled their way to where I could get a few bales to them. We lost a few calves but no cows that I can remember. One thing: if I found a cow out there bawling for a calf, I had one for her. If there was no calf to be found where she was bawling, I just brought her in and went to the house porch or barn, where there were many waiting to be adopted.

The sun finally came out from behind the clouds, and the water started running. With all that snow, at least there was one thing I did not have to worry about: the cows had no trouble finding something to drink.

We were snowed in plumb solid; there was too much snow for the road graders to even move. Sometime toward the end of April or early May, they ploughed, opening the road with a D8K Caterpillar.

When it comes to their calves, most cows are plumb intelligent with the mothering instinct; other times, they can be plumb stupid. After that storm started clearing up, an older cow, maybe seven or eight years old, had her calf right close to the winter field fence on the east side of the horse pasture. She was a Hereford cow.

When the sun came out, the reflection of the snow on her white teats caused them to get sunburned and sore, and she would not let the calf suck. The calf was up, strong and healthy and, as my trench trail in the snow was getting packed down in the bottom from much use, I headed her and the calf to the corral. There was a doctoring chute in the corral, where I was going to grease her teats and then feed the calf.

Well, I got her in the chute and greased her teats with bacon grease. Bacon grease is best to start with, because the calves like the salty taste and just glom onto the teat and go to sucking. After I was done, I turned her loose with her calf, but no way would she let him suck. Next day, he still had not sucked, so it was back in the doctoring chute to grease her teats and feed the calf.

This went on for three days; she was healed up so she was not sore no more, but no way would she let the little guy suck in the corral. She acted as if he did not belong to her. I was scratching my think pot, trying to figger this out—why would she not let her own calf suck, now that her teats were healed up?

After giving it some thought, I had to try something. I got the big black mare out, loaded the calf up on her—the cow did not seem to give a damn—and headed back down to where I found them by the winter field fence. I unloaded the little guy and, with an old piggin' string, tied him to sagebrush by his hind leg so he could not go anywhere. I gave him about three feet of slack.

Then I went back and got the cow, heading her down the trail for the calf. I was hoping for the best.

When we got in sight of the calf, she started to bawl, ran over and smelled him, and he went to sucking and she was licking him. The cow was plumb sociable, so I sneaked over and untied the little guy. He did not miss a beat. His tail was swinging forth and back. They were mother and son once more.

What mystifies me is why she would not claim him in the corral. He must have smelled the same in the corral as he did out in the field. The only way I could find out was to ask the cow, but she was not saying.

With the sun out nice and warm every day, the water was just boiling down them coulees. It did not take too long for all that snow to settle and melt. The hills in the calving field were getting bare.

I moved the cows out of the horse pasture into the calving field. They hit for the good grass on the bare hills. That kept them fed until the rest of the field bared off. Besides that, there was no trouble with sunburned teats from snow reflection when they went to calving on the bare ground.

The weather stayed good, and calving went well. The grass came fast, after all that moisture. The calves had grown like weeds, and branding time was upon us in no time.

It was on toward the latter part of June, when the boss lady decided we should brand. We passed the word to the neighbours to come and help. In that community everybody helped everyone else with branding; that way, everybody was assured of a good branding crew.

I moved all the cows and calves back into the horse pasture so they would be handy for early Saturday morning. Some of the neighbours brought their horses to help me put the pairs into the branding corral. They were there early, around two o'clock in the morning. We wanted the cattle in the corrals and branding done before the day got too hot. Besides that, we could lay in the shade, eat and drink beer when we were all done. Never got too hot for that.

Well, we were sitting on our horses, ready to go before daylight, when from behind me a fella named Jim said to the fella beside him, "We're going to have a rodeo here before we're done." The other fella said, "How do you figger that?" Jim said, "Look at old Danny's eyes; he's mad about something, and he'll likely blow before we get back."

Talk about making my day. I was sitting on Daniel, fully aware of what Jim was talking about, but did not know anyone else had noticed. I was going to do my best to talk Daniel out of any notion to buck and get the hump out of his back so maybe the saddle skirts would come down level again.

We took off; Daniel started to relax, and we had enough daylight to see. All went well, and just after sun-up, we had the herd down on the level by the corrals. The leaders were shy about going in the gate, as the rising morning sun was throwing shadows from the gateposts on the ground. The cows just stood and looked at the shadows and thought they might be dangerous. Some of the boys at the tail end of the herd rode carefully up to hold the leaders in case they spooked. They just sat, patient-like, until the leaders decided it was safe and started going through the gate.

Meanwhile, the back end of the herd came to a standstill; I was all alone, riding drag. A calf broke back, wanting to go back to where he sucked last, to find his mommy. Daniel was working like a clock; he loped off to the side, came around in front of the calf and put him back in the bunch.

We just got the first one back, and another one broke back; we got him back, and I was hoping them leaders would hurry through the gate and get out of the way so I could get the drag end moving before a whole bunch of calves decided to turn back and look for their mamas. The drag finally got moving, and the boys came back to give me a hand.

At the last minute, a third calf broke back. Daniel loped to the side, around the front of him, lay his ears back and ran him back into the cowherd. By then, three-quarters was all in the corral.

Jim had it figgered right: just as that calf got with the cows, Daniel blowed his cork. Caught me plumb unaware, as I thought, by now, he had gotten over his mad.

Well, he poured it on, and I was up there cussing, begging and pleading for him to stop and trying to pull his head up. He knew he could buck me off. I knew he could buck me off, but be damned, I was going to make him work for it. A guy's got to try his best, and I thought, this time, I was going to ride him till he quit, and I figured I was doing just that.

I felt the saddle slip sideways; I had not thought to tighten the cinch, especially after he took to me. Well, I did not want to wind up under his belly, so I turned loose and he bucked me off. I hit the ground and buried my nose in the grass so I would not get my head kicked off. I knew he would not jump on me, and after a bit, I heard his hoofbeats fade away.

I looked up and saw him run up to the cattle, with the saddle sitting over on his left ribs, and stop. One of the boys caught him and brought him back to me. I straightened the saddle, climbed on him and we helped put the drag end of the cattle in the corral. He went back to working like a clock.

One of the boys said, "What got into Danny? He was working good all morning." I said, "He still had a mad on, I guess." Jim said, "Damn it, I was so busy watching them cows, I missed the rodeo."

Branding went plumb smooth; the boys took turns heeling calves, and some of the big kids helped, too. They wanted to

At the Milk River Cattle Co., Art on the head and George Douglas on the tail: "A good wrestling team makes big jobs a little easier."

learn, and this was the place to do it. With a little practice before we were done, the kids had dragged in quite a few. I was running the branding irons, another rancher ran the vaccinating needle. One fella tended the fire, and we had three pair of husky young fellows flat-assing calves. By a little after midday, we were done. We let the cows and calves back in the horse pasture, took care of our saddle horses and headed for dinner that the women had set up in the shade of the trees by the house.

Now it is near impossible for a good branding crew to choke down that good grub when their throats are still full of dust from the branding corral. Being as the boss lady had anticipated that to be the case, she had a washtub full of cold water sitting there in the shade with the bottom half of the tub decorated with full bottles of beer. That was one time when nobody needed halter-breaking to be led up to see what was in that tub.

Come Monday morning, I proceeded to put the cowherd into the summer field, and then a week or so later, I turned the bulls out. Things were going good, but I had gotten the uneasy feeling that there were domestic difficulties in that family outfit and somehow it could involve me, and I had no idea why.

One morning, I had the old Chevy two-ton truck backed up to the chute to haul a bull out to the heifer field, when the boss lady's son-in-law came down to the corral. We visited a little bit and he told me what an excellent job I was doing looking after the ranch. Then I near fell on my ass when he added that they did not need me anymore.

Apparently, they had some kind of meeting, and he had been stuck with telling me the glad news. To this day, I am not sure what it was all about. I told the wife, and we went to town on the lookout for another job, which I would need in a couple of weeks.

While in town, we ran into a rancher we both knew well, and he told us he had a friend who had a big cow outfit down on the Milk River that needed a good hand. He phoned his friend, and his friend wanted to talk to me. The rancher handed me the phone, and after a little discussion we agreed to an interview. Two days later, we had a new job and a better deal than we had before. The way it turned out, the boss lady's son-in-law had done us a good favour. It has been said that every cloud has a silver lining. Somehow, I really believe there is a lot to be said for that old saying.

In a couple of weeks, we would be moved to our new home along the Milk River. There were a few things that I had started that the boss lady asked if I would finish before I left. I agreed, as I had time before I had to start my new job on the first of the following month.

We had about 100 miles to move, so I borrowed a one-ton truck with a flat deck and grain box to move our furniture and belongings. It only took a couple of days; my sister-in-law was good enough to bring her truck and horse trailer and moved our two horses, Daniel and Star.

We were off on a new venture, and it turned out to be a very good outfit to work for. We lived on the big ranch and worked for them exactly 10 years to the day, at which time we bought a small place of our own, but that comes later in the story.

When I first started working for that outfit, the whole crew was busy building fences. Some of it was page wire. Of course, I was just added to the fencing crew. This was the first of August, and, as the haying was contracted out, our own crew tended to other things.

After a few weeks of fencing, I was starting to wonder if this outfit spent much time on horseback. It turned out, at the time, this part of the ranch was where they ran all the dry stuff. Yearling steers and heifers, two-year-old heifers for replacement stock and some to ship and all the two-year-old shipping steers. They had two more ranches quite a few miles east, where all the wet stuff was. Mama cows, calves and, of course, bulls.

After weaning, all them big calves was trucked over to grow up where I was working. A damn big outfit, all told, and well run.

One day, we came in from fencing and one of the boys who had been working at the corrals that day informed us that the boss told him we had to start gathering the two-year-old steers for shipping. He said, "I already wrangled the horses and got them fed and watered in the horse corral, ready for morning." The big steers was about nine or 10 miles east, down the river.

The next day, we rode the horses down there to an old vacant ranch on the south side of the river. We fed and watered them in the old corrals there. One of the boys came and got us with the old army Jeep, and early next morning, we piled into the old

Jeep and went back to our horses. After saddling and graining them, we got a good, early start to herd them two-year-old steers home before it got too hot.

In those days, cow outfits did not have horse trailers sitting around, as nowadays—we did it the old way. By taking the horses down the day before, it was much easier on both men and horses. Another thing: we might need fresh horses when we started gathering and moving them big two-year-olds. They had been on that range all summer, and you never knew when the whole 500 of them could spook and run.

As it turned out, it became a long day, gathering the big field and trailing them 10 miles home. It was also an uneventful day as the cattle handled well, and as all four of us knew the business of trailing cattle, we had them in the home corrals by early afternoon.

After grabbing a fast coffee, we all headed for the corrals. All hands and the cook, and the boss and his brother, as they were partners. After looking over the two-year-olds, they had decided to cut off 100 head of the tail-enders and keep them over for next year.

The corral setup was good, so things went well and we had them all sorted pretty well by suppertime. It had to be done that day to be ready for the big trucks that would be there to load about sun-up the next morning.

We had an early breakfast and were waiting for them trucks, but not for long. There were more than a dozen cattle liners in the yard ready to load, so we got right at it. The first one backed into the chute, and we loaded as many as he could handle. When his truck was full of two-year-old steers, he would pull out of the way and the next one backed in. In this way, the loading went fairly fast, as the loading chute and corral facilities were of the best in design and construction.

By midmorning, 400 two-year-old steers were on their way. Those cattle liners carried close to the same number of head as a railroad stock car. They loaded right at the home corrals, eliminating the long trail drive to the railroad.

In earlier times, that same ranch used to have to trail their steers roughly 50 miles to the railroad at shipping time. Modernization is a big help at times, with cattle liners and trucks and horse trailers, but there are things, in my opinion, that tend to get too damn modern. The outfits that make the old ways work in cooperation with these modern so-called efficient ways have the best operations, as far as I can see.

Mind you, not too many of the boys complain about hauling their horses 20 miles to the job in trailers, instead of riding that distance, doing a day's work and then riding home. It is sure a whole lot easier on horses and men and just as efficient, even when you have to trail drive a bunch of cattle a long ways home.

You only have to ride one way when you trailer the men and horses to where the cattle are. It is also damn nice to be able to shut the gate on a trail drive 20 miles from home, after moving from one part of the range to fresh grass on another part, then loading your horses in trailers and climbing into a truck seat and going home.

In years past, when you shut the gate on the trail drive after a long day and then had to ride home 20 miles, it tended to separate the men from the boys, figuratively speaking. Also, back then, some of them poor old ponies were not holding their heads too high by the time the home corrals came in sight, usually in the dark of moonlight, if we was lucky.

However, I do think this modernization has tended to make us all a little lazier. It's kind of nice to be spoiled that way, though, especially when the weather is bad or sometimes downright ugly. Yes, some of the new ways do have their good points, when you think of it.

Anyways, after all those two-year-olds were gone on the trucks, I and one of the other boys moved the cutbacks back on the range. Roundup was just around the corner, and we had to start getting ready.

CHAPTER 19

THE MILK RIVER RANGE

The weather was still nice, and we had another week or so to finish the fencing project we were working on before we gathered and shipped the two-year-olds. We carried on with fencing until we had it done, as we were actually rebuilding the fence around the horse pasture, which also served as a holding field for cattle from time to time.

Actually, it was a case where we would maybe only have time to round up, say, half the cattle in a big field in a day. We would throw our gather into the horse pasture and finish gathering the remainder of the big field the next day. We would split the yearlings, two-year-olds, calves and so on into separate fields to make it easier to ship a few loads if need be. Whatever the boss had figured out. Actually, the procedure worked very well.

The horse pasture fence was done and had to go over the fence around the big winter field to be ready for the cattle, when they got onto the winter range. The winter field was some eight or ten miles down the river to the east. It took a little time, as there were numerous big coulees that the fence crossed. Some seemed close to a quarter-mile deep.

The fences on this big outfit were, in general, in very good shape, having been periodically replaced with treated posts as the old-time cedar posts slowly rotted. Even so, the winter field had to be checked, as through the course of spring, summer and fall there were times when a herd of wildlife, like elk, deer or antelope, might have the fence broke down right in the bottom of one of those big coulees.

Those places were worst, as you could in no way get down those steep coulees with a vehicle, or a team and wagon, for that matter. It was a case of hauling tools and materials to the top of the coulee and wrestling it down from there by hand.

Getting the posts and tools down wasn't so bad, as it was steep enough in most cases that a guy could throw the fence posts down, then slide down some more himself and repeat the process several times till they hit the bottom. We would then fix the broken fence with hand tools as usual. No newfangled machine-driven post pounder there. A 14- or 16-pound post maul with a three-foot handle, powered by a sweating cowboy who reluctantly tried to make his hands fit around that hardwood handle. Hands that was far more accustomed to a rope and a pair of bridle reins.

They do not often show those things in the movies, where some good-looking cowboy lopes across the silver screen rescuing some beautiful woman in distress. I often wondered if that silver-screen cowboy had ever fixed busted fences in any deep coulee.

Now back to reality. The fence was fixed; we had to get back to the old fencing truck with the tools. Standing at the bottom looking up, it seemed like an awful long ways to the top where the truck was sitting, looking about as big as an overgrown apple box with wheels on it. Most of the time, them big coulees was about as steep as the roof on a hip-roofed barn, and we had to pack the tools, post maul, crowbar, hammers, staple bucket and wire stretcher up with us. Nobody has ever figured out how to make them tools fall back up to the top like they fell down.

It was all in a day's work, so we very slowly divided the tools between the two of us, resting often on the climb back to the top. We were mighty glad that we had a mile or two of level prairie to check the fence until quitting time. We had probably a mile or two to drive around the head of the coulee and come back along the other side, to where the fence came out. That was okay; we need a little rest anyway.

It was worse when a person was working alone, driving those posts in the coulee bottom by hand, fixing the fence and then having to make two trips to the top to lug the tools back. By the time you got to the top with the second trip, you had a tendency to think you should have gone to school longer and become a doctor or a lawyer or maybe even a politician, instead of settling for a cowboy career.

Speaking from experience, I think cowboys must have short memories. In the spring, when the weather is beautiful, sunshine and blue skies and the new calves are playing in the green grass, a guy will sit there on his horse and think, this is the life. I would not trade it for anything. I know I am one of those guys. You never think of fences with deep coulees or hauling feed when it is cold enough to pop the knots out of a jack pine plank.

That day was beautiful; I was at peace with nature and the world. Well, the fences around all the winter fields were gone over, the days were getting shorter and roundup time was upon us. There were quite a lot of cattle to gather and sort out, to be put in their own various fields. We spent a few weeks gathering and sorting and trailing different bunches to their designated winter fields, some of which were eight or ten miles from the home ranch.

It had snowed just enough to settle the dust, by the time we were done. The east ranch weaned their calves and sent them over to us, close to 2000 of them. It took many cattle liner loads, but being as the weaned calves was about half the size of a grown critter, each liner loaded quite a few head.

We fed them in the feedlot until they quit bawling for their mamas then turned them into the hayfields on the frozen, dry, second-growth alfalfa to graze. After the second-growth alfalfa was frozen and the sun turned it somewhat brown, there usually was no problem with bloating. At least, we did not have any bloat problems.

These calves would eventually go to their own winter field, along the creek, where there was plenty of shelter. As they were young and needed a little extra care, they needed to be trained to eat range pellets. While the grass lasted in the hayfields, we would start hauling range pellets to them. A small amount to start with, to get them accustomed to the grain in the pellets and to acquire a taste for them.

Before many weeks passed, when they saw the feed truck coming, all we had to do was holler, "Come, calves," and they'd come on the run. We kept them on the hay meadows on full grain feed for a couple of weeks so that all of them came for their grain before we moved them into the big winter field along the creek.

After they were moved into the winter field, there was miles of range to scatter out, and they divided into smaller bunches. We hauled range pellets out to the winter field, and when we seen calves, we would holler, "Come, calves," and everything in hearing distance would come to the truck. We would take a rough count on each bunch we found and, as the feed was all in bags, we were able to figure out easy how many bags to put out for each bunch. So many pounds for each calf, divided into the number of pounds in each bag, times the number of calves, equals the number of bags.

We would just run the range pellets into the truck track in the snow, and the calves would clean them up as if they were in a trough. We would carry on until we would find another bunch, call them to the truck, repeat the whole process and keep doing that until we had the whole winter field covered and the big calves all fed.

On this big outfit, they really looked after their grass. It was the sensible, efficient way to do it. Lots of grass fed cattle well, and good cattle paid the bills. Grass was one of the most important necessities for good ranching business. The ranchers are the stewards of the range, as wildlife also has the benefits of the ranchers' good management.

On this big outfit, they had enough range that the winter fields were emptied in the spring, the gates were shut and the fields would grow undisturbed all summer. When the cattle were turned in during fall, the wild grass was matured, cured and deep like a hayfield. The big stock looked after themselves with all that grass and came out in the spring in damn good shape.

As the calves were young, they were fed range pellets to help keep them in good shape over winter. The second winter, as big yearlings, they did fine on their own without range pellets.

There was always lots of grass. When the cattle came out of the winter fields and were put on the summer range with green grass coming, they went right to growing and gaining weight. A very efficient method of taking good care of the range grass, for wildlife and the cattle business as well.

The cattlemen have been operating this way for more than 100 years, since the buffalo roamed the prairies, and I believe the range is in better shape now than it was then, overall. I think if the so called "range experts" and government agencies leave the cattlemen alone to keep on managing the rangeland so efficiently, there will always be grass and shelter for both wildlife of all kinds and cattle. That in turn keeps the environment in good shape with feed and clean water, two very necessary things for both wildlife and the livestock business.

We fed the tail-ender calves at home in the feedlots. They were the poorer-doers and late-born calves, the ones that was too young or not big enough to go in the winter field. As the

winter slowly passed, we hauled range pellets to the main
bunch in the winter field and fed our feedlots at home.

The winter was going good, and then the weather turned
cold. We were hoping that it was going to be just a short spell,
but as the weeks came and went, it just hung on. Seemed like
one day after the other, it just got a little colder. One day it hit
−50°F (−46°C). There were three of us working, so two always
went together with four-wheel drive trucks with range pellets
for the calves. The other two boys had been going to the winter
field for the last while, and I took care of the stock at home.

One evening, about the middle of January, they pulled back
into the yard. I was all done feeding at home, so we all went into
the cookshack for a coffee before I went home. I lived about four
miles from the main home ranch, where I had a feedlot corral
with about 130 calves to feed as well as the bull herd. The bulls
(some 90-some odd of them) had all been hauled over to the dry
ranch, where they was fed for the winter. Where I worked, this
part of the ranch had all the dry stuff, leaving the east ranch
with the cowherd of 2500.

While we were having coffee and warming up a little, I asked
how the calves in the winter field were doing. One of the boys
said they seemed fine but had been pretty well in the same
places in the field for the last three days. They did not seem to
be moving around much in search of new grass. Seemed like
they just ate their pellets and stayed put, waiting for the feed
truck to show up next day. I said, "My God, those calves have
quit rustling, with all the snow and cold weather."

Big calves are good winter rustlers, digging into the snow for
the good grass, but if the winter is tough and cold they can get
to the point they just quit looking for grass and wait for the
range pellets. They are young and, unlike the big stuff, just do
not seem to have the staying power. When the other boys told
me this, I knew we had to get them home on feed.

The boss was away on a business trip, so that night, I got him on the phone and told him. I suggested we would have to get the calves home as soon as possible or we could have some losses. He said it was impossible for him to get home right away, so I should use my own judgment and do what was needed.

Next morning, the other two boys asked what the boss said. I told them and we proceeded to get them home. We were lucky, in that the calves would come to the feed truck, so we put a load of pellets on and used that to lead them. We went right through the field and then started back, calling them as we went. They followed very well; I rode behind, keeping the drag end moving, heading for the river valley on the north side of the winter field. It took us all day to get them off the high, flat country into the river bottom.

With them following the feed truck and me riding drag, we got about 1700 of them lined out. When the feed truck went over the hill into the river valley, there was a string of calves a half-mile long and about 15 yards wide ahead of me, going over the hill.

As only two of us went out to bring the calves in, the third man fed at home and then met us with a load of hay at the bottom of the hill on the river. By then, it was dark. He had followed the river road along the river with the big four-wheel drive truck, and we fed them there to keep them until morning.

We had them about halfways. There was good shelter along the river. With a little bit of hay and −30°F (−34°C), they would not move.

First thing next morning, we went down the river with some more pellets on the feed truck and, again with me riding drag, we got them to sheltered feed ground along the river, close to home. George met us with another load of hay; we fed them just before dark and went home.

From then until spring, they were fed all they wanted. It kept George and Bob busy as hell, with all them calves and the home chores to do. I had some damn cold riding to do, as there was little bunches of calves that we'd missed in the first gather scattered out in the coulees and the creek brush all through the winter field. They had to be brought home.

Then it snowed some more as it warmed up to about 10°F (–12°C). It quit snowing and dropped back to thirty below (–34°C); now I had about another foot of snow to contend with.

I would feed my feedlot calves and bull herd and head for the home ranch by about 10 o'clock in the morning. Bob had my horse in the barn and fed, so I would just saddle up and head out. Two lucky things that tough winter: the calf winter field came down to within a half-mile of the home ranch buildings, and I had a garage to keep the little international Scout four-wheel drive in—both where I lived and at the home ranch.

I would put a gallon of oats and my lunch in a gunnysack behind the saddle. I had not found any calves by about one o'clock, so I headed for the creek, dug a pocket into the snow and fed my horse her oats. I then dug the snow away and built a fire out of dry, dead willows that I could break off. I took my knife and found a small green, frozen, forked willow to toast my sandwiches over the fire. That was an absolute necessity, as, by then, the sandwiches were frozen as hard as a cast iron sleigh shoe. Most of the time I ate them burned black on the outside and the middle still froze somewhat.

Them burned, half-froze sandwiches and that warm fire sure was fine on them winter rides. As soon as I found a small bunch of calves, whether five, ten or whatever, I would head them for home. In that snow, you could not gather, just take the first little bunch you found, head them into the trail your horse had made in the snow and trail them to the home ranch.

Next day, I would repeat the same procedure and eventually, after a great many cold rides, I had them all home. It took me at best three weeks. It is slow going, when you are working alone and can bring in only a few head a day. I had on all the warm clothes I could carry, but in that weather there was times I near froze my ass off.

We figured we had pretty well all the calves, but as the ranch had bought a new Arctic Cat snowmobile, the boss said, "I'll try that rig out and check the field to see if you got them all." That worked well, as the wind and cold weather had hardened the snow so the snowmobile went over it. When he got back, he had found one bunch way up in the southeast corner of the winter field that I missed. About 30 head. The rest of the field was clean.

We decided to get them the next day. They were about six miles from home. The snow was deep enough that we had to plough a road to bring them in. The ranch had a small Allis Chalmers Cat that was kept in a heated garage so it would start when we needed it. With all the snow, we sure as hell needed it. It had an eight-foot blade, which was fine to plough a trail for them calves.

Come daylight, the boss fired up the little Cat, heading south, ploughing snow. I fed my feedlot calves and the bull herd and then headed for the home ranch, saddled up and struck out on the snowploughed trail. The trail was good so I could trot right along. Thankfully, there was no wind.

Even with a three-hour head start, the Cat had only got to within a half-mile of where the calves was. When I caught up, it was slow going in all the snow. The boss was cold, driving that rig. There is not anything colder than driving a Cat with no cab when it is –20°F (–29°C). No heater in the Cat. I was good, as I had been able to travel at a slow trot keeping my horse and me fairly warm from travelling.

When I caught up, he stopped and produced a lunch he had managed to keep from freezing on the Cat and two or three big Thermoses of coffee. That hot coffee and sandwiches that were not frozen was a meal fit for a king, for both of us. Especially the coffee—it rather thawed us out, so the blood went to circulating again. After the warm lunch, 20 below (–29°C) did not seem so cold.

Well, the boss ploughed his way right into the middle of that little bunch of calves and turned back along his trail toward home. I rode around and gathered the calves onto the ploughed trail, and they followed the Cat, with me behind, keeping the stragglers moving.

We had six miles to go to get home, and it was getting on toward nightfall, which at that time of year came early. The calves travelled well, with deep snow on each side; they were glad to follow the ploughed road. It was dark before we got back. The lights at the home ranch yard were sure a welcome sight. Mission accomplished, you might say. We finally had the calves all home. Lucky, too—the winter got worse after that.

Jack must have been one cold cowboy after herding that Cat all day, ploughing snow. I was cold enough, but driving an open Cat in that weather is way colder than riding a horse. That is ranch business for you. The weather does as it pleases, and we live with what we get and work with it. By the first of June, them cold old trips would be just a memory and soon forgotten.

Spring finally came, and Bob and I rode east to the winter field, to see how many losses there was. There still was snow on the ground, but it was melting fast. Much to everyone's satisfaction, we found only one old cow that had not made it. With the brush-covered flats along the river and the deep coulees for shelter, all the rest of the cattle came through in real good shape.

We could see cattle trails in what snow there was left, where the cattle worked their way up out of the coulees, on good days, to the grassy flats above. The wind had blown the snow off the high ridges, uncovering the good grass. On the good days, they would go up and graze, returning to the shelter along the river and in the coulees at night. If the weather was bad, they would stay in the sheltered area until it quit storming.

Spring roundup was not far off, and the yearly process of moving and sorting cattle and fencing, irrigating and eventually haying began. Later, fall roundup and another winter were looming on the horizon. We would again come full circle.

That fall, the ranch decided to quit using the place I worked for as a straight dry field and hauled 500 cows from the east ranch. The trucks just unloaded them right into the winter field, north of the river, with a portable chute and no corrals. This worked fine, as there was no calves involved. The calves had been weaned and hauled over a couple weeks previous. The cows would stay on the north side of the river and be moved to the south side to the calving field just before the ice went out, while the ice was still strong enough to hold them crossing.

The river was very low that winter, maybe six inches of water under the ice at the crossing, so there was no danger if the cattle did break through. Crossing on the ice was much safer and easier than to wait until after breakup, as the river would get fast and deep with the snow runoff.

It was early enough that there were no new calves to contend with. Getting cows out onto the river ice can have its problems, even with snow on the ice. Seems like they are just naturally nervous if you try to crowd them onto the ice, even if it is perfectly safe.

To help this situation, I hauled a half dozen bales down to the crossing whenever I went down to check and cut water holes, and made a hay trail across the river. I started doing this in January so the cows would eat their way, forth and back, across the river ice and get used to it. By the time it came to move them across, we had a regular packed road across the ice.

About the middle of February, early one morning, Bob and I went down with some salt for the south side calving field. We came back and looked at the crossing; the weather was warming up. Looking at the ice, I said to Bob, "We've got to cross the cows today, this afternoon. The ice is softening up." We headed for home, about four miles, saddled our horses, had a quick lunch and headed across the river to round up them 500 cows and hopefully get them across.

Luckily, the north winter field was only eight square miles, so we got them to the river just before dark. We had them all bunched at the crossing, on the north side—they was not at all wanting to cross, as it was getting dark. It looked like we may not be successful, as only two of us could not do much crowding. With that big a bunch, they might try to break back. We sure needed more help, which we did not have. The other man in our crew had to go to town that morning. None of us knew before he left that we had to cross the cattle that day.

It was getting darker by the minute, and we were holding them at the crossing, where they were milling about some. Our only hope was that some of them that had been feeding on my hay trail would decide to lead them across. That was what I was banking on.

We held them there for about an hour or so; it was getting plumb dark, and then a full moon came up over the horizon. We had light. One old cow saw the crossing, headed out and crossed, with the rest of the herd slowly following the leader. We just kept the drag end going, real easy-like, as they needed time, but kept on moving across in a steady line. They was all across, and as the last part of the drag was coming onto the south side, the shore ice broke and the last few climbed out amid chunks of broken ice and water. We had succeeded.

We rode home four miles in the moonlight, getting to the ranch about nine o'clock. A good day, well spent. After taking care of our horses, I had a coffee with Bob before heading home, four miles with the truck to where I lived.

Art's birthday; a celebration with his children, Julie and Irvine.

While we were drinking our coffee, the phone in the cookhouse rang. It was my wife, plumb upset and worried that we had got into some trouble, as she had phoned several times before, with no answer. I had phoned before we left to gather the cattle that I would be a little late, not thinking it would be this late. It is tough on a ranch wife when these things happen. All they can do is wait and worry, which is sometimes far worse than where we was. At least Bob and I knew we were okay and what was going on. Anyway, both her and our two little kids were glad to see me back. They could go to sleep and not worry about Dad.

The next day, the river ice broke; spring was on its way early that year, unlike the tough winter previous. When we took a count later, we had only missed 14 head, which calved where they were and stayed in the north winter field until the river went down later in the summer.

CHAPTER 20

GOOD PARTNERS

Spring was on its way, but something had come up and George had to go, leaving Bob and me to look after things for a while. The boss right away went looking for a new man. Bob and I would need some help, now that we had 500 cows to calve out and spring roundup coming.

Toward the end of April, I was going across the yard at the home ranch to close the gate into the west hayfield. Right where the road crossed a creek, coming into the yard, I met a car. A cowboy was behind the wheel, and he had his wife and two little girls with him. He stopped and asked if the boss was home. I said, "Yes, he's at his house working on the books in the office." The fella was a plumb stranger to me.

After a few hours, I saw the car pull out. The boss came over to the shop where Bob and I were fixing something. He said, "I got good news, the man who was just here was looking for a job, and I hired him. He is a damn good man; he worked for us some years ago, before he was married. He'll be starting the first of May." That was music to my ears as the cows were calving, and spring roundup was upon us.

Wes started on the first of May, and it did not take too long for us to realize that Lady Luck had sure smiled upon us the day he drove into the yard and got a job. He was one of the best range and ranch cowboys that I have ever rode and worked with. He was a hell of a good man around horses and cattle and done a damn good job of everything else that needed doing.

Art and Wes Newhouse: "See the Ross Ranches sign? This is the Milk River Cattle Company."

The fact that he drove in and got the job just when we was needing some experienced help seemed almost as it was something that was meant to be. A very pleasant fellow to work with, an attractive, pleasant wife and two beautiful little girls. It was the beginning of a lasting friendship between our two families.

Spring roundup was upon us, so we got right at it. We were east in the winter field, gathering yearlings to put into a small holding field for the night and then trail them home to the summer range. We had to hold them at the home ranch corrals for a day or two, to separate the steers and heifers.

While we were rounding up the winter field, Bob nearly got hurt. He and Wes were bringing a bunch of yearlings down the steep road from the top flat into the holding field on the river bottom. The road followed the top of a high ridge that sloped down to the river, with a deep coulee on each side. The cattle were going well, when, all of a sudden, a few yearlings headed down into the coulee on the left-hand side, where Bob was. Bob was riding a chestnut mare, a good pony, but she did not have much more for withers than a mule. It was one of them times things happen so fast a person does not have time to stop and tighten his cinch.

The mare dived over the side to turn the yearlings. The slope was steep enough that she was pretty near standing on her head, so to speak. The cinch was a little loose, no withers on the horse, and Bob and the saddle slid over her head. She stopped, of course, but Bob and the saddle just kept going as the mare stuck her head between her knees and backed out of the cinch.

By that time, the cowboy, still with the saddle between his knees, hit the bottom of that steep coulee. He had a few tender spots here and there. I think he hit his head on a rock on his way down because his head was a mite sore, but nothing broke. We made him feel better by telling him he was lucky that his head hit the rock, or he might have really got hurt.

We had the old Jeep truck at the old buildings at the corral in the holding field, so he did not have to ride all the way home. We all left our horses there for the night on feed and water. We went back with the little Jeep truck the next morning and moved the yearlings back to the home ranch corrals.

Bob was hurting badly enough that day that he could not ride. He was tough, though, and was back on a horse in a couple of days. Wes and I went back to trail them 500 or 600 yearlings eight miles home by ourselves. We would go back and get the truck and Bob's horse later.

The yearlings trailed pretty well, except we had a couple of high-headed runners in the bunch that tried to slip into every side coulee they saw. That is where experience counted. Seemed like Wes anticipated them trying to get away up them side coulees before they thought of it themselves. It was a pleasure riding with such a good hand; we covered those eight miles along the river uneventfully and corralled the herd in the home ranch corrals in good time. Bob was back on horseback, and we continued calving cows and getting spring roundup done.

All went well, and the summer slipped away before we knew it, with branding, fencing, riding and other general ranch activities. Before we knew it, fall roundup and weaning and shipping was upon us, all events falling into place like well-oiled gears on an old horse mower.

Another winter was arriving. We were ready for it, though, at least workwise. Keeping from freezing, well, you're never really ready for that. Just live with it and look forward to spring. I think that is why winter seemed so long—even if the days were shorter, they were harder to endure. Summer seemed to go fast, but I guess working and living in the warm summer weather in solid comfort, compared to the winter, made it seem that way. Time went fast when you were warm and comfortable and having fun. We did not even think of winds strong enough to blow the bridle off your horse or thunderstorms that seemed like someone was shooting at you and missing. I do not remember ever being hit; I am still here.

Then there was the dry prairie heat, hot enough to fry an egg on a flat rock. We enjoyed it all. Whenever we would kind of feel like complaining, all we had to do was think of last winter and the next one coming up and count our many blessings that summer was there.

Christmas week, Wes and his family were invited to spend Christmas with Mary's mother and dad over in southern British Columbia, about a three-hour drive over the Alberta–BC border from the ranch. Bob was having Christmas with me and my family right on the ranch, so we told Wes to go ahead, we could handle things till he got back, as the winter was fairly moderate, only around –10°F (–23°C). We could handle things until after New Year's, for that matter, and it was okay with the boss man.

There was about 500 long yearling steers in the winter field across the river, just north of the ranch buildings, which were right next to the river, on the south side. The river was frozen solid, and it had snowed about six inches on the ice. It did not take that bunch of steers long to figger out that them haystacks at the buildings would be a whole lot easier to feed on, instead of digging grass out of them six inches of snow, even though the grass was nearly a foot deep. They also found that with six inches of snow froze to the river ice, it made for safe and easy walking.

Over the river they came, back to the feedlot corrals they had been fed at the winter previous. This happened mid-afternoon, between Christmas and New Year's, so Bob and I saddled our horses to move them two miles east to the next winter field and fresh grass.

We got them back across the river ice and headed east, when a few head turned north over a ridge. Bob went after them, while I kept the main bunch heading down along the river. Bob never came back, and I figured maybe he needed help, so as the main bunch was stringing out along the river, I went to help him. I rode up onto the ridge and did not see anything. I rode north a little farther and seen the cattle had turned east toward the main bunch—but no Bob. I rode over a little hill. There was his horse, standing with an empty saddle and something dark lying beside him on the snow. It was Bob.

I rode up quick-like and said, "What the hell happened?" He said to me, "My leg is broke. I just got them damn yearlings turned, and old Patches stepped in a badger hole covered with snow and fell. I couldn't get out of the way fast enough, and he fell on my leg on the frozen ground." I said, "I'll have to leave you here and go back to the barn and get the four-wheel drive and get you home."

It was not all that cold, only about –10°F (–23C), and he had on lots of clothes. It was lucky we were only about a quarter mile across the river from the barn. I caught his horse and headed for home on a high lope to put the horses away and get the truck. The cattle would have to wait; there was a fence along the south side of the river, and the stacks were fenced, so they could not really go too far. Lucky there was not much snow; I crossed the river ice with the truck and was able to drive right to him.

Then I had to get him into the truck cab. He was no light-weight, maybe 170 pounds and pretty well helpless. Besides that, I had to be careful not to break the leg worse wrestling him into the truck cab. I got him up on end on his good leg, where he could stand holding onto the side of the truck. Then I got a piece of binder twine and tied his broke leg onto his good one, so the broken end could not dangle. With him reaching in from the passenger side and grabbing the steering wheel and me pulling like hell from the driver's side, we managed, between the two of us, to get him into the cab and got the door shut.

He was lying on the seat half upright with his feet resting on the floorboards on the passenger side and hurting some. I had to get in to drive, so we managed to get him raised up enough that I got under the steering wheel and got the door shut. He let a yelp out of him. I said, "You hurting bad?" He said, "A little, I bumped my foot on my broke leg against the side of the truck."

I put the truck in low gear, crossed the river ice and got him to the yard. I ran into the cookhouse and phoned a neighbour who had a car with a big back seat to take him to the hospital. With the neighbour's help, it was sure a lot easier to get him out of the truck and into the car. When that all happened, Bob and I was at the home ranch all alone, as everyone else was gone. It turned out his leg was bad broke, as the bone had splintered some and was broke in two places.

It looked like maybe I would be a busy boy, with Bob in the hospital, but Wes showed up the next day, so everything fell into place. It was a good thing that everything went well with shipping and roundup, getting ready for winter the past fall. With Bob laid up, Wes and I had to keep everything going workwise. That was okay, as we were well ready and organized for winter before Bob got hurt.

We did not know it at the time, but it was going to take a long time for that broken leg to heal. I guess the doctors had to practically screw the splinters and pieces of bone together to get it set properly. Poor old Bob was destined to be in a cast until the end of July.

Of course, the doctors changed the cast from time to time as the healing progressed. The last was a walking cast, which was much better, as he could get around better. Better for all of us, as his humour sure improved when he was able to throw them damn crutches away. It had been a long haul for him. However, when it was finally over, he seemed to be good as new after his leg strengthened up when the walking cast was finally removed.

Wes and I had handled the work quite well, as it had been a good winter. It took longer for spring roundup with only two of us. We just had to gather smaller bunches at a time and then, of course, had to keep an eye on the cows calving. That, too, went well. Mind you, having the experience by then of having been ranch cowboys for years was in our favour, as we did not make too many bad moves, thereby using our time to the most advantage. We got to all the necessary things as they came along, mainly looking after the livestock and fences. The rest would be caught up on, now that Bob was back in harness.

By the time Bob was in the saddle again, it was not long until shipping time, so everything was back on course, with a full crew of all three of us.

Gathering cattle at the Milk River Cattle Co.: "We are closing the gate, and we are done for the day."

After shipping the two-year-old steers, it was the usual fall roundup, sorting and weaning and moving the cows and yearlings to their various winter fields. We also had to get that year's crop of calves established on grass and grain pellets to be ready for the oncoming winter in the feedlots.

After they were weaned, the ranch ran them on the frozen, dry second-growth alfalfa on the hayfields until it was grazed off. We got them started on grain pellets at the same time. That way, when winter hit, it was easy to round them up right at home, sort them out in right-sized bunches to fit each feedlot and go to feeding steady. Of course, all the time we hoped it would be a nice winter, so we would not freeze our asses off.

As usual, the winter dragged along slow, but spring eventually came, as it always did, and the round of ranch events started again for another season. Another thing that helped the work tremendously was that the boss pitched in whenever he could. He had to go away on business trips quite often. He was on several boards, and he had a lot of business meetings to go to, some far enough away that there were times we did not see him for a week or so at a time. He always did the irrigating on the hayfields himself every spring and was good at it.

The ranch had to flood irrigate with ditches and diversion boxes, to turn the water where it was needed. It was sure okay with us that he tended the irrigation water himself. None of us was madly anxious to learn that fine art, as it involved running a shovel and wearing them fancy, high-topped gumboots.

Well, I guess I was destined to learn something about the art of flood irrigation before too long. One morning, the boss came out and said, "Art, you're going to have to take over the irrigating till I get back. I got a phone call last night from one of the big companies where I am on the board of directors that I have to come to a meeting; I have to leave right away. I'll be gone for a week or so." I said, "Holy smoke, I've never run a muck stick in an irrigation ditch in my life, but okay. I'll try to keep the water going in the right places."

The boss just grinned and said, "You'll figure it out, there is nothing to it. Just put the wet water on the dry ground and you have it made. I'm even going to help you a little before I go." He went and got his high-topped gumboots and said, "Good thing you and I wear the same-size feet. That's all the time I got to give you any help; I've got to go."

After a little, I was somewhat able to figger out how he done it by observing the layout of the small ditches coming away from the main flow of water. Actually, I made out fairly well as the hayfield was watered.

When he got back about a week or 10 days later, I was willing to give him back his gumboots and shovel. When he came in for dinner, he said, "You did okay. I suppose now you had so much fun you'll want the irrigating job steady." Well, I said, "I wouldn't think of such a thing as depriving you of all the enjoyment of playing in the water; besides, you're much better at it. Think of how much more hay you'll get by tending it yourself." He grinned and said, "You've got a point there," and I got the hell gone to do something else before he might change his mind.

I guess I let my irrigation knowledge go to waste, as I've never run an irrigating shovel since, nor any other watering device, except one time I got a pitcher of water and irrigated the wife's flowerpots in the living room.

At that time, the ranch contracted out all the haying, so I never even had to cut the hay that I so diligently watered. I did not mind that at all, because, by that time in my career, my ass fit a lot better in a saddle than on a mower or swather seat. As the years slid by, one season giving way to the next, the routine was pretty well the same every year.

Then Bob got to looking at some of the faraway hills, craving to see what was on the other side, and decided he needed to see some new country. Bob was a single fella, and when the urge hits a fella to move camp, it does not take too long to make up his mind. Wes and I used to do that, too; that is, until we got married. Every once in a while, the urge would still hit us. Of course, nothing came of it. By then, we both had two kids.

Common sense told us just to scratch our itchy feet, never mind wearing the itch off our soles by looking for something over the next hill that might not be there. Besides, it's tough climbing a hill with a kid hanging on each hip pocket and trying to lead a wife who is not halter-broke and don't want to leave.

When Bob left, we just told ourselves that was the best ranch we had ever worked on, that was home. I suppose we secretly envied him, his freedom when he left, and I am sure there must have been times he envied us a little, having good wives and kids. We had it all, except a ranch of our own, but we were both determined to remedy that somehow, and in time we both got a toehold, but that is another story.

Bob had been there about six or seven years. We fell back into the routine we had used when his leg was broke and managed quite well. Of course, everything was caught up workwise before he left, so we had a clean slate to work on. Actually, we did okay, just the two of us on the crew. It maybe took a little longer to gather and move cattle, but by then, we were familiar with every side coulee and trail over the whole ranch, so we could rather keep a step ahead of a trail herd's desire to turn off where they were not supposed to.

When it came to sorting cattle, the boss done that pretty well himself in the home corrals. We just swung the right gate off the sorting lane for the right cut to go into the corral when he hollered "in" or "by." It worked very well. There were times, like at a late weaning when there was snow and 30 below (–34°C), that watching those sorting gates was not exactly fun or comfortable, but then what is, when it's that cold?

The seasons kept rolling around, year after year. Wes and I wound up with just us two on the crew and the boss helping when we needed it. I guess there were not too many good men floating around, and we were better off by ourselves than steering a greenhorn around who did not know what to do. Having by this time years of experience and working very well together, we never let ourselves get in a bind.

A few interesting things happened now and then. We was both breaking and training horses for other people off the ranch, just to supplement our income and have a few spare dollars. Seems like them growing kids needed many things, especially after starting and going to school. Not that they were asking too much, but on a cowboy's wages, there were times when you had to stretch that paycheque like a tarp strap on a grain truck, to keep those little extra things coming. The money we made after supper, riding and training young horses for people off the ranch, made quite a difference and helped with little things the women and kids needed.

Usually, if I rode a green horse to work, Wes rode a well-broke one, and when he rode a green horse, I rode a broke one. That worked well both ways; the young horse would be more settled and quiet and worked better with the broke horse as a pilot. Not to mention it was safer, as it is possible for a green horse to blow up 10 miles from home and set a fella on foot. Luckily, that never happened to either of us. It can even happen that a broke horse will bury his head between his knees and take to you.

One day, we got done sorting the yearlings. Taking the steers from the heifers, we were moving the yearling steers just a short ways into the horse pasture for overnight, right alongside the main road heading away from the yard. The grade had been built up pretty high so the snow would blow off, and the year-lings were following the side of the hill. We were both riding well-broke horses.

Just before we got to the wire gate in the horse pasture, right beside the cattle guard on the grade, three head climbed up onto the grade and were going to cross onto the other side. I loped over to the grade to stop them, and Shorty, my horse, just jumped from the level ground right up onto the grade. Right there, I guess it was about two-and-a half to three feet high. He just landed up on the gravel road on top of the grade, bogged his head and went to bucking plumb serious, like a rodeo bronc. I looked at the gravel road; I had no intention of being bedded down there, so I grabbed the cowboy saver and hung on and rode him until he quit.

Wes rode up and said, "You rode good." I said, "Yeah, I was pulling leather to beat hell; that gravel road made up my mind to stay on top." Wes said, "I wonder what got into Shorty, he's plumb gentle." Then he said, "Get off, Art, easy-like." I looked at him and he said again, "Get off easy." So I carefully stepped off.

What happened was the strap between my front and wide leather back cinch had broke. The back cinch was hanging a little loose, and when Shorty jumped up onto the grade, the wide leather strap swung back, so when he landed on the road he was flanked like a rodeo bronc. For a minute or so, it made him think he was one and got serious enough that I had to ride some to stay on him. To this day, I check my tie strap between my cinches, regular. That could have happened on a side hill coulee, steep as the roof of a house, and in a place like that it could have ended in a bad way. However, all is well that ends well.

There were times, too, when being short-handed moving a sizeable bunch of cattle, we had to depend on our imaginative influence and inventive intuition to cope with some hard-to-figure-out way to make it work. Cattle, being cattle, are at times unpredictable. Lady Luck was a welcome ally. The cattle's unpredictability sometimes worked in our favour and some-times not.

Come shipping time, we'd gathered 500 head of two-year-old steers and had them in a small field close to home, awaiting the day the cattle liners were scheduled to haul them away. Just a matter of a few days.

Well, the boss was negotiating with the cattle liner outfit, and because of their busy schedule, they did not let us know what day until the last minute. It turned out they made up their mind one evening and said, "We'll be there at eight o'clock in the morning, day after tomorrow." That was okay; the steers were in a small field along the river, only two miles from the shipping corrals.

Only one thing was uncertain: they were across the river. The river was small but wide, a good solid bottom to cross, in about a foot or so of low water. However, cattle are unpredictable; I have seen times they would not go and get their feet wet, never mind crossing. Two men do not have much of a chance forcing 500 head into a crossing in the open prairie, no matter how good the crossing is. We had one day. If they wanted to cross the river, no worries, it would only take a short time.

But if they refused to go into the water, with only two men on the wide-open crossing, there was enough of them and not enough of us. We could wind up not getting them across at all, especially if they started to scatter into small bunches. The trucks would be there at the appointed time, come hell or high water. We had to figure out some way to make them want to cross or possibly spook them across. With only two of us and all those cattle, spooking them into the river was just a dream. Making them think they wanted to cross was a faint hope. Cross they must, to get to the loading corrals; there was no other way.

Well, we left the corrals early, to give us all the time we might need, and rode across the river. If all went well, we should be back with the herd long before noon. The fact stared us in the face: there was just the two of us. It seemed too much to expect that them 500 steers was going to string across like a bunch of milk cows waiting to be juiced.

As we were riding up the steep, grassy slope from the crossing, Wes said, "How do you suppose we should work this?" I said, "I don't know, hope like hell they'll want to cross, I guess."

Then I thought something I had not thought of until just then. We had never had to cross at that particular place before, at least, not since we had been working for the outfit. The small holding field was fenced with page wire all along the north side. The river curved to the south, forming the other fence, so to speak. The page-wire fence went right down the hill, across a little brush flat and right into the river. It just came to me that, if we were really, really lucky, we could bring the herd of steers along the page-wire fence. Once they dropped over the edge of the hill, if we spooked them good enough, they might stampede across that narrow little brush flat and be in the river before they knew it. Once the leaders crossed, the rest would follow.

I explained my thoughts to Wes and asked him what he thought. He thought for a bit and said, "I think that might be our best bet; we just might pull it off. Let's give it a try; we do not have anything to lose, and we might win."

We rode slowly through the grazing steers at a walk, to not excite them. We started moving them to the crossing nice and easy along the fence, grazing them along, and they started bunching up along the fence as the drag was catching up with the leaders. We took our time, and they were ambling along plumb quiet and contented-like. By the time we eased them along the fence and they spilled over the top of the hill, they did not run at all.

As soon as the leaders hit the bottom, it was time to wake them up, as the last of the drag was starting down the hill. The leader was just about at the little brush flat, the river not more than 50 yards away. This better work, I thought.

We had been working our way along the fence, and we very quietly and unobtrusively had untied our slickers from the backs of our saddles. It was time.

Them steers sure came to life on that slope when a couple of wild-eyed, yelling maniacs on fiery-eyed horses came boiling over that hill, waving their slickers over their heads and making more noise than a crowd in a hockey arena. Those poor old steers woke up so quick from their drowsy peace of mind that they just ran down that slope wide open to get away from they did not know what.

It seemed like our plan was going to work, until I seen the leaders head down the river. They were far enough ahead that they were not spooked enough to not see the water, and the rest of the herd followed. Lady Luck was with us; about 300 yards down the river, a big hog's back was sticking out of the ground. Do not ask me why it was there, sticking up out of the prairie only about 15 or 20 feet from the riverbank, and the cow trail was between it and the river. I seen at a glance that if those leaders got by that hog's back, all would be lost. I yelled to Wes, who was behind them, "Give 'em hell, I've got to leave you."

I rode for the far end of the hog's back, passing on the opposite side from where the leaders were following the cow trail on the run. Shorty ran as he had never run before. He was a good horse and knew as well as me we had to beat them or we would be in real trouble.

We came around the other end of the hog's back on the high run, and talk about timing—we met the lead steer about 20 feet before he came out the other side. Shorty came a-charging, I was screaming like a banshee and waved my slicker practically in his face. He stuck his hind feet in the ground like a well-trained rope horse, his eyes stuck out of his head like a pair of apples. The hill was on one side of him, this crazy maniac on the charging horse was in front, and the riverbank was only about four feet to the water. He made up his mind a whole lot faster than I am able to tell it and jumped into the river and crossed, with the rest of the herd following his lead.

The rest of them likely figured if he could cross, so could they. Anything to get away from those two horseback fellows who was usually so quiet but had now gone plumb crazy. We just kept the drag going across. By now, all we had to do was stay in sight to keep them going. Just seeing us was all the incentive they needed to foller the leader.

We just sat on our horses in the shade of the hog's back, as both us and the horses needed some air. Besides that, we wanted them to settle down again, which they did right quickly. Cattle nowadays tend to be more gentle and quiet down quick after a little scare.

There was a fence close by across the river, and they quickly went to grazing in the smaller area. When we saw that, we rode into the river so our horses could drink and stand in the water and cool off. Then we rode slowly up to the herd; they did not spook at all. I do not really know how or what a cow critter thinks, but I would bet they sure wondered what got into them two cowboys back there.

"Well," Wes said, "I guess it worked." I said, "Ya, by the skin of our teeth. If Shorty and I would have been two jumps slower, it could have been a different story." Then we both had a little laugh when I told him how that lead steer had looked when Shorty and I came around that hog's back. I said, "I wonder if his eyes have gone back into place in his head yet."

We slowly and carefully moved them through a gate into a small pasture up the river, close to the corrals and buildings. We sat and day-herded them until they quit grazing and had a drink out of the river and started to lie down in the grass. We made sure they was watered and fed and content so they would not take a notion to try to go back across the river.

We left them there on the river flat and kept an eye on them until about suppertime, so they would not have to stay in the loading corrals any longer than they had to. We were able to go and have a coffee as we had them bedded down by the river by 10:30 in the morning. We went back and checked them, then came in for dinner and went and kept an eye on them there on the river flat until we put them in the corral for the night.

It had turned out to be a good day; the weather was very nice. The next morning, by eight o'clock, there was 15 or 16 cattle liners in the yard.

CHAPTER 21

THE GRAZING RESERVES

We had all them cattle liners loaded by midmorning, and the boss followed the liners out to their destination. The steers had to be weighed coming off the trucks. The boss and the cattle buyer who bought them were there to supervise and to help. Wes and I were left to our own resources. As there were a few head here and there to clean up and put where they was supposed to be, we thought we would just as well get that done.

When we had gathered the winter field during spring roundup, we had somehow or other missed an old cow. We knew she was there, as someone had driven by during the summer and seen her. Now, this was September, so this old granny had been alone for quite a spell. She was a dry cow, no calf, and being alone had not exactly improved her disposition. She was not wild at all, just kind of on the fight if we tried to move her.

We were riding along in the next field and saw she was fairly close to the gate, where she would go into the field with the rest of the herd. Wes said, "Lets get her, she'll never be handier." We opened the gate, which, at her age, she must have gone through many times. As we rode down to ease her through the gate, we soon found out she was set in her ways. She had been living alone long enough; I think she must have liked it because, instead of heading for the gate, she decided to go to war. Wes and I were both good on horseback. He was riding his best horse, a gentle, papered stud, and I had not ridden old Daniel for some time, but that day I had him.

Well, we dodged around, keeping out of her way and trying to ease her toward the gate, without much luck. The gate was only about 200 yards away, but the old cow had bogged down and stood her ground, full of mad, refusing to move except to fight, which is often apt to happen when an old cow has lived too long alone and figures she's the only bovine critter left in the world. Wes said, "Let's just leave her, the rest of the herd will be back in the winter field in about three months. She will mix with them, and we will be sure to get her, come spring. We've got more important things to do than stand here arguing with her." I said, "Sure, it ain't that important."

Then I thought of something. Old Daniel had handled worse cows than her, and I was just curious enough to see what he would do alone. I said to Wes, "Let me try her alone." He looked at me as if maybe I was not thinking right and said, "If two of us mounted, good as we are, can't get her attention, how in the hell do you figure on getting her alone?" I said, "I don't know, I'm going to put this old horse of mine on her, then drop the bridle reins slack and let him have her on his own. I just want to try and see what he does." "Okay," Wes said, "I'll get out of the way and see what happens."

I turned old Daniel loose on her; it was his play. He manoeuvred around and managed to get her broadside. I figured the cow had won, when, all of a sudden, he laid his ears back and flew straight at her. He hit her up front on her left rib cage with his right shoulder and knocked her flat on her side. Her eyes rolled back in her head, her legs seemed to stiffen out, and I thought we maybe killed her. I sat on Daniel as he stood beside her, and finally she rolled up on her belly. She lay there for maybe a minute and got on her feet. Talk about memory improving fast. She right quickly remembered where the gate was and walked through it like a well-broke milk cow. She had no desire to argue with the bay horse anymore.

Well, as usual, fall roundup was coming up. We went over the fences in the winter field and started getting ready for winter, same as years previous. Winter came and went.

About spring, roundup time was half over. Wes got a phone call from his brother, who had bought a piece of rangeland in southern Saskatchewan. He had a good job with an oil company, which he wanted to keep. He offered Wes the use of the land. I do not know what the arrangement was, but Wes gave his notice after spring roundup, moved down there, went to building a barn and corrals and acquired a nice house trailer to live in. He got himself a bunch of cows and was getting into the cattle business. It seemed this cowboy and his family had their toehold and was getting on their own.

That same spring, a quarter section with buildings came up for sale, about seven miles northwest of the ranch. The wife and I decided to buy it. The price was right; it was not big enough to make a living off, but with me working and what the place was capable of producing, we should do okay. We would have a home of our own.

A month after Wes left, I gave my notice, and in a couple of weeks, we moved up there. I spent a month fixing things, as it had been vacant for a time. I then went riding on fall roundup for a big provincial grazing reserve about 30 miles down the river. Their roundup was around the middle of October, when the patrons took their cattle home. We started moving cattle as close to the loading corrals as possible so they would be handy to gather and ship home when the time came. It was a fairly big grazing outfit, running something like 4000 or 5000 head during the summer—in other words, a large community pasture.

All went well; it was well organized, and the farmers trucked their cattle home at the appointed time. During roundup, we had missed a cow and calf in the river brush about three miles up the river from the buildings and did not find her until all the other cattle had been trucked home. We tried to get them, but they holed up in the river brush, and on them flats, the brush was thicker than the winter hair on a jackrabbit. The manager of the grazing base said to leave her, one of those days it would snow, and she had to leave tracks. We would get her then.

We went to building and repairing fences. There were a lot of miles of wire fence to check, with cross fences for various fields. I guess the whole grazing lease would be well in excess of 100,000 acres.

One night, in the latter part of October, it snowed about an inch. The manager came out to the bunkhouse, where Larry and I lived, right after breakfast and said, "Let's try to get that cow and calf today. With this snow, she has to leave tracks, and if all three of us go, we should surely get her and the calf."

We saddled up and headed upriver the two-and-a-half or three miles, to where she was holed up on the brush flat with her calf. We picked up their tracks real easy and tracked them to a big brush patch on the flat, where they went hiding when they heard us coming. Larry said to me, "Hold my horse, and I'll go in on foot with Joey (his dog) and flush her out."

I was standing there holding our horses, when the brush started crackling and the cow and calf came out of there on the high jump, with Joey on their heels. I hollered to Larry to come and get his horse, and I stepped up on Rusty and took after her, to keep her in sight as she was hightailing it across a big, open flat to the brush on the other side.

Rusty pulled up beside her, and we tried to turn her to keep her in the open. Rusty was just a little horse, maybe 900 pounds soaking wet. He crowded his shoulder into her and tried to push her into turning, but to no avail—she outweighed him by 300 pounds. I could see she was going to get away, so I jerked down my rope and hung a loop on her. I was right close, so I dallied up in the middle of my rope. Rusty stuck his hindquarters in the ground, the cow reared straight up, came to a stop and went to fighting the rope. I got her just in time, on the edge of the brush; three or four jumps later, she would have been out of sight.

Everything held, but I was in a precarious situation. It was one of those times when I did not have time to tighten my cinch before going after her, never figuring she would have to be roped, anyway. The saddle was sliding up onto Rusty's neck, with her fighting the rope. All I could do was hold Rusty's head up, so his neck would stop the saddle. I sure did not want to lose her then, and thinking the other two guys were close by, I sat there hollering for help to get one of their big horses tied on to that cow.

No answer. I hollered again, still no answer, and my situation sure was not improving. Rusty was cool and tending to the business of hanging onto that cow as if it was all in an ordinary day's work. If he realized I was holding his head as high as possible to keep the saddle from going over his head, he did not let on. As far as he was concerned, we had her, and she was not getting away.

The cow finally ran out of wind with the rope choking her and stopped pulling on the rope and just stood there catching her breath. I was in no better shape to do anything: my saddle was still loose, Rusty's head was still up, so it was a stalemate. What happens when she gets her breath back, I wondered.

I was looking around, hoping there was a tree or stump I might tie her to, but how? If I gave her any slack, she would start fighting again. Then I noticed a scrubby little poplar tree standing right beside my right stirrup. It was only eight or ten feet tall but had about a four-inch trunk at the ground level.

I figured if I could tie the rope to it right against the ground, it might hold.

I had the reins in my left hand, and my right was holding the dally. I had to try it before the cow got her wind back, right then, while she was standing still. I very slowly stepped off on the right-hand side, bringing the reins around the back of the saddle horn to keep them tight enough that Rusty did not move. On the ground, I passed the rope over to my left hand; I was now holding the reins and the dally in the same hand. When I roped the cow, I had dallied in the middle of my rope. The long, loose end was dragging on the ground.

Right there, it was a good thing Rusty was a little horse. I could reach up to hold the reins and the dally with my left hand and reach low enough to get the tail end of the rope around the little tree and secure it with three half-hitches around itself. I had her tied to the tree. I pushed the rope right to the ground with my foot, threw my dallies and led Rusty out of the ring of fire on the run. If that cow started circling, I sure did not want him tangled in the rope.

As we were getting out of the way, I had visions of that little tree coming out by the roots and follering the cow into the brush. I got Rusty far enough away onto the open grass, and when I turned around, that little tree was swaying and shaking like a cyclone was working on the top of it and an earthquake underneath. I ran over and grabbed the trunk about four feet off the ground and managed to hold it straight when the cow hit the end of the rope, so she wouldn't bend it out of the ground. I had to watch the cow as well; she did not seem to be on the fight, but after all that, she might blame me for the situation she was in and go on the warpath.

She had the rope partly wrapped around a three- or four-foot sagebrush and came toward me. I let out a yell; when she turned back, the rope completed the wrap, and she pulled that big old sagebrush right out of the ground. That probably saved the little poplar from being pulled out as she decided she was halter-broke right quickly after that.

After the excitement was over and the cow quieted down, I got to wondering where the other two guys was. I heard voices on the other side of the brush island, on the open flat that hid me and the cow from view. It was Johnny and Larry coming; they had found my tracks, even though by then the snow had all melted.

I heard one of them say, "I think Art's got her," meaning that I knew where the cow was. The other one said, "There's his horse, I wonder where he is." I stepped over closer to Rusty and said, "I'm right here." Johnny said, "Have you got the cow?" I replied, "Yes." He asked, "Where is she?" "Right here, I've got her tied to a tree," I said. They both laughed, figuring I had lost her and was making a funny.

I said, "Don't laugh, I'm serious. Come and see for yourself." They rode from behind the brush patch and looked. One of them said, "I'll be darned, do you know where the calf is?" I said, "Not really, I was too busy keeping track of his mother."

We got the rope transferred to Larry's big bay mare, a good horse, no danger of her getting away. With Johnny on one side and me on the other and Larry behind with the rope dallied to the saddle horn, we herded her home. We put her in the corral with some other cows for the night.

Next morning, she was turned out, went back, got her calf and was back with the other cows by four o'clock that afternoon. She was not alone anymore and came back to the company of the other cattle. She was the last of the roundup; Johnny phoned the owner, who came and got her, and the three of us went back fencing, until the weather turned bad and there was snow in the air. Riding the summer range was over for that

Sweetgrass Hills, Montana, as pictured from Coutts, Alberta: "I looked out at those hills for a lot of years."

year. Larry and I loaded our horses and went home. Johnny, being the manager, lived there permanent.

I had done some fixing on the house and barn on the place we had just bought the previous summer. It was a hard winter that year, but it finally passed and spring was in the air. Now I needed a job to go with the little ranch, and as luck would have it for me, there was a smaller pasture close to the Montana border needing a rider. I contacted them and went to a director's meeting. We came to an agreement, and I left there with the rider's job in my hip pocket.

That was more than 20 years ago, and I am still riding for them today, except for one summer. After 19 years on the Community Pasture Association ranges, I left and drove a horse-drawn tourist carriage in Banff for Warner Guiding and Outfitting for one

summer. I have been back on the Community Grazing Association lease for two years since.

The first year I was back was a typical southern Alberta
summer, too dry and intermittently cool and hot. It was hard on
the grass and water holes, but we came through with fairly
good grass left—dried up but still nourishing. That native grass
cures on the stem when it dries up. The water holes were low
but in good enough shape. They should last another year, with
a little runoff and rain showers to keep their water levels up.
Well, things do not always turn out the way we hope.

The following winter was a very easy winter, with not much
snow and no runoff to speak of. Some places had some very
heavy, good spot showers that filled their water holes. No good
general rain, though, and no good spot showers on the lease
I rode. It was a damned hot, dry summer, hitting over 100°F
(38°C) most of July. August seemed to be shaping up likewise.

I have only seen one other summer as dry in the 20-odd years
I have rode for a grazing association: that was the summer of
1988. That summer in 2000 sure seemed to try hard to outdo the
summer of '88. It must have been 100°F (38°C) or better in
the shade.

Southern Alberta and Montana are experiencing many difficulties on the range, with the hot, dry weather and the problems
of grass fires to add to the rangeland misery. That doesn't take
into consideration the plight of the dirt-farming community, as
they stand by and watch their crops wither and dry up, building
up to a glum financial future. Ranchers and farmers are a tough
bunch, though, and will weather the difficulties.

Maybe next year there will be lots of rain, and the water holes
will likely be full again from a good run-off. Maybe the range and
grass will be tall and green and the crop fields will be waist tall,
with long heads of grain. Those two dry years will be memories
of the past, only to be remembered as a conversation piece in

the bunkhouses and bars. As the stories are told, they will likely not lose anything in the description of how dry it really was.

Yes, it appears, at times, that this is a "next year" piece of country, especially in agriculture. Mind you, I suspect conditions like this have been happening since time began and maybe sometimes in the past, even worse. I cannot really comment on that, I cannot remember that far back.

Riding these grazing association leases are, as a rule, a safe kind of riding job. Working alone, as I have been doing for all these years, though, reminds a fella to try not to let his guard down. When something does happen and goes wrong, it is usually unexpected.

At times, the odd bull can be a major problem. Bulls nowadays are not halter-broke generally and are not handled with horses very much, as in times gone by. Consequently, some bulls seem to resent horses and at times figure out that they do not have to run from a horse.

This usually happens when a bull goes on the prod. Most of them are okay. When a bull is on the prod, refuses to be handled and comes for a horse and rider, you have no choice but to get out of his way. There is more than enough strength in one of them bulls for him to get his head under a horse and actually bodily throw horse and rider up in the air and pile them up on the prairie. Knocked down and lying on the prairie, with a one-ton bull on the fight and after your hide, is certainly not a spot a horse and rider want to be in, so you run to get out of his way.

Right now, the bull figures he is in control and, of course, usually gets still harder to handle. If he is impossible to get, you get a truck and someone on one of them four-wheel drive machines. Usually he handles fairly well with the gas-driven outfits he is used to. In very isolated cases, even then, he can be pretty impossible.

Usually, a difficult bull can be brought in with a bunch of cows, but I have seen the odd one quit the cows and defy anyone or anything to move him. That is about the time the thoughts of a contraption referred to as a tranquillizer gun come to mind. A dart in the ass filled with slow-down serum usually does the trick, and he is docile enough then to load in a trailer. When it wears off, he is in the home corral waiting for a one-way ticket to market.

I have been lucky down through the years, not getting hurt bad enough to be laid up for long or in the hospital, except twice, I believe. One time, at roundup time in this grazing association, a 1400-pound cow tried to stop my clock by attempting to push me through a five-rail fence made of two-by-sixes. She got out of the corral and was coming down the sorting lane. Someone hollered, "Stop that cow," and as I was standing right by the open cross gate in the lane, I just swung it across the lane and stood there holding it. I was backed up against the plank fence on the side of the sorting lane.

Now, pretty well all of these farm-raised cows in the grazing lease are gentle. So was this one, but she was plumb aggravated and, seeing me holding the gate across the lane, she turned and hit me in the belly and chest and went to pushing me against the fence. It was a terrible feeling; she was big and strong, the fence behind me did not give and, for one terrible moment, I thought I had hit the end of my trail. Then the cow eased off, pushed me again, not so hard, and dropped me on the ground. Had I been standing in front of the gate, the gate would have swung back.

Without thinking of the cow being half on the prod, I was backed up against the side of the sorting lane. I was feeling a bit roughed up. Someone said there was blood coming out of my mouth. I figured I could be hurt internally after all that pressure, so I asked one of the boys to look at my bleeding mouth and see what he thought. He looked close and said, "You've got a cut lip that's bleeding some." That sure made me feel better; I was never so glad to have a cut lip as then. It was not serious.

A rancher and good friend got a hold of a pickup truck and took me the 50-some odd miles to the nearest doctor. He was a good driver, and that truck, I think, made it to town faster than it had ever been driven before. I did not feel too terrible, but he kept looking over at me and pouring the juice to that truck. He told me afterwards that he thought he was losing me, by the colour of my face as we came over the bridge in the river bottom. It was no wonder that old engine was screaming, pulling up the hill leaving the river.

As it turned out, he got me to the doctor in record time and, after a thorough examination and x-rays, it turned out I only had one broken rib and two that was badly cracked. Somehow, too, that old cow had managed to bend my two floating ribs on one side, which sure did not improve things any. The doctor said, "You'll heal up pretty good in a month's time. You're not hurt internally, except for damaged ribs." Upon hearing that, we both relaxed, and the rancher took me to his daughter's house for dinner. I even had a good appetite, after the doctor told me I was not in any danger of kicking the bucket. I will be forever grateful to that rancher, though, for seeing that I got cared for. We have been good friends ever since.

Just like the doctor said, I was able to handle bales, very carefully I must admit, and feed cattle again after a month or six weeks. After spending a couple of weeks sitting half upright, day and night, on the sofa, it was nice to get back in a harness again. For some reason, I could not lay down for two or three weeks after I got hurt. My ribs would hurt too much, like a bad toothache. Sitting propped up with pillows I was relatively comfortable, so I slept that way.

The other time I got hurt a little, a bull ran into the side of my horse and very near wrecked my leg between his head and the horse. He hit us hard enough that he knocked little Rusty sideways about three feet. Rusty stayed on his feet and was not a bit hurt. More than I could say for my leg, which I thought was broke.

I very carefully stood up in my stirrups, and it took my weight. I could not feel or hear any bones crackling so concluded that nothing was broke. I got the bull into the corral with a small bunch of cows that was handy, took care of Rusty and limped to the cabin to size up my leg. It was badly bruised, starting to turn blue, and by morning had swollen some. It hurt but was bearable, so I rode for three days until we gathered the rest of the bulls. It was bull roundup time.

I went to see the doctor after. He said, "That's a hell of a looking leg, but there is nothing broke." He wrote me a prescription for some kind of antibiotic pills, told me to get some Epsom salts to put in warm water and soak it.

This went on for several weeks, and it did not help much. I was not good for much, as my leg had stiffened up so I could not ride. After roundup, where the riding was done without me, another doctor looked at it and found one spot where the leg was going bad and put me in the hospital for a week on an intravenous. He fixed up the bad spot and got it to healing good, and it turned out as good as new after a few months. He was a damn good doctor.

These things can happen to anyone, and I am sure at one time or another, practically every range cowboy has had similar experiences only never wrote about them. I would not neither, as it sounds like I am whining about these things, but far from it. It is just to illustrate honestly what a working cowboy is all about. We take the bad with the good.

Since then, things on the grazing lease have been good. Only two bulls at separate roundups have been a problem. One had to

Julie and Irvine Hagen, pictured in 1994: "A couple of years later, Julie got married and became a Blackmer."

be tranquillized with a dart in the ass filled with slow-down serum. He got a one-way ticket to the bologna factory. The other one would come for a horse when it got within 200 yards, with murder in his eyes. We finally got him with one of them little four-wheeler machines and a truck. It really helped that he was following a cow in heat and she handled well and was quite willing to go home. Nobody got hurt, mainly because after previously handling those bulls on the warpath, by then, we were head-shy enough to keep well out of their way.

The long, hot summer was slowly winding down. No moisture in sight, as far as rain was concerned, and it was so dry, like one fella said, "The antelope are kicking up dust ahead of themselves when they go to running." The water holes were still hanging on, and the cattle were doing surprisingly well on the bone-dry grass. Thank goodness the native grass cures on the stem when it dries up, retaining the nourishment in it.

Well, there is not much left to say about the rangeland experiences of this cowboy. The kids are all grown up and on their own. I got divorced about 15 years ago, and I am thinking just maybe I have rode far enough. Mind you, I still like my horses; cowboying has been a good, healthy life. I enjoyed it and will miss the horses, cattle and cowboying, if I quit doing it.

Maybe a fella should take it easy and find a grazing lease, half as big, where you only have to look after 500 pairs, instead of 1000. That could lead to laziness, and a fella could become fat and pot-bellied. I will have to give this some thought, as I like the idea of being slim and in shape.

I have a sideline enterprise. I am trying to do something in the country music field. I have already produced two country western albums, *The Hills of Home* and *Cowboy Country*. Have to see how the country music turns out, while I am making up my mind if I should ride a few thousand miles more. It will be kind of nice if the music turns out. A fella should not have to run from any fighting bulls or cows on the warpath. It would be nice to be noticed singing songs, instead of swearing at a bunch of ornery bovines and bad weather.

CHAPTER 22

HORSES I'VE KNOWN AND ADMIRED

This story of my lifelong experiences as a working cowboy and range rider would seem cut short and incomplete if I did not write this last chapter and give credit to horses in general and especially horses I have known, worked and rode. Down through the ages, horses have been the lifeline of civilization. North America would not be the country it is, as we know it, if it had not been for the horse and his counterpart, the mule. For that matter, there have been few places in the world that, at one time or other, have not been positively affected and greatly improved, certainly constructively progressive, with the help and use of horses.

It has been said that through the ages of the dim and distant past, many people have left their footprints in the sand. Right beside the peoples' footprints are the tracks of horses, helping those people accomplish whatever they had to do. It goes without saying that horses in general deserve far more credit than they have received for their contribution to the march of civilization, which has brought the modern world to the way we know it today.

I can give only a small example of my relationship to horses and their contribution to an everyday cowboy's life on a personal basis, relating to horses I have known and worked with, as well as horses I have known of that have been associated with other people. I am going back to my boyhood to try to relate to horses

I have known in the sequence of time since then, starting with a horse named Darky.

A big, black workhorse of, I think, Percheron and Shire or Clydesdale breeding, Darky was a gentle, very intelligent horse with three white stockings. His left front foot was black. He had a pure white blaze on his face. He was a logging horse, as those days, pretty well all logging was done with horses. He would work very well anyplace he was asked to, but skidding timber was where he really excelled. Skidding timber, he worked single with no bridle, only a halter, with the halter shank tied loosely to the top of the hames on the harness. In other words, he handled those logs down hillsides or on the level entirely on his own.

My dad was in the logging business, producing peeled-cedar telephone and telegraph poles. These poles were cut and peeled by hand in the bush and were skidded out with usually a big, single horse, to where they could be loaded onto sleighs in the wintertime and were hauled to and piled on a landing on the riverbank. Usually in September, they were put into the river to be floated probably close to 100 miles downriver, where they were pulled from the water, loaded onto flat cars on the railroad and sent to their destination. They wound up holding telephone and telegraph wires.

Getting these peeled poles from the stump, where they were felled and peeled, to where they could be piled was where the single skidding horses came in, and there were a lot of good ones them days, working without bridles or reins. The men who worked these horses cut the narrow trails in the bush and, of course, hooked the horses onto the poles.

Old Darky was a master at the skidding business. It was a pleasure just to watch him work. I was a big kid at the time and saw him work for myself. If the end of the pole was stuck behind a stump or exposed root on the worn skidding trail, no sweat—he would look back, turn sideways, then pull the log sideways to get it clear. If that did not work, he would try the same on the other side and, when the end came clear, would continue down the trail.

Occasionally, the tops of the logs would get stuck under an exposed root where the dirt and mud had worn away. In those cases, Darky still was not beat—he would try both sides, and if neither side worked, he would turn back beside the poles, pull them backward and then sideways to clear them and continue down the trail. My dad claimed that old Darky could take two telegraph poles down the hillside and get stuck less than my dad could driving the mare, and could get unstuck better.

In the wintertime, the peeled cedar poles were frozen, and one might shoot over a hill. That old horse would watch those logs and go so slow, you had to hold up a stick to see if he moved. As soon as those peeled cedars dipped over the brow of the hill, he just turned up the hill and kept them from running too fast by backing down with the trace against his leg until the logs stopped at the bottom, then continued down the trail.

He was my dad's pride and joy and part of the family. When we kids were small, we would get to ride him in the yard a little bit. That made our day, even if it was only 100 yards. He was so careful when little kids was on his back. No one ever fell off.

One time, Dad was in town and a bunch of the teamsters was drinking coffee and telling of their good skid horses. Dad did not say anything, but a friend of his who knew that big black horse spoke up and said, "I know you boys have some wonderfully good skid horses, but none of them can match Louie's old Darky." Someone said, "What makes you think he's so much better than ours?" Dad's friend just said, "There's only one thing old Darky can't do when it comes to skidding poles." The fella said, "What's that?" and Dad's friend said, "Darky can't hook himself up."

When Dad came home and told us, he seemed to neither agree nor disagree with that opinion, but we could see the pride for his old black horse in his eyes. That was a long time ago, but I can still remember Darky very well. Every so often, you hear the remark that some man is a man among men; well, Darky was a horse among horses, without a doubt.

Back in the winter of 1936, there was lots of snow and a cold spell that hung on, if I remember right, for a month or better, where the thermometer would register 30 or 35 below Fahrenheit (–34°C or –37°C) most every night. During this time, Dad hauled some loose hay from up along the river. He pulled into the hay shed about dark, unhooked his team and watered, unharnessed and fed them in the barn for the night, leaving the hay to be unloaded come daylight the next day.

It was still cold enough to pop the knots out of a jack pine plank when he went out to do the barn chores come morning. When he was done, he came in for a cup of coffee and said, "Looks like we got another horse on this outfit." Well, it was Saturday, us kids were home from school and I piped up, "What kind of a horse?" Dad said, "There is a little two-year-old bay mustang stud eating off the load of hay I left last night. I don't know if he belongs to anyone—no brand or mark of any kind on him."

Us kids got excited and asked, "If no one owns him, can we keep him?" The thought of acquiring a nice little horse we could someday ride was very appealing. Dad said, "Sure, I'll find out if anyone lays claim to him." Nobody did, so Dad talked to the Mounties and was told, as far as they knew, if no one claimed him and paid for his winter's feed in a certain period of time after it being advertised, he could keep him for the feed bill. No one did and that is how Bill, as we decided to call him, became part of the family. I will just give him honourable mention here as I have written quite a bit about him in the beginning of this book. He was the horse my sister and brothers and I learned to ride on, after Dad got him broke.

Well, time goes on; I was about 17 and working the bush, making a little money. Come spring, the annual rodeo on the reservation took place, kind of a sports day and rodeo combined. In the bucking string that was gathered in from the bush range was a beautiful sorrel stud with a white diamond on his nose and another larger diamond on his forehead, the two joined by a narrow white blaze on his face. The bronc riding was won on him that day.

He belonged to an elderly Indian gentleman living on the reservation. I wanted that little sorrel horse so bad it hurt. I was sure I could train him to become a good horse, but he was not for sale. Come fall, I was told that he had been gelded and that Richard was willing to sell him. I did not lose any time finding out, and Richard told me the price would be $55.

Come next spring, no one had bought the sorrel and, during the winter, I had worked and saved my money. I had the $55 and then some. I threw the saddle onto Bill and rode to the village where Richard lived, about six miles. His daughter answered the door, and I asked her to tell her dad that I had the money and wanted to buy the sorrel. She said, "Come on in and talk to Dad."

Well, Richard could talk hardly any English, so his daughter translated my words to him in the Indian language. I offered him $50; I could not resist the urge to try a little horse dealing. When his daughter told him, he looked me right in the eye, shook his head and said, "Fifty-five dollars or no deal." The horse-dealing urge left me in a hurry. I said, "Okay," and gave him five ten-dollar bills and a five. He could not read or write, but he could count money. After counting it slowly and carefully, he put out his hand. We shook hands, and he said, "Deal. Your horse now." He spoke to his daughter, and she said, "The horse

Art and Dusty, pictured in front of the Hazelton Hospital: "I stopped by to visit my sister Louise; she was a nurse at the hospital."

is running out on the open range; you go ketch him when you want him and he's yours."

I had my sorrel horse, and he turned out to be a great little horse, a really good walker. Not to say he did not give me a run for my money getting him broke. He turned out nice and gentle. I really liked him, even though he bucked me off flat on my ass on a big spruce stump while I was breaking him. I called him Dusty.

Then there was Mike, my sister's big sorrel gelding. This is the horse that let me keep on living by not dragging me when I was so badly hung up in a stirrup. He certainly deserves honourable mention here. I have written about this incident in the early part of this book. Without a doubt, I owe my life to that old sorrel gelding for standing still so patiently, without ever moving, while I struggled to free my foot and fall to the ground.

About this time, there was a small strawberry roan workhorse in the valley where I was raised. He belonged to a cowboy from Nebraska, a friend of ours, and was known by the name of Dutch. Dutch was a gentle, well-broke driving horse. I myself mowed and raked lots of hay with him and his teammate, a black, part-thoroughbred mare called Lady.

Working in harness was okay, but Dutch drew the line when it came to being ridden. He was one of the best bucking horses I have ever seen. He was never in a bucking string and only bucked at a very few small rodeos. Nobody really wanted him in those small bush rodeos, as whoever drew him knew there was no chance of winning on him. He was practically unrideable.

This was in the '30s and early '40s, and, those days, quite a lot of good riders came our way looking for work. Upon hearing of the strawberry roan, I believe practically all of them tried him with the same result—lying full length on the ground, kissing Mother Earth.

A top rider from the Cariboo Country came to live in our valley. This man apparently could ride with the best of them, having won a winner-take-all purse in a bronc-riding contest in the Cariboo Country just before coming up our way. There were 53 entries in that contest, and in them days, there were lots of top riders and rank broncs on the range. Winning something like that would, I think, be a credit to any rider's ability.

Someone mentioned him winning that contest. He just grinned and said, "Lucky, I guess." "Well," the fella said, "there's a horse here in the valley you can't ride." The bronc rider said, "Let's try him and find out." They went up to Fred's place and said to the Nebraska cowboy that they were there to ride Dutch, if that was okay. Fred just grinned and said, "Sure, bring your saddle out to the big corral."

Fred caught Dutch and put a jacket over his head so he could not see, and would stand still while being saddled. They got him all rigged out with no trouble. Harry, the bronc rider, stepped up on him, got all set and said, "Pull the coat off his head and let's see if he can buck." When Dutch saw the light of day, he dropped his head and poured it on. Harry done okay for a few jumps, until the roan horse was warmed up. When Dutch went to sun-fishing, Harry and he parted company. The strawberry roan had won again.

I saw him buck at the reservation rodeo, one of the very few times he was ever put in a contest. He bucked his rider off in the contest in a matter of seconds; I think he lasted three jumps. Then someone came up with the idea that the rider who won the bronc riding that day should take him out in exhibition, for a pass-the-hat-around purse from the crowd. They asked the winner and he said okay.

They led Dutch into that shotgun chute to be rigged out. He did not seem to mind at all, as if he knew what the outcome would be—which he probably did. No one had ever successfully ridden him yet. He was more interested in looking over the shotgun chute gate at a bunch of horses grazing on the far side of the arena—the arena being a grass-covered, fenced-in baseball field with the shotgun chute off to the side of home plate. That was the way it was in many small rodeos in them days, in that part of northwestern British Columbia.

The rider climbed over the chute and settled in the saddle. He nodded his head, and the gates swung open. Dutch took his time, stepped out a yard or so and buried his head between his knees. The man aboard was a good rider, but about the fourth or fifth jump, he was in trouble. Dutch was just warming up and went to sunfishing. I have never seen a horse do it like that before or since. He would go way up in the air and roll around on his side (I saw the sun shine on his belly) and still come to earth with his feet under him. By this time, the rider was on the grass watching the action.

As far as I know, he was never successfully rode. That was a time before hardly anyone had bucking strings as a business. Most ran in a bunch of range horses in that part of the country. I suppose that is why Dutch's ability never came to the attention of anyone in the bucking horse business, and no one tried to buy him for a rodeo bucking horse.

While on the subject of good bucking horses, I think we must not forget the great bucking horse, Midnight, the only horse I know listed in Guinness World Records. He was never successfully qualified on in his entire rodeo career and was retired as the world's undefeated champion bucking horse at the age of 17 years.

Time marches on, and some years later, in the summer of 1950, I went down in the Cariboo Country to work on some of the big cattle outfits. In the fall of that year, I got a job on the roundup crew on the Circle S Ranch at Dog Creek in British Columbia.

During the last part of the roundup, we had to wean the calves. This outfit ran close to 3000 head, counting everything: yearlings, two-year-olds, cows, calves and bulls. There was close to 700 or 800 cows. There, I saw one of the best gate horses work that I have ever seen.

We put the whole cowherd in the big, main corral. There was a wooden gate leading out of the corral into a small holding field, where the cows were let out after being weaned. The calves were held back in the corral to be later put on feed and water. The cows and calves were all together in the big corral, and we were about ready to start letting the cows out and keeping the calves in.

There was seven of us, all told, one of us being a very pleasant Indian cowboy named Gilbert. He was riding an 1100-pound white mare that looked like she may have had some Percheron in her ancestry, along with mainly mustang. The cow boss said, "Gilbert, will you watch the gate?" Gilbert said, "Okay, let me go down to the creek and cut me a willow." Coming back from the creek, he was walking along, peeling the bark off a willow stick with his jackknife—a stick about three-and-a-half feet long and about as big as a fork handle. I think the rest of the boys probably seen him work before; they never said anything.

I was still a mite green and curious as hell. I said, "Gilbert, what's that willow for?" He just grinned and said, "When you guys are pushing the cattle at me, to the gate, the calves want to go with their mothers. Once in a while, a calf will try to duck under my horse's neck, too close for her to stop it. When that happens, I just shove this shiny, peeled stick down in front of his nose. When he sees that, he'll stop, and she will have time to get in position and turn him back."

The cow boss said to us, "Pair up, you fellas. We will work in pairs and bring small bunches of cattle to Gilbert. Try not to crowd him too hard. We have to keep them coming through to be done before dark. You ready, Gilbert?" Gilbert just grinned and said, "I'll open the gate, then I'm ready." He got off his horse, opened the 14-foot plank gate leading from the corral into the holding field and tied it back to the fence so it would stay open. He got on his horse, rode into the open gate hole and turned the white mare back into the corral facing the cattle, grinned and said, "Bring them to me."

The white mare was shod with ice corks, as were all the horses, and when the first bunch of cows and calves were pushed slowly to him, he and the white mare went to work letting the cows out and holding the calves. The ice chips were flying around the little mare's feet as she danced forth and back, covering that gate hole, working mostly off her hind feet. Gilbert was a superb horseman and rider and looked like he was grown to her back. He never once threw her off balance when she dived sideways with precision-like speed to stop a calf. The pair of them working was just beautiful to behold.

We brought the cows to him, and he let the cows out and held the calves back. It seemed that he hardly reined that little mare. It took most of the afternoon, the little mare dancing forth and back with precision-like accuracy. When we were done weaning, out of 635 calves, Gilbert and his little white mare only missed one calf. One of the boys rode out, dropped a loop on him and led him back to the corral.

I said to Gilbert when we were done, "That little white mare of yours is the best gate horse I've ever seen. She must be the best in this part of the country." He grinned and said, "She's purty good, all right, but not as good as old Black Jack on the Alkali Lake Ranch." The thought occurred to me that if that was the case, old Black Jack must be one hell of a horse.

I never knew Black Jack, but curiosity took over. I started asking cowboys who worked for Alkali Lake Ranch and anyone who might know of this good horse if he was as good as his reputation. Upon my asking questions, I was somewhat surprised that even a lot of folks in the little town of Williams Lake had knowledge of old Black Jack. Quite often I had asked someone in town if they ever heard of the black horse, and the answer would be, "Oh yes, that Alkali Lake Ranch top horse.

I do not know him personally, but everyone seems to think he is the best in the country."

Seems he was a top horse, no matter what he was asked to do, but watching the gate when sorting cattle was his specialty. I asked a friend of mine who had worked for the ranch if he had ever ridden this good horse and was he as good as everyone said he was. Chuck grinned and said, "I've rode him some, and he can back up everything that's said about him. He's the best I ever sat on."

He said, "I'll give you a small example. One day we had brought the weaned calves into the corral to be worked on, vaccinations and such. When we were all done, the cow boss opened the gate to put the calves back in the feedlot. We just rode around the back of the bunch, easy-like, and they headed for the feedlot through the open gate. Well, in the tail end of the bunch, two little renegade calves ducked back. The cow boss said, 'We'll come back and get them, let's keep the main bunch moving.'

"The main bunch went through the gate," Chuck continued, "and all five of us rode back, slow-like, got behind the two calves, and they started up the fence with us guys riding abreast behind them. As they were going good, we was visiting and not paying too much attention. After all, with five riders abreast behind them, there was not much chance they would try to break back. I was riding next to the fence on old Black Jack, and if we were too complacent and not watching, that black horse was on the job.

"All of a sudden, for no reason, those two calves ducked back, one heading for the opening between me and the fence, the other for the opening between me and the next rider. Black Jack had one coming at him from both sides. It happened so fast, I do not really know how, but Black Jack dived at the one by the fence first, turned him back, then snapped like the buckskin popper on a bullwhip and stopped the other one. When he stopped the second one, he lifted me right out of the saddle. When everything stopped and the calves were again heading for the gate, I was standing by the fence holding one rein. Lucky I landed on my feet." He added that old Black Jack was some kind of a horse, one of a kind and could back up any reputation given him and then some.

About a year before this all happened, I was working on a haying crew for the summer on a ranch north of Kamloops, close to the small town of Heffley Creek. One of the boys on the crew was a young, very handsome and very likeable Indian fella who was the ranch's full-time hand. He had a very good friend living in the Kamloops area, also a top hand and Indian bronc rider by the name of Gus Godfrieson. One weekend, he came home from town with a folded-up newspaper in his hand and a wide grin on his face. He came into the bunkhouse and said Gus had rode Snake. I asked if he meant Gus qualified on Snake to the whistle. He just grinned and handed me the paper.

There, on the front page of the Kamloops Sentinel, was a big coloured picture of a man riding a bucking horse, and at the top of the page, in big, black letters, was the heading "Godfrieson Rides Snake." To the best of my knowledge, this was the first time Snake was ridden.

You see, at that time, Snake was the top bucking horse in Kelsey's rodeo string from Washington State. The mighty Snake and his counterpart, a black mare known as Devil's Dream, always left some cowboy kissing Mother Earth before the whistle would blow. Whether Devil's Dream had ever been qualified on before this or not, I do not know. If so, it was very seldom.

When news of Godfrieson riding Snake successfully came out on the front page of the Sentinel, I think the whole city of Kamloops and surrounding area was very proud that their own home-range bronc rider had been the first to do so. Gus riding Snake was an admirable ride on an admirable bucking horse by an admirable rider. As a point of interest, some years later, Mrs. Godfrieson, Gus's wife, was chosen as Canada's Mother of the Year.

I worked for the Cariboo Cattlemen's Association Feed Warehouse at Williams Lake before coming to Alberta. The rancher's cattle representative working for the Association was a fella who had been cow boss on the big Douglas Lake Ranch out of Merritt, British Columbia, and he knew the quality of live cattle better than anyone I have ever known.

Slim had a five-year-old roan mare he left at the ranch and figured she'd make a good rodeo bronc. I asked if she had ironed out a lot of riders, and Slim said she was only halter-broke and no one had ever tried to ride her. I asked what made him think she was the makings of a good bucking horse, if he had never seen her buck. Slim just grinned and said she come from good bucking stock. That mare's mother and the great bucking mare in Kelsey's string, Devil's Dream, were full sisters. If she even came close to her famous aunt, she would be hard to sit on. He did not think there was any doubt about whether or not she would fire, coming from that bloodline.

In due time, he went back to the ranch and got her. One day, he said, "Let's you and me take that mare down to the rodeo arena and try her out." I told him I would help rig her out if he wanted to ride her. He said to try her out. I told him, "Hell, no. I'm too old; you're the one who's got to try her." To him, this seemed like a good joke. The way he was laughing, I did not want any part of her.

In the first place, with a plumb green bronc, you do not know what they might do. In the second place, the idea of trying out Devil's Dream's niece just did not seem a good idea without any pickup men standing by. Besides, Slim was only 10 years older than I was, and I do believe he could ride a tougher horse than me. With that thought in mind, if he did not want to try her, I figgered I would pass. It got to be kind of a joking matter between us. Slim would say, "Let's try her out." And I would say, "Sure, if you do the riding." This went on for a time, and then the Williams Lake Stampede was upon us.

Slim talked to Kelsey, and the roan mare went into the bucking string. I had entered the bronc riding, and another rider and I went down to the corrals to see what horse we had drawn. Gil found his right away, a big black gelding with a number 10 painted on his hip, a good horse that could put him in the money, if all went well. We could not find mine, number four. We knew that horse had to be in the corral, so we kept looking.

Finally, Gil called to me that he had found number four. I went to look, and the roan mare I had been reluctant to try for weeks was wearing number four on her hip. Lucky me, I was destined to be the first rider to get on the direct niece of Devil's Dream. I felt sure I had drawn a money-winning horse, if I could ride her. I would give it my best shot.

When they called my name, Gil and a couple of other friends rigged her out. She was good and quiet in the chute. I got down on her, took a long shank and a deep seat and nodded my head. The gate swung open, I got her started high on the shoulders and we were out in the arena. I was doing fine, but she was just getting warmed up. Slim thought it right when he said she was bred to buck, and she would fire well. She was firing, all right.

About six seconds out, she threw one at me I could not ride and we parted company. Them days, we rode 10 seconds before the whistle blew. I was never so glad to be bucked off as I was then. I was lying on the ground watching her go as she tried to sunfish with the empty saddle. She had no trouble sunfishing; the sun was shining on her belly, but being new to bucking, she failed to get her feet under her and landed flat on her side. Had I been on her when that happened, I could have hit my head on the ground and gone to shake hands with St. Peter.

She got up and went back to bucking. One more sunfish landed her flat on her side again. She got up and, being spent, crow-hopped down the arena. She went back to Washington State with the bucking string. I walked back to the chutes feeling that it was one time to be glad of losing my entry fees.

It was after that my friend George and I headed for Alberta to try out some of the prairie bucking horses, with not much success, but we managed to stay healthy. There were many good bucking horses in those prairie strings, some of which stand out in my memory:

Stormy Weather, a big, gentle sorrel, about whom that I heard an announcer say, "Watch this, folks. This horse has bucked off his last 52 riders. A great bucking horse."

Blue Bill, practically unrideable, who my friend drew at Saskatoon, Saskatchewan. Blue Bill won, but not without a lot of effort.

Old Farmer, who would try to tear the chute apart if he got mad. I drew him at Saskatoon, and he was in good humour, but I blew a pedal on him before the whistle. You guessed it; I took a feed of Saskatchewan soil that day, when he ploughed my face into the arena.

I quit riding bucking horses before too long and did some calf roping. However, I went back to what I was good at: working.

Many years have passed since then. I have been riding mostly gentle horses on the job, except occasionally one would spook at something and try to unload me. Some have succeeded, but I have never had to walk home...so far. I have always managed to come home with my horse between my knees.

Well, there is not much more to say. I have surely got to give honourable mention to my good bay horse, Daniel Boone, that I had so long ago and written about previously. As lease rider for a grazing association for the last 20 years, I have had some good horses that have been with me a long time. Like me, the years are adding up on them, too, but we are still good for a day's work.

Art and Danny at the Elkwater roping club: "With Danny, I never went out after some cattle that I didn't come home with."

There is old Boomer, who I raised from a colt. A pure Appaloosa, about 1300 pounds. A big, gentle horse, he's been my strong right arm on the grazing lease for years, working and doctoring cattle, big enough to stretch out any cow by the hind

Boomer, retired in this picture: "I raised him from a colt, and he was my strong right arm. He passed on at the age of 28."

legs on the prairie, and he works the rope good. He knows what he is doing, any place you put him.

There is my daughter Julie's big sorrel horse, Casey, a direct great grandson of old Three Bars, on his sire's side. A great travelling horse and very active. He works the rope well, and if you ever get in a position where you have to pass and turn back a runaway critter, you had better have a good hold on the cowboy's safety post, when that critter turns back and Casey turns back with him, or you will likely get a taste of prairie wool. With the power, speed and know-how of that big sorrel horse, you have to have a deep seat and lots of riding ability.

Julie's horse, Casey, which I used out on the Writing on Stone Grazing Reserve for a number of years: "One of the most powerful horses I ever sat on."

Then there is little Rusty, now fully retired, at 28. He has earned every day of his retirement. He belongs to my son, Irvine. He has had him since he was 11 and Rusty was four. They have done a lot of ranch work and cowboyed hard together.

Last, but not least, is my registered sorrel quarter horse, Handy. A trained calf horse, good at everything he does, is how he got his name. His registered name, You Hard Cider, is too long-barrelled to use everyday. If you see or have a copy of my latest cowboy western album, *Cowboy Country*, that is Handy with me and my good cow dog, Jake, on the cover.

My working cowboy career has been long and interesting. Not much monetary wealth, but the personal wealth acquired in an occupation that has kept me healthy, happy and optimistic outweighs the monetary aspect. There have been many hard

Art and Handy on the Writing on Stone Grazing Reserve, taken during a photo shoot for the cover of his album *Cowboy Country*.

miles that have passed under my saddle but many good ones, too. When you get out on the open prairie under the blue sky on a quiet day, the spring grass is green, the wildflowers decorate the green carpet and birds sing in the early morning sun, it seems like it must be what heaven is like. A fella feels like he is part of it all. Nature at its best.

If you are riding in rough, hilly or mountainous country and break out of the time on the open in the high country, you can see for miles, sometimes over a landscape that is still the way God made it, in the first place. Lakes and meadows, timber, rock bluffs and running creeks, cattle here and there, along with deer, elk, coyotes, birds and flowers. A mental picture that stays in your memory forever.

Art on Julie's barrel horse, Spitzy: "This photo was taken by a Danish photographer, looking for a story."

It has been said that cowboys do not like to walk much. Well, that is partly and basically true, but at times like this, when everything is leisurely, peaceful and beautiful, it is very nice to get down and lead your horse for a ways and limber up your hind legs. Walk to the edge of the high country hills to admire the miles of valleys, river, lakes and creeks that come into your view from the top of the world, so to speak.

I myself, and I'm sure most range riders like me, quite often get off and lead our horse up steep and difficult hills. After all, the old pony needs a little break occasionally. It is hard enough climbing those steep places with an empty saddle, never mind packing a man. Sometimes, too, we will get off and lead our horse down into river or creek ravines that are deep and steep, for us both to get a drink.

If, someday, somewhere, you come upon the tracks of a pair of high-heeled boots with spurs trailing in the sand, look closely. There will be the tracks of a good horse beside them.

Stop and listen for a spell, and with a little imagination, you might picture a working cowboy and his horse and hear the owner of the tracks in the sand say, "Come on, *compadre*, let's you and me walk down to the creek for a drink and then head home. It's been a long, hard day."

THE HORSE BETWEEN MY KNEES

I've rode these western ranges for 40 years or more,
From the rolling windswept prairies to the Fraser River shore.
I've rode many miles a-horseback, I've always aimed to please
And I've always had a lot of faith in the horse between my knees.
Out along the mighty Fraser, where the cold north winds do blow
The night was dark and stormy, as we plowed on through the snow.
I said a little prayer as we struggled through the trees,
But he never once did fail me, the horse between my knees.
When it's roundup on the prairies, with many long miles to ride,
The winds are hot and dusty and sweat stains streak your hide.
A scary bunch of cattle, running at full speed
I could usually always turn them with the horse between my knees.

There have been many arguments with horses young and green
I've had my share of buck-offs when they would let off steam.
But they always stayed and waited, as if they aimed to please
And I've always managed to come home, with my horse between my
knees.

They were backed up in the roping box, the crowd was quiet and low
Nine seconds was the time to beat in the big rodeo.
The gate cracked quickly open, the rope cut though the breeze
He made a running dismount from the horse between his knees.

The run was quickly over, the rope was still held tight
The announcer said, "Did you like it, folks? That was done up right.
The time is eight and seven, give them a hand if you please
Half the credit does belong to the horse between his knees."

There have been many inventions, can put a cowboy's mind to strain
Motorbikes and motor trikes, and four-wheel all-terrain.
But when the chips are down and dirty, and a cowboy is in a
   squeeze,
Nothing ever will replace, the horse between his knees.

There are things about my horses, some folks don't understand
When the cards are dealt against me, they are still my winning hand.
At the risk of sounding mushy, if you listen, please
I will always love and cherish, the horse between my knees.

© Art Hagen
Published in the *Western Horseman*, June 2000

Art Hagen

Art Hagen was born in 1923 in the picturesque town of Hazelton, British Columbia. Raised in the Kispiox Valley, he moved south to work as a ranch hand in the Caribou Country and the southern interior of British Columbia. He then found his way to southern Alberta where he married, had children and continued as a ranch hand and range rider until he retired at the age of 80. Art is a musician and songwriter with two albums out, The Hills of Home and Cowboy country. After spending many of his later years living in Valleyview, in the Peace River Country of northern Alberta, Art passed away in September 2014 at the age of 92. He lived a long and full life as is evidenced by this story of his life as a cowboy and ranch hand in the early days of western Canada.